The Children of the Peo|

Writings by and about CUNY students on race and social justice

Rose M. Kim, Grace M. Cho and Robin McGinty, Editors

Printed on acid-free paper

© 2022 DIO Press LLC, Lewes, DE

https://www.diopress.com

Cover Art: Painting ("New Chapter" by Kibrom Gebremedhin) is courtesy of owner Rose M. Kim.

Book Jacket: Book design is courtesy of Kibrom Gebremedhin.

ISBN 978-1-64504-238-9 (Paperback)

ISBN 978-1-64504-239-6 (Hardback)

ISBN 978-1-64504-240-2 (E-Book)

Library of Congress Control Number: 2022931026

ACKNOWLEDGMENTS

Our book *The Children of the People* emerged from *Autoethnographies of CUNY*, a public humanities project conceived by faculty co-leaders Grace M. Cho and Rose M. Kim, two of the book's editors. Funded by the Andrew W. Mellon Seminar on Public Engagement and Collaborative Research, a platform directed by Kendra Sullivan of the Center for the Humanities at The Graduate Center, the seminar supports the institutionalization of public humanities practices and pedagogy at CUNY and across New York City through community partnerships, public research projects, policy development, curriculum enhancement, and expansive creative, cultural, and collaborative works with a social justice thrust. We are thankful to the Center for its institutional support and encouragement throughout the course of this project.

The editors are also thankful for the inspiring CUNY faculty, colleagues, and students that have deepened our commitment to the value of critical thought and rigorous scholarship and its revolutionary potential to help change the world.

We appreciate all the alumni who responded to our public call for essays on race and social justice, and are especially grateful for the contributors to this volume, who patiently and graciously worked with us.

We also want to thank the College and Community Fellowship and Asian American Writers' Workshop for their collaboration, and Bushra Rehman for teaching her *2 Truths & a Lie* Workshop for CUNY students and alumni.

Finally, thank you to the staff at DIO Press for your enthusiasm for this project and for bringing it into the world.

Table of Contents

Foreword

MICHELLE FINE

"You've been CUNYied": a (self) mocking recognition that erupts when students find weird, enraging, unexpected fees attached to their already too high tuition bills; when faculty or staff receive checks late or for amounts much smaller than anticipated; when program staff are thanked by administrators, "You have been amazing, a life saver, but with austerity, well you understand, it may be just one more month."

CUNY is like a lover you should—but can't—leave. You know they will break your heart, but there's a magic, seduction, and often a betrayal. But then a student who shines; a class that sings; a policy victory; a book you take to bed that you never would have known about....

You know it will be a struggle; there may be a diploma, or full-time job, or promotion—or not.

You are nourished by the energy, the protests, the histories, the wild ideas just voiced in a classroom by the person with full body tattoos, pink hair and piercings, sitting next to the Afghan war vet, next to someone with an UNDOCU-QUEER t-shirt, next to someone deeply religious—debating *the uses of anger* by Audre Lorde.

Something keeps us hanging around. It's certainly not the pay or the security.

CUNY the institution is entangled, always, in a struggle of Thanatos (death wish) and Eros (desire). Haunted now and always by racialized austerity politics, managerial governmentality and carceral logics, CUNY is threatened from without and molding from within. And yet the children of the people—students, staff, faculty—breathe solidarity and radical possibilities in every generation, living the good fight. And, as a friendly amendment to John Lewis, in this volume, writing the good fight.

In reading *The Children of the People* during quarantine, and in the midst of draconian cuts to CUNY and energizing protests for Black Lives across the world and on our campuses, it is easy to conjure CUNY as colluding in racial capitalism and the gentrification of the city. The institution casts away elders, cuts adjuncts, dangles jobs for college assistants, throws people off insurance during Covid-19—disproportionately staff and students of color, contracts with lousy software companies, invites the NYPD, CIA and FBI onto campus, threatens to sell buildings (John Jay and The Graduate Center) in the midst of pandemic, bows to anti-Palestinian ideologies, and invests in PATHWAYS ripping through beloved intellectual, pedagogical and labor commitments. Just to name a few of our recent institutional betrayals…

And yet CUNY is also peopled, a pulsing throb of desire, freedom dreams, journeys, dead ends, love affairs with people, ideas, books and movements. At once a mirage and a sanctuary, at times a police state and an immensely frustrating bureaucracy, here we engage with/we are the children of the people. Droning on in an endless loop, we repeatedly hear a marketing campaign promoting "CUNY as an engine to economic mobility" and yet even louder voices can be heard from generations of lusty protests and uprisings—for trans justice and insurance for graduate students, free tuition and adjunct parity, for racial justice and remove the cops, for women's studies and Students in Solidarity with Palestine, welfare rights, instate tuition for undocumented students, queer justice, open admissions, free tuition again, and one more time—remove the cops.

Generation after generation we rise, collectively, maimed and motivated, hilarious and weary—a mosaic of educators and students and staff, together. We gather (and caravan) in awkward and sometimes in-tension-all solidarities, huddled in the PSC, publishing long ago in campus newspapers and now tweeting, fighting for the soul of public higher education. And we pass evenings with our own children and elders, lay in bed with dying grandmothers, sitting at tables with our mommas doing homework in the kitchen, witnessing fathers who launched the good fight for faculty governance at CUNY, worrying about relatives in countries far away, chanting through Trustee and City Council meetings, boarding buses to Albany protests, proud to be a part of the "revolting" CUNY diaspora.

We can no longer be "surprised" by the neoliberal moves of management and we must be prepared to engage, always, the struggle that is CUNY.

This is a volume of writers who have been stung by CUNY. Smitten, enraged, brilliant and passionate. I know and love many of the editors and writers. I adore that the essays were crafted, sculpted, in a collective, in a writing hive. How else to describe CUNY but a hive of conflicts and desires, a cauldron of love and struggle, a borderland in the language of Gloria Anzaldua, where we come together—lives, inequities, struggles, wounds and desires—to ask the question that Robin McGinty and writers ask, "What is freedom?" Where we imagine and insist unapologetically that public higher education must be accountable to the people of the City, designed to carve paths toward collective freedom dreams.

The three stunning editors—Rose, Grace and Robin—live lives, build nests of families/friends and communities, write scholarship, publish with critical edge, organize and even in a pandemic, they ZOOM pedagogies of *fierce* love. In this volume, curated with care and wide-open arms, they pry open and reveal the affective CUNY core, exposing the messy contradictory desires that entangle at the abused and abusive, still-beating heart of CUNY. We meet educators and students who engage as if another world is possible, knowing well the corduroy grooves of oppression and hunger, rage and thirst, that circulate through students/staff/faculty—their very CUNYied bodies.

The essays provoke, conjure old struggles and touch, softly and delicately, our most protest-weary organs, stimulate our wants (hesitant to believe, again), moisten our tear ducts, resurrect our buried memories and seduce suppressed hopes tucked beneath our CUNY fatigue. The essays carve a journey back-across-forward, to remind, remember and rekindle what CUNY has been/might be/ never was. Perhaps tomorrow.

In the language of Stefano Harney and Fred Moten or Patricia Hill Collins, these essays and poetry are written of course by outsiders within, working in the undercommons, carving maroon spaces in hollowing neoliberal sites of racial austerity. But that's not quite right either…these essays sprout unapologetically, demanding audience, refusing shadows and closets and insist on being heard as erotic texts of resistance, penned as the great grandchildren of Audre Lorde, Toni Cade Bambara, Adrienne Rich, writing/teaching/protesting in the legacy of unnamed protestors at City College demanding Black studies, those who fought for open admissions, the women at Hunter who struck for welfare rights, the Muslim students who organized to oust the NYPD in-filtrators at City College, the students who demanded a women's center at John Jay and Asian American studies at Hunter College, Eddie Ellis and the formerly incarcerated collective who built the Center for NuLeadership at Medgar Evers, and Vivian Nixon and comrades who carved College and Community Fellowship at The Graduate Center, both exiled when their radical vision caught fire (and headlines). CUNY is a site that loves to be radical chic until a trustee, or the *Daily News*, or the Governor, or real estate develop-ers or the NYPD or management decides that standing for justice is inconvenient to the neoliberal machine.

And yet, in the language of Maya Angelou, we rise. We write, we teach, we resist, we hold our students, we cry and we link arms, again, to name and enact the response-abilities of public higher education.

CUNY: an institution of magic and cold heart, white suprem-acy, neoliberal betrayals, long lines in registrars' offices, closed courses, neoliberalism and austerity, radical (and not at all rad-ical) faculty, outstanding bold students, wonderful/over-worked/under-paid staff who break all the rules to help us get by, tears and joy. Across five boroughs and 25 campuses, there burns a passion, a lava of radical desire, that moves underground and erupts across and within our academic homespaces.

These essays are penned in that ink of rage and desire. You will hear the be-*longing* in each piece.

It's kind of hilarious that Rose, Grace and Robin organized the chapters neatly into three sections: *"life," "organizing and activ-ism," and "teaching and learning,"* as if these were distinguish-able at the City University of New York. Maybe in more privi-leged settings.

But once you are CUNYied, these three spheres bleed into

each other.

We at CUNY are not good at boundaries. And we are proud of it.

The writers in this volume are old New York, immigrants and indigenous. A few have been accused of "acting white" and many have embodied all the anxieties of the imposter syndrome. We are DACA and we fear/know that our classrooms (and ZOOM spaces) are under surveillance. We are careful not to wear hoodies or fancy shoes, and many cross the street when police turn the corner. Boldly, we are formerly incarcerated, name our disabilities, remind readers of our days in foster care, survive without official documents, spent time in psychiatric facilities, attended private schools, have a trust fund, live in shelters for the unhoused…

In a language that renders lives as full and wonderous, relational and solitary, burdened and joyfully light, the CUNY authors tell us about mothers/fathers/grandparents/siblings/uncles who died too young. We learn that you were "bright," "the one who studied," "loved to read," were "plucked from my neighborhood school to be the only XXX in my private school" and yet you remember from where you came.

As children, and now, you picked up the pieces of families/communities/the diaspora in the ashes of racial capitalism. When young you watched elders sacrifice in silence so you might succeed. You learned to code-switch and make white/rich/powerful people comfortable, part of the unspoken deal of navigating education. And then at CUNY you sharpened your wit and organizing skills, and learned to make trustees and bureaucrats (often white/rich/powerful people) uncomfortable by design.

You always made your family proud…except when you slept with/brought home/married/had a child with someone of the same sex, the "wrong" race, class or political persuasion. Another perk of CUNY—vibrant dating opportunities.

Political as kids, you grew into students and faculty who insist, even into Covid-19, that CUNY stretch the corners of higher education into prisons and detention centers, into food pantries and sanctuary spaces.

In this volume writers recover historic memories of courageous movements borne in, mobilized at and sometimes purged from CUNY: Welfare Rights Initiative, open admissions, no tuition, SEEK, 1969 renaming of City College as Malcolm X-Che Guevara University and later University of Harlem, the movement to BAN the BOX, in-state tuition for undocumented students, the BMCC DREAM team, struggle for Third World Studies, the 1991 CUNY STRIKE and occupation of the Graduate Center, "Operation Budget Storm," teach-in's in Madison Square Park and Bryant Park, the 2016 fight for CRAASH (Coalition for Revitalization of Asian American Studies at Hunter College) and the bodacious College and Community Fellowship project built by and for newly released women to nourish "the historic desire of newly freed people to be educated." Banished just a few years later.

We who have been CUNYied embody curiosity, dare to dream and insist. Alone and with others. You sit by yourself in parks to read and you protest en masse to remove police on your campuses. Then you pick up the kids/siblings/nieces/neighbor's child from school, or translate in court for a relative, go home and argue with your uncle or sister, a police officer who works in corrections. We resist categories even as we insist that Black Lives Matter.

We are deeply and intimately embroidered into others' lives, across generations, with our kin, our students and our collective dreams. But we are not simply sweet.

As kids, we fought—with neighborhood girls, with racist teachers, with security guards who wanted to discipline/criminalize our rage. As adults, we fought with doctors who ignored the DNR from a grandmother, with administrators who insist on enforcing policy with racialized impact, with administrators and trustees who privilege power over people.

At CUNY, we fight the defunding, the neoliberalization and the vocationalizing of the academy, the silencing and censoring, the moves to privatize, and we fight hard to create conditions where thought, dialogue, dissent, protest and imagination might flourish.

In our separate spaces, across boroughs and zip codes, we sleep with words of Audre Lorde and Adrienne Rich, the ghosts of elders who nourished us, teachers who saw us, students who have disappeared, as assignments pile up, deserving feedback and dignity.

In our classrooms, our scholarship and on the streets, we dare to carve the questions, hold the tensions, feel the rage, kindle the yearnings, soothe the disappointments, and build very fragile solidarities among the *children of the people*, in the soil of always-under-assault CUNY. We critique the institution, even as we build its soul.

What is freedom?

Sitting on a park bench, reading through the pages of *The Children of the People,* and laughing out loud when we meet an immigrant student from China in Constance H. Gemson's essay, *Adjunct Blues and Class Notes*, who asks innocently:

What is red tape?

Ha! Give that student their diploma now. He's been thoroughly CUNYied.

In the midst of Covid-19, racial uprisings, wretched racialized austerity, a steady stream of police murdering people of color, the screams of children in detention, the death of John Lewis and Ruth Bader Ginsburg, the fires, hurricanes and fear of evictions/deportations, we bear witness to the grotesque display of inequities and the precarity of abolition dreams. In this moment of despair, it is easy to surrender. But written with desire and chutzpa, sharpening the skills of insurgency, *The Children of the People* insists that we mourn and critique, but then imagine and mobilize for a *just* CUNY, always in struggle. A CUNY worth fighting, and worth fighting for.

Thank you, Rose, Grace and Robin for a luscious read, a call to affect and action, a reminder that CUNY is an idea, trapped in an always inadequate, resource-starved and sometimes toxic institutional body, occupied by generations of those who yearn, deserve, demand and write with a fever.

Editors' Introduction

ROSE M. KIM, GRACE M. CHO AND ROBIN MCGINTY

We write this introduction in May 2021, well over a year since the Covid-19 pandemic upended daily life with the imposition of quarantines, shifts to online workplaces and classrooms, and mandatory social distancing in public, a situation only recently abating with rising numbers of the vaccinated. Furthermore, the pandemic has laid bare the economic and racial contradictions that divide us. In the past year, while 76 million Americans lost work, creating widespread food insecurity and fears of eviction, especially among people of color and immigrants, the collective wealth of American billionaires increased from $2.95 trillion to $4.56 trillion during the same period (Collins). As the federal government continues to refuse entry, imprison, and deport undocumented migrants fleeing desperate situations, often the results of U.S. military interventions, such as in El Salvador, Guatemala, and Honduras, it overlooks their widespread employment as "essential workers" in various sectors of the U.S. economy, e.g., agriculture, construction, and hospitality.

Similarly, on April 21, almost a year since Minneapolis police officers suffocated 46-year-old George Floyd to death, igniting the largest mass protests against systemic racism and police brutality in the United States and around the world, police officer Derek Chauvin was convicted of second-degree murder, as three others await trial in August. Yet even as protestors celebrated the conviction, they mourned the fatal shooting ten days earlier of Daunte Wright, 20, in a routine traffic stop, just miles from the courthouse; in the 24 hours following the verdict, at least six people were fatally shot by police, including Ma'Khia Bryant, 16, in Columbus, Ohio (*Associated Press*). On May 4th, the Mapping Police Violence database reported there had been only six days in the current year where police did not kill someone. This seemingly endless litany of senseless deaths has fueled the demonstrations for racial justice and calls for defunding the police that continue unabated across the nation today. Meanwhile, a right-wing, white supremacist movement, vitalized by the 2017 march in Charlottesville, VA, and the Donald Trump presidency, challenged the legitimacy of the 2020 presidential election, even inciting an assault on the Capitol on Jan. 6th, and has also been pushing legislation to limit voting rights and the teaching of critical race theory (Goldberg); there also seems evidence of a growing multiethnic, fascist movement, according to the *ProPublica* documentary *American Insurrection* (2021).

This historic moment has exposed the massive fault lines around race, class, gender, and immigration status in American society, raising a multitude of questions: Who gets access to good health care, or any health care, for that matter? Whose jobs provide a living wage and legal protections that support one's self and loved ones? Whose jobs are a form of "social death" (Patterson) or "slow death" (Berlant, 2007). How is one's chance of getting arrested, and then dying at the hands of police more determined by one's skin color or state of mental health than one's actions? While these stark inequities are not new, white middle-class Americans are only now waking up en masse to this reality and joining the fight.

As the nation's largest urban university and the fourth largest public university system by enrollment, perhaps no other institution in the United States can teach us as much about the gaping divides that have been exposed as can the City University of New York (CUNY). For more than four decades, faculty and staff have struggled to provide a quality education despite waves of neoliberal, austerity-driven cuts to the essential budget; meanwhile, our students, growing up under the post-9/11 regime of defunding essential social services and building up the military and police, can teach us about how they survive and thrive despite these constraints and cutbacks; how they strive to learn and grow; and all that is at stake for them, their families, and this nation.

Our collective student body, numbering 270,000 and representing 25 campuses across five boroughs, is one of the most diverse in the nation and heavily represented by immigrants or by the children of immigrants from all over the world, like New York City itself. Many are essential workers or the children of essential workers. In an April 17th op-ed in the *Daily News*, Michael Yarbrough, assistant professor of law and society at John Jay College, wrote of our students, "They are the still-beating heart of metro New York City, the people who make the region run every day—crisis or not." While politicians and the news media hail these workers as "heroes," as a group of Brooklyn College faculty noted in *City Limits*, "the term 'hero' can be a rhetorical sleight of hand—a form of praise (and applause every evening at 7:00), but not actual material recognition—no guarantee of living wages, health care, safe working conditions, or a fully funded education" (Theoharis et al.).

As we write this introduction, CUNY has laid off around 2,800 contingent faculty members in anticipation of state budget cuts, leading many to lose their health insurance, sometimes after decades of service. Ben Lerner, Distinguished Professor of English at Brooklyn College, wrote in a *New York Times* Op-ed, "After years of being brutalized by Albany, CUNY has apparently so thoroughly internalized the backward logic of austerity that it responds to crisis by attacking itself." The future is further uncertain, with a 3.7% drop in enrollment system-wide, a decline of more than 10,000 students, likely reflecting the difficulties of transitioning to online education in a digital divide, as well as the economic strain of the pandemic on students and their families (Sandoval).

At its core, CUNY was and remains an institution designed to serve the public. In 1849, Horace Webster, the first president of the Free Academy, said of the radical social experiment that would become City College, and later, CUNY: "The experiment is to be tried, whether the children of the people, the children of the whole people, can be educated, and whether an institution of the highest grade, can be controlled by the popular will, not by the privileged few, but by the privileged many" (qtd. in Medina). While CUNY has served generations of working-class and immigrant New Yorkers, it wasn't until the student-led movement for open admissions in the 1960s that CUNY began to educate Black and Brown people in significant numbers, thus coming closer to its stated purpose of educating "the whole people." Today, roughly 75% of our 270,000 students are nonwhite and nearly 50% come from households earning less than $20,000 a year. About half are first-generation college students. They tend to have jobs, while living at home and commuting. They have children, or help to take care of younger siblings and elders. Our students represent the populations hardest hit by the pandemic.

On March 11, 2020, when CUNY announced the decision to

shift all classes to online instruction, for many in our communities, it would already be too late. In the weeks immediately after the shutdown, we—Grace, teaching at the College of Staten Island, and Rose, at the Borough of Manhattan Community College—tried to adjust to teaching from home as New York City quickly became the global epicenter. We felt the devastation wrought by the pandemic in our classes. Unlike students at private liberal arts colleges who were mourning the loss of their campus experience, our students were facing challenges of a far greater magnitude. They struggled to continue school, as many did not have adequate access to technology, or lacked their own study space. They juggled responsibilities of caring for children and siblings whose schools and childcare centers had closed, while also trying to help their family make ends meet. Virtually all our students reported job loss, illness, or anxiety and trauma related to their own status as an essential worker. One had become homeless. Several had lost family members. It became apparent to those of us teaching at CUNY that not only was New York City a global epicenter, so was CUNY. Echoing our experiences, our colleague Michael Yarbrough, cited earlier, described how the virus had torn through the families of his students. In one class, 25% of his students had contracted the virus; over 60% had family members who had fallen ill; and another 25% were mourning. Indeed, by the pandemic's third month, *Inside Higher Ed* reported that CUNY had been the hardest hit university in the United States, and as of this writing, at least 52 faculty and staff have lost their lives to Covid-19 complications (Valbrun, In Memoriam). There is no current accounting of student deaths, but one can only imagine that the numbers are equally grim.

While this picture of how the pandemic and its economic consequences unfolded across our university in the spring of 2020 may be dramatic, it is perhaps more the rule and less the exception. As Yarbrough and others inform us, a mere 15% of American college students live on campus, while the rest have experiences similar to those of CUNY students, in that they live with their families and hold jobs. They, too, are being asked to shoulder the burden of "efficiencies" as the boards of public universities across the United States are downsizing faculty and cutting essential services.

With the election of President Joe Biden, and a Democratic majority in the House, and Senate, if including Vice President Kamala Harris' role as a tie-breaker, a significant amount of federal aid, more than $2.6 billion has been allocated to New York colleges as part of the American Rescue Plan Act of 2021; of that amount, $836 million will go to CUNY. Hopefully, this aid will reach those who need it most. Yet, even as this aid is welcomed, it must be remembered that CUNY has suffered a series of devastating cuts in a decades-long trend to defund public higher education. Since the 1976 fiscal crisis in New York City, CUNY, like public education more broadly, has been steadily starved of resources. As our colleague Matt Brim wrote in *Gotham Gazette* on May 6th, almost two months into the quarantine amid threats of budget cuts, the crisis is "not a novel crisis," but rather, a crisis that has been decades in the making.

We argue it is the culmination of a neoliberal, white supremacist agenda to gut the social safety net and to corporatize and privatize public services. In the post-Civil Rights' 1970s, as tax dollars began to be diverted from schools, affordable housing, community mental health centers, and social services to the military-industrial complex, the prison-industrial complex, and other corporate interests, CUNY became one of the innumerable casualties in the assault on public life. This decades-long shift of taxpayer dollars from public to private, from CUNY and other vital public goods to the carceral system and the militarization of society, is the largely unacknowledged substrate of media portrayals of the campuses' crumbling facilities, corrupt administrators and "underachieving" students.

While CUNY faculty have published a slew of op-eds, student voices have been largely unheard. One exception is Michael Villanova, a CUNY undergraduate and self-described "working class kid from the Bronx," who published a critique of Governor Andrew Cuomo's cuts to CUNY in *The Riverdale Press*. Asking "why, during a pandemic, does Gov. Cuomo think it is necessary to gut funding for the 'greatest engine for social mobility'," Villanova eloquently answers:

> For CUNY students, this is nothing new. The steady cuts to CUNY over the years have left buildings with ceilings caving in, broken elevators, and classrooms moldy and overcrowded...
>
> Whenever I hear people say they want to return to the way things were "before" the pandemic, I wince. "Before" was a utopia for the well off or ignorant. In reality, "before" was bearable for essential people who made the city run, and the students who believed in that "engine" to a better future...
>
> So you will have to excuse me and fellow CUNY students—many of who have taken to the streets recently—when we do not share the same thrill for Cuomo (whose approval numbers have soared in the past few months), or any other New York establishment figure, when our chances at a better life are snatched from our hands.

The CUNY students that have taken to the streets have put the fiscal crisis squarely in the context of racial justice and the Black Lives Matter protests by calling to "Fund CUNY Not Cops." This call for structural change and for investment in the institution is also a call to reclaim some of the funds that have been taken from higher education and given instead to New York State's vast prison industrial complex. According to the Center on Juvenile and Criminal Justice (1998), New York State was already ranked 45th in the nation in per capita higher education spending in 1995, when prisons began to receive a bigger share of public funds than higher education.

The protests to "Fund CUNY Not Cops" also speak to how the decades-long assault on CUNY is intertwined with the Black Lives Matter movement. CUNY is and has been an engine of upward mobility not only for working-class and immigrant students, but also for Black students. The most recent demographic data available show that CUNY educates over 60,000 Black students a year, more than any other university in the country and more than the top five largest Historically Black Colleges and Universities combined (Fraser). The defunding of CUNY is another powerful, though less obvious, force of institutional racism that renders Black futures less important, that makes Black people more valuable to the state as bodies in prison than as educated, actively engaged citizens. If we really want Black lives to matter, then the education of Black students must matter. If we really want to solve problems of racial injustice, we must understand the experiences of CUNY students. And we must financially invest in their education.

This year throughout the state's 2021-22 budget process, CUNY Rising Alliance, an advocacy coalition, has been calling for a "New Deal for CUNY." The proposed legislation, introduced by Brooklyn State Senator Andrew Gounardes and Bronx Assemblymember Karines Reyes, would increase the number of full-time professors to meet the national average, raise adjunct salaries to equal full-time professor salaries, and increase the number of mental health counselors and academic advisors. Most significantly, the plan would provide free tuition to all in-state undergraduate students. One hopes CUNY—students, faculty, and staff—will receive the public support it rightly deserves. Whether or not it happens, CUNY will probably carry on, as it has. The stories in this volume are testimony to the burning desire to learn and to build a better world, even as one is struggling for basic survival, even as one is struggling to breathe; that is, in part, CUNY's history.

Despite the multitude of challenges of being a CUNY student, each year at graduation, more than 50,000 students complete their programs of study, many gaining entry to competitive jobs and graduate programs. Often, a select few students are profiled as high achievers despite the governmental neglect of their campuses and communities, which goes unreported. As Linda Luu, one of our contributors points out, these narratives have "reduced individuals to their hardships in the face of structural violence to tell a neoliberal tale of aspiration and success." Our book does not want to do this. Rather, *Children of the People* seeks to paint a fuller picture of the student experience and the structural context in which our students live and learn.

We contend that despite massive divestment from public education, despite the historical role of institutions of higher education as gatekeepers for the privileged, CUNY continues to be a vital space of radical possibilities for teaching and learning. Perhaps, as Stefano Harney and Fred Moten propose in *The Undercommons: Fugitive Planning & Black Study* (2013), it is a case of faculty and students having a "criminal relationship" to the university, being "subversive intellectuals" and taking what we need to survive and thrive in desperate, unequal times. Harney and Moten (2013) say of the American university:

> [I]t cannot be denied that the university is a place of refuge, and it cannot

be accepted that the university is a place of enlightenment. In the face of these conditions one can only sneak into the university and steal what one can. To abuse its hospitality, to spite its mission, to join its refugee colony, its gypsy encampment to be in but not of—this is the path of the subversive intellectual in the modern university. (26)

So, more than 170 years after the founding of the Free Academy, we revisit Horace Webster's experiment from the perspective of the students. Although it's impossible to represent "the whole people" in one collection, we wanted to include a broad spectrum of experience. Our contributors are current and former students from community colleges, four-year colleges, and graduate programs; the faculty and staff who have contributed to this collection are either former or current students themselves, as are the three co-editors, and have done intensive work with students. We also strove for generational diversity to capture a feel for CUNY through the decades.

In the spirit of polyvocality, this collection of writings is composed of various forms—scholarly and personal essays, memoir, poetry, and performance—but they are all autoethnographic, making observations about social justice and race that are informed by the writers' lived experiences. This book was inspired by our participation in the 2017-2019 Center for the Humanities' Mellon Seminar in Public Engagement and Collaborative Research at The Graduate Center. As part of our work in the "Autoethnographies of Public Education and Racial (In)Justice" seminar, we organized two projects. One was an autoethnographic writing workshop for a dozen past and present CUNY students, led by writer Bushra Rehman at the Asian American Writers' Workshop. The other was the commissioning of an original theater work by The Theater for Social Change, an ensemble of formerly incarcerated women who earned their college degrees post-release, guided by Nina

Angela Mercer, cultural worker and doctoral fellow in theater and performance at The Graduate Center. Both projects culminated in public events. Other essays were written in response to a call for papers reflecting on education and social justice by past and present CUNY students; from 76 submissions, we selected twenty. Additionally, the essay by Lavelle Porter, "Dear Sister Outsider," is a reprint from poetryfoundation.org. We chose to reprint this piece because of the way in which it speaks to Audre Lorde's legacy at CUNY and her ability to continue guiding us through her words.

The book is divided into three sections: (1) Life; (2) Organizing and Activism; and (3) Teaching and Learning. The first section Life offers windows into the complex, intersectional lives of past and present CUNY students, including one who was a student, and is now faculty. The second section Organizing and Activism addresses political barriers encountered by students in public higher education, and how that oppression necessitated political mobilization, whether fighting cuts to educational funding or pushing for new disciplinary studies. The third section Teaching and Learning addresses how faculty reflect on their own learning, grapple with social inequalities in their classrooms, and strive to teach critical consciousness and civic engagement, despite administrative pressures to emphasize occupational training.

The common thread running through the essays is a critique of the key narratives promoted by the dominant culture. Refuting the idea of a color-blind and meritocratic society, our contributors analyze the indisputability of racism and white supremacy, and problematize assimilating into the "American Dream." They critique U.S. militarism and imperialism; the prison-industrial complex; and the neoliberal logic whereby college is regarded as a vehicle for job training rather than of critical analysis, self-reflection, and broader civic engagement. They question the notion of meritocracy in a society riven by inequalities of race, class, gender, and nativism, and describe lives fueled by rage over injustice and filled with the love and sacrifices of family and community.

Although the essays were all written before the seismic shifts of 2020, they now have heightened relevance. They reveal the ways in which CUNY is both a microcosm of our social problems and a key to solving them. Now, as before, students must navigate personal struggles that are emblematic of larger social struggles. Now, as before, student protest and radical classrooms are the life-blood of the institution. Through their writings, our students and faculty illuminate not only the emancipatory potential of the nation's largest urban public university, but also the possibilities for a just world.

References

Associated Press. (2021, April 24). 1 verdict, then 6 police killings across America in 24 hours. *U.S. News & World Report*. Accessed May 15, 2021.

Berlant, L. (2007). Slow Death (Sovereignty, Obesity, Lateral Agency). *Critical Inquiry*, Vol. *33*(4), pp. 754-780.

Brim, Matt. (2021, May 6). Not a novel crisis at CUNY. *Gotham Gazette*. Accessed May 30, 2021.

Center on Juvenile and Criminal Justice. (1998). *New York State of Mind? Higher Education vs. Prison Funding in the Empire State, 1988-1998*. https://pdfs.semanticscholar.org/3803/5e3479fb-81781ce124d0498e8b469945b622.pdf. Accessed Aug. 19, 2020.

Collins, Chuck. (2021, April 15). Updates: billionaire wealth, U.S. job losses and pandemic profiteers. https://inequality.org/great-divideupdates-billionaire-pandemic. Accessed May 15, 2021.

"In Memoriam." The City University of New York. https://www.cuny.edu/memorial/?fbclid=IwAR2EZN-fzBG7SnX7CmgyUMDu2eflLzFpGYea_v2bmOulFyp2px-IZECr33dM. Accessed Aug. 19, 2020.

Fraser, Jessica. (2018, August 24). Largest HBCU in the nation: Top 10 Black colleges by enrollment. *HBCU Lifestyle*. https://hbculifestyle.com/largest-hbcu-by-enrollment/. Accessed Aug. 20, 2020.

Goldberg, David Theo. (2021, May 7). The war on critical race theory. *Boston Review*. http://bostonreview.net/race-politics/david-theo-goldberg-war-critical-race-theory. Accessed May 19, 2021.

Harney, Stefano and Fred Moten. (2013). *The undercommons: Fugitive planning & Black study*. Minor Composition/Autonomedia.

Lerner, Ben. (2020, May 26). The backward logic of austerity threatens America's most vibrant campus. *The New York Times*. https://www.nytimes.com/2020/05/26/opinion/cuny-cuts-ben-lerner.html. Accessed

May 26, 2020.

Mapping Police Violence Database. https://mappingpoliceviolence.org/. Accessed April 28, 2021.

Medina, Douglas. (2014). Open admission and the imposition of tuition at the City University of New York, 1969–1976: A political economic case study for understanding the current crisis in higher education. *New Political Science*, Vol. 36, No. 4, December.

Patterson, Orlando. (1982/2018). *Slavery and social death: A comparative study*. Harvard University Press.

Sandoval, Gabriel. (2020, August 7). CUNY fall semester enrollment drops as financial outlook takes toll on students and staff. *The City*. https://www.thecity.nyc/2020/8/6/21358031/cuny-fall-semester-enrollment-drops. Accessed June 1, 2021.

Theoharis, Jeanne, Alan Aja, and Joseph Entin. (2020, May 13). Spare CUNY, and save the education our heroes deserve. *City Limits*. https://citylimits.org/2020/05/13/opinion-spare-cuny-and-save-the-education-our-heroes-deserve/. Accessed 19 Aug. 2020.

Valbrun, Margjorie. (2020, June 23). Lives and Livelihoods. *Inside Higher Ed*. https://www.insidehighered.com/news/2020/06/23/cuny-system-suffers-more-coronavirus-deaths-any-other-higher-ed-system-us. Accessed 19 Aug. 2020.

Villanova, Michael. (2020, July 11) Cuomo's CUNY Cuts Put Students' Futures on Line. *The Riverdale Press*. https://riverdalepress.com/stories/cuomos-cuny-cuts-put-students-futures-on-line, 72167. Accessed Aug. 18, 2020.

Yarbrough, Michael. (2020, April 17). What CUNY teaches us about the coronavirus, and vice versa. *Daily News*. https://www.nydailynews.com/opinion/ny-oped-what-cuny-teaches-us-about-the-coronavirus-20200417-a3632rnkmjadldaoutmzyrrimy-story.html. Accessed Aug. 19, 2020.

LIFE

allegiances

SYLVIA BEATO

and on those mornings when we opened the door wide to the garden green humid air of august endless the whirring of the fan a song so ancestral we blinked like baby jellyfish in air and soon the high whistle of the kettle and soon the comfort deep of the inkwell mug as we **promise to give up loyalty to other countries** and yet what do bones know of the places that come before them *el día que tu naciste* what do they remember as the tongue memorizes the 13 original colonies *fue el día más feliz de mi vida* while in the corner of the mind we whisper our truths to the open book of myths *al hijo de Regina se lo llevaron* the book that **promise[s] to defend the Constitution and laws of the United States** *y nunca se supo lo que le pasó* and in response we unhinge our mouths to the papaya tree at the edge of el balcón over which possibilities are early and doubt has boiled the skin of the plantains away *seguro que se lo mataron, el pobre* what else besides our sleepy lashes muddy and slow what else besides this folktale of the frontier *y te juro que Regina nunca se recuperó* where we **promise to obey the laws of the United States** from nothing out of no one into something that "fundamentally changed the course of human history" that **promise[s] to serve in the U.S. military (if needed)** call upon we the people to bounce on the board then dive *por eso te ruego, hija mia, no te metas tanto en política* into becoming a singular **promise to serve (do important work for) the nation (if needed)** and dashing the lullaby languages loud stories and their heroes *al fin y al cabo, todos son ladrones y todo es mentira* to replace it all with narratives that keep running over ~~there has to be another way~~ you say ~~there has to be a different change~~ but quiet guard these mornings hush hush as we wake and we look and **promise to be loyal to the United States** and look into one another - *mira* - all is still for a moment we understand *porque no hay nada tan sagrado como la vida* and we kneel down for it

Education, My Refuge

JAIME RODRIGUEZ

I am a 27-year-old, visually impaired Hispanic man of humble beginnings. I have seen and experienced my fair share of social injustice, having grown up in the projects in a crowded city and having attended underfunded schools in an underserved community. This essay details my journey into academia while battling social stratification and injustice and explains how the City University of New York has helped me to rise above what I was born into and allowed me to blaze my own path.

I grew up in a tiny two-bedroom apartment in the Gowanus Houses, one of the many housing complexes run by the New York City Housing Authority, which serves the city's lowest-income residents. As a community of working-poor individuals and families, not much was expected of us and the chances of us managing to change our social location was low. While reflecting on my personal experiences in my introductory sociology course at the Borough of Manhattan Community College (BMCC), I learned that one's social location is a leading indicator of the outcome of a person's life. I learned how it helps determine our role in society, our social class, and any benefits or conflicts we may face in life. I also learned how it determines how easy or difficult one's social mobility will be. It was then that I understood that I, like the majority of my neighbors, occupied the lowest rung on society's ladder.

I was the second-born of four children. My siblings and I grew up living with our great-grandmother. Our mother suffered from addiction and was in and out of jail for various offenses and our fathers were completely out of the picture. And, as many people in our predicament were—and are—we faced food insecurity and the omnipresent threat of eviction. Having grown up in poverty, I dreamed of a day where I could escape the struggles I faced on a daily basis. But where I lived, education was something that people didn't seem to want or respect. As children, both at home and in the neighborhood, we were praised for being street-smart as opposed to book-smart. Simply reading a book or talking about enjoying school was enough for my peers and the people on my block to ridicule me for being a nerd.

It wouldn't be until much later when I began studying sociology in college that I would understand why my friends and family felt the way they did regarding education. I came to realize during my studies that the people that surrounded me felt disenfranchised by many aspects of their daily lives—economically, politically, socially, and educationally. That is to say, they felt the privileges and benefits afforded to the middle class and the wealthy were not extended to them. I came to understand the world was stratified in a way that forced them to worry about survival instead of education. So, pursuing an education to escape the forces that oppressed them wasn't as much of a goal as working hard to put food on the table.

For me, however, school was a refuge from the cruel world I was accustomed to. I spent the majority of my free time there. I enjoyed the company of my like-minded peers and the attention of my teachers. Being praised for good work became my goal. These teachers whom I looked up to gave me hope that one day I'd be able to change my circumstances. This pattern I had fallen into—spending all my free time at school—continued to high school. With the encouragement of my teachers, I obtained good grades in the hope that I could move away to college and away from my family.

But at the same time, as I was dreaming of my college experience, I was simultaneously drifting away from my peers and my community. In my neighborhood, to become educated was to alienate yourself from the community. It meant leaving behind everything you'd ever known for pursuit of something foreign and new. Everyone scoffed at my aspirations of collegiate life and told me I was acting "white"—as if to say that utilizing proper speech, an advanced vocabulary, and having an interest in education somehow betrayed my cultural identity.

By committing myself to the pursuit of a formal education, I was deviating from the approved "cultural capital" practiced in our community. According to sociologist Pierre Bourdieu, "cultural capital" is a currency of cultural knowledge as opposed to dollars, of resources that expresses one's social status and degree of power in a stratified society. Cultural capital is the social assets (manners, skills, and behaviors) that people practice to navigate their life opportunities and experiences, and also expresses one's social status and degree of power in a stratified society. And in the eyes of my neighbors and peers, I was refusing my rightful place in my community among other racial minorities in the struggle and pursuing a status in a world where I didn't belong. A place where they thought they weren't welcome. I had begun to use a different form of cultural capital as I delved further into academia, one that was foreign to my community.

I'd come to understand that the racialization ascribed to my community had caused most people in my immediate proximity to identify themselves, their race and ethnicities, by the struggles their families had endured over the generations. To them, this newly used cultural capital, though they didn't understand what that was, and my desire to escape the drudgery of poverty, were white aspirations. I was a Brown kid who spoke and behaved too white for the other Brown kids, and they shunned me. But even so, I wasn't white enough for the white kids to accept me either. They looked down on me for being the only Hispanic kid in their class, and I was degraded and spoken down to. I began to feel like an outlier in my community, though I maintained my belief that a college education was my ticket out of the hardships of my life. It was at that point that I decidedly left that part of my life behind me.

As my high school career progressed, things at home got steadily worse. My great-grandmother had passed away and my mother had come back to care of my siblings and me. The abuse, lack of food, and rampant drug use by the adults in the home was at an all-time high. Eventually, my mother was arrested on drug charges and incarcerated, and shortly after that, my stepfather, who had been taking care of my sisters and I, passed away unexpectedly. With nobody left to care for us, my sisters, and I, aged 13, 15, and 17 with me being the middle child, were left to our own devices, living completely unsupervised and with zero income to support ourselves. When I think back on this time, I like to say that the inmates were running the asylum, and that was entirely true.

I was about 15 at that point, and, as the most responsible member of my family, I took it upon myself to take care of my siblings. We had fallen through the cracks of society. Nobody had noticed that we'd all suddenly stopped attending school; nobody had bothered to check if we were okay. When I mentioned earlier that I had attended underfunded schools in an underserved community, I wasn't being facetious. Nobody had noticed us missing. The school system in my neighborhood was overburdened. I wonder how many children like my siblings and myself fell through the cracks and how many of those didn't make out as well as I had.

After about six months, my mother finished serving her sentence and was released. And the misery at home became increasingly unbearable. My only choice at survival was to officially drop out of high school and move away to work, get my GED, and pull my life together. But what I hadn't anticipated when I dropped out of high school was that the GED test I had banked on wasn't accessible to my visual impairment and that I would be stuck waiting in educational limbo until that changed.

After being stuck in that limbo for several years, after so much struggle, the test was finally made accessible and I obtained my GED; I immediately started planning my future. I was on my own when it came to researching and applying to college. Nobody in my family or friend groups had ever attended college. Nobody had even graduated high school or gotten a GED; I was truly on my own. But I understood that obtaining a higher education had a long history of empowering those who were negatively impacted by societal strain, and potentially gave people the knowledge and skills required to not only survive and thrive but to positively impact their communities; a goal similar to the one that Townsend Harris had when he founded in 1847 The Free Academy, which later became City College.

Searching for colleges and the best ways to fund my education, I understood that I wouldn't be able to afford much. I had no help and I didn't know where to start, but before long, I found myself pondering the possibilities. My ultimate goal was, and still is, to attend Columbia University, the school previously attended by my idol, President Barack Obama. Knowing I wouldn't be accepted with a GED and no formal education, I sought out an education at the City University of New York (CUNY). I discovered that the tuition rates were lower than many schools in my area and that as a citizen of New York, I'd get a quality education at an affordable price. I eventually settled on BMCC. I knew that I'd feel comfortable and at home there, as the student body was extremely active and diverse. I was excited when I was accepted.

As a first-generation college student, I was nervous and didn't know what to expect. I had already started life behind the eight ball, so to speak. The only thing I knew going in was that this was the first step in achieving the life I so desperately wanted, a life free from poverty and abuse. My dream was to work hard and to prove myself so that in the future, I might, in turn, help those facing plights similar to mine.

When I first accepted my position at the school, I was nervous about attending. It wasn't just the average new student jitters, though I had that, too. It was the fear about where I was going in life and if this school was right for me. It was also about the quality of the education I had received and if I was even worthy of being in the classroom among kids that were fresh out of high school. I was a 25-year-old former dropout. I wondered how I'd manage a full-time course load with my visual impairment as a major obstacle.

But once again, in CUNY's great tradition of uplifting and diversifying its student body, I discovered the Office of Accessibility; a comprehensive support system for students with disabilities. And suddenly, my visual impairment wasn't such a daunting obstacle to overcome. With their support, I felt confident in my abilities to enter the world of academia. I was excited, since the prospect of a college education had been all I had really ever wanted.

It wasn't until I reached college that I fully understood how the worries that burdened me so much were also the burdens for far too many people like myself. For those living at or below the poverty line, as my family did, the disparities between social classes are quite apparent. In my neighborhood, the majority of residents were poor, undereducated people of color, with dreams of escaping "the hood." And with the ever-increasing wealth gap, the only avenue left for minority groups and those living in poverty was education. I also understood that obtaining an affordable, quality education was outside the realm of possibility for most, as it was certainly out of reach for me without the assistance of others.

My first semester was nerve-wracking but fascinating. I had so many questions and reservations about attending school again, and I felt like the weight of the world was on my shoulders. I signed up for CUNY's Accelerated Study in Associate Programs (ASAP). That was meant to assist motivated students in completing their degrees faster, and I took to my college experience like a duck to water. I took four prerequisite classes to start and I passed them all with flying colors. I learned that at CUNY people like myself could thrive. I may have a disability, but I learned that it didn't define me or hinder me because CUNY had a diverse student body, full of people with disabilities, like myself. For the first time in my life, I felt like I was in control of my education. With the help of my ASAP advisors, the Office of Accessibility, and my own drive, I was able to graduate from BMCC with a nearly perfect GPA, and an appreciation for the school system that provided my affordable, quality education.

I am proud to say I hold an associate degree; the first in my family to hold such an honor. I realize that without CUNY, this would not be possible. As just one student with a dark and troubled past, I am in no way representative of the whole; however, I believe that there is a disproportionately large population of people coming from circumstances similar to mine who have and will continue to benefit from attending institutions of public higher education. This community has used CUNY as an opportunity to change its circumstances. Meanwhile, CUNY has allowed me to grow as a person and to find out who I am and where I fit in society, as I mingle with my professors and classmates of various backgrounds, all who have a story of their own, some quite similar to mine.

In my opinion, public higher education is a beacon of light in a dark world. It shines through the darkness and gives light to people who wouldn't be able to change their circumstances without it. It takes the impoverished and those whose intersectionality would prevent them from attending school or affording a public higher education. It gives them the social capital to positively affect their social mobility, thus improving their lives.

For all its faults, CUNY is an invaluable institution for those of us who were disadvantaged but have retained hope for a better future. It has provided me, and so many more like me, the tools and opportunities we needed to break the molds we were born into. And by utilizing our lived knowledge of the world and combining it with what we've learned in our college experiences, CUNY has allowed us all a way to shape our society into a more just and equitable place for all by giving us the springboard we needed to launch ourselves into the future we shape for ourselves.

On the Election of Donald Trump and Saving Ourselves

MAYA GARCIA

I can vividly remember the election of Donald Trump. The endless months leading up to that fateful November, the long list of celebrities lining up in favor of a certain Mrs. Clinton and priding themselves on the civility and sophistication of their candidate, the ongoing jokes about the stupidity of each and every Trump supporter, all the friends I unfriended or unfollowed online if I found any opinion that even remotely disagreed with my own—all of those memories are crisp in my mind like it's still 2016.

I was then a college freshman at Brooklyn College—more energetic and enthusiastic than I am now, and probably too excited about voting in my first election. The Democratic Party had already disappointed me that year, whether it was by ignoring and sabotaging the support of Bernie Sanders, a candidate I felt actually saw and heard me. Not to also mention the ongoing racism from the Democratic Party—anybody remember the racist comments referring to the Latinx outreach as "taco bowl engagement" from a leaked email from Debbie Wasserman Schultz, the then-chair of the Democratic National Committee. Like more than an ample amount of Americans, I was simultaneously excited to vote, but upset about the choices I thought I was forced to choose from.

And yet, despite all of this, I, like so many other Americans, knew with almost certainty that I would be ringing in the first Woman president by sunrise. The thought of living under a Trump presidency felt like a joke.

I can also remember staying up until 4 a.m., stress-eating hummus and old bagels as I watched the map of the United States slowly turn more and more red. I can remember the way my old friends and I sent panicked messages back and forth in our group chat, the way I could hear my roommate screaming at the crack of dawn in her devastation.

Devastation. How many of us were devastated? How many of us felt lost, disappointed, tired? And how tired?

How many of us failed quizzes that next morning? I personally failed my ear training quiz after giving up halfway through, too exhausted and upset to even think straight. For context, I was a music education major at the time because, apparently, I love to make bad decisions. When my professor returned our quizzes the following week, he did so with a note about how I could "Do Better!". Looking back on that moment, I came to an epiphany: Maybe I didn't really want to do better—maybe I just wanted to go back to bed and forget that the past 24 hours had ever happened.

A few days passed, and I remember wanting to hold each person a little closer, wanting to stay at home longer, to make sure that I wasn't alone so often. I remember hearing story after story about these tragic hate crimes: women getting their hijabs getting ripped off on the subway, men being run over and killed for speaking Spanish, people being told to go back to their own countries, etcetera, etcetera. The list went on and on (as it still goes on), and I remember feeling this kind of passion that hadn't been there before.

I swore to myself that I would take this tragedy and learn to be a better person: to be more politically active, go to more protests, and be kinder to each person I interacted with.

Trump had been president for a year and a half when I first started writing this piece, and I now feel...numb.

But not in the way I was when he was first elected, no, not that kind of numb. As college students under the Trump administration, we do not cry because we feel that our country has betrayed us—we cry because we have realized that it was never really there for us in the first place. By "we," I mean the people I call my comrades and my friends—those of us who are poor and working-class, who come from immigrant families, who are queer, who are people of color, who are women, those of us who identify as everything and nothing at all, who have felt this country's hatred for them first-hand and sometimes decided that we hated it right back. We have all realized that this country was never really there for us in the first place, and for this, we cry.

Because in the time that Trump has been president, I have realized that he has not planted a seed of hatred that has quickly sprouted and spread within this country, but that he is just another branch in the long-standing, white-centric standards of capitalism that allow for this kind of nonsensical violence to continue. My peers would write about how the election of Donald Trump signified a turning point in American history, one that made it clear that this country did not care about marginalized communities. And yet, did it ever?

Since Trump has been president, I have realized that the Democratic Party wasn't as wonderful and delightful as I had thought it to be, that maybe no politician or public figure can be a messiah in this crazy, barbaric world. That maybe the people who said that Hillary Clinton was just as bad as Donald Trump may have had a point.

Since Trump has been president, there has been a surge of people who have suddenly decided that they actually want to care about marginalized communities. And I'm not just speaking about those of us who were too young to realize how corrupt the world was, but about the people who have lived through the strife and struggle and sorrow of so many communities and only now have decided that the political sphere is a problem because the president is more openly bigoted than previous presidents have been.

I want every American to know that immigrant communities have been worried about family separations for years, that detention centers are absolutely nothing new, that ICE has stood as nothing more than terrorism for over ten years now. It's strange to see people I know, people I've called close friends, talk about the inhumanity of Trump's immigration policies when they used to shudder and react in shock when I told them about my formerly undocumented immigrant family members. A strange time, indeed.

What is it to be a college student during the Trump administration?

If I'm completely honest, finding an easy answer for that question is difficult, simply because the Trump effect means so many different things.

The Trump administration means fear. It means fellow students, friends, the very people I've shared my struggles and trials with going to school while fearing that they will lose the two-year deferral from deportation provided under the federal Deferred Action of Childhood Arrivals (DACA). It means listening to those same students explain those anxieties during town hall meetings where I feel like I can do absolutely nothing to help. It means those same people being worried about returning home to empty households; it means being stopped by policemen and security guards for not passing some imaginary, specific social quota; it means listening to men joke about sexual assault while I keep my head down and leave as fast as possible.

The Trump administration means fear for so many different reasons, and yet, I can't act like these anxieties were only born in the past two years—I know for certain that policies like DACA were only seen as the halfway point to helping undocumented people. That those people that have been deported and killed under Democratic and Republican presidents alike could care less about who was leading the country at any given moment. That Hillary Clinton has a long-standing tradition of attacking Black communities and befriending people she called corrupt on the campaign trail, and yet, having Trump in the Oval Office still amplifies all of these fears.

The Trump administration means constant vigilance. It means that I try not to stay out too late anymore and that I'm constantly watching my back. It means that my Muslim classmates have to specifically ask people not to record the things they say during student meetings for fear of surveillance. It means that my parents have told me to be careful more times in the past two years than they did for all of high school. It means taking all the precautions necessary to avoid becoming a victim: not wearing hoodies, not wearing fancy shoes, not going to convenience stores too late. It means crossing the street when I see anybody that may be at odds with me; it means avoiding walking home alone at all costs; it means making sure I never ever get lost, it means making sure my phone never dies—it means all of these things, and then some.

It means cynicism. It means desperation. It means survival at all costs. It means that the Trump presidency has made things like hope or change seem impossible, despite how much I can read or research about the ideal world I want to live in. It means not wanting to get out of bed some days.

It's still strange to imagine that years from now, long after I've left Brooklyn College and all that remains of my undergraduate experiences are memories, that the 2016 election will soil them— that all of the wonderful experiences that come with the college will automatically be synonymous with my hatred of the administration and capitalism, the history and culture of the very country I was born into.

I can vividly remember calling my mother early, early in the morning on November 9th; it was 4 a.m. for me, right after Trump was officially announced president, but only 3 a.m. for my mother. We both shed tears that night. It seems strange to have been crying over something like a newly elected president, but at the same time, those tears felt right. Like they belonged.

My mom started college around the same time that Ronald Reagan was elected president in 1980—another election that she swore she wouldn't make it through. She can specifically remember how it felt like the world was ending when he was elected, how she couldn't believe that a country could ever vote for somebody so hateful.

And even though I hated hearing about how upset my mother was when we were around the same age, in some ways, it's comforting to know that we both realized how deeply we hated our presidents at the same age. She survived her college years under a horrible administration, and I knew I would, too.

I called my mother at four o'clock in the morning, and we both cried—we cried about betrayal, of all the people who were inevitably going to be hurt by the Trump administration, of this country that has yet to love us back, but I won't ever forget what she said before I had to say goodbye. She told me that when Reagan was elected, people also didn't know how they were going to survive. And yet, despite believing that she wouldn't survive the Reagan years, it was through dancing and finding community that she learned to cope.

So maybe 40 years later, there's something to be learned from that lesson. That may be all we can do sometimes is dance and find community. Find a community of people who live on the outskirts the same way I do—whether that be through race, sexuality, gender, economic background, or country of origin. Being a college student has provided me with communities of people who understand my struggles, who wholeheartedly understand what it is to live in a country that refuses to love us back. After that, all we can do is dance and realize that no country, no president, no politician, can really save us—that when all is said and done, we must save ourselves.

Mirroring Ngin-Ngin

ALISON MEI WONG

Growing up as a mixed-race Chinese-German-American born in the Bronx, New York, my appearance often unsettled people. Strangers passing on the sidewalk would take a double look at me, their eyes deglazing from the floor, before asking, "What are you...? No, no, where are you really from?" to try to understand why I looked different. They often found it difficult to put me into an aesthetic category. I struggled to answer this question. After responding that I was born in the Bronx, and not in China or Germany, they would look satisfied, as if I had fulfilled their curiosity.

But I often began to question internally, "Who am I really?" after answering these questions. When I would share my experience with my sister, the other half-Asian in the family, she would laugh in disbelief.

"That never happens to me, and it has nothing to do with how you look—who are you even hanging out with?" she said.

"But it's not just people I know—it's random people, like the crossing guard or an interviewer for a job," I said.

"No, that just happens to you," she said.

While my father was born in Hong Kong, he has lived in New

York for most of his life. My mother, born in Queens, has been a lifelong New Yorker. There weren't many conversations discussing identity between us, but there were multiple times where I felt confronted with these questions. One time when we went to Chinatown for dinner, a Chinese tourist stopped my father and spoke to him in Cantonese, pointing at a map. My father, seeing the man, began shaking his head saying, "I don't speak Chinese" in English. The man on the street became even more flustered, shaking his head, laughing a bit in disbelief. We began walking away, and I asked my Dad why he had lied. "Just didn't feel like it," he said.

When we arrived at our usual restaurant, we were seated around a circular table, each seat set with a small white plate, a glass, and a pair of chopsticks. My grandparents called for the waiter, detailing the menu, and simultaneously, a waiter came around the table, dropping off pots of tea. Before leaving, he came to place a fork beside my chopsticks, as well as in front of my mother's and my sister's plates. While I eyed the fork, noting it as a gesture of hospitality, we would only use the chopsticks during dinner, leaving the tines as clean as they came.

During family gatherings, I felt disconnected as I couldn't communicate with my Chinese grandparents. When we were at my grandparents' house, my grandmother, *Ngin-Ngin,* as I called her, would often ask me a myriad of questions, "Alison, how's school? How are you with your homework?" All in English. But after those initial questions ended, we were held in loud silence, her eyes searching for English words, putting them into sentences, meticulously monitoring her speech to translate out the Cantonese. Following the silence, I'd run off nervously to speak to my aunt who spoke English. Years later, I wondered why I hadn't learned how to speak Cantonese or German, like some of my friends who attended Chinese school growing up. When I asked my parents why they didn't enroll me, my mom once said, "It wasn't fun. German school didn't teach you anything; it was…felt like a wasted Saturday."

Yet despite feeling different, I felt most comfortable in Ngin-Ngin's kitchen. There, I could just sit next to her in silence, watching her hands smashing ginger and flicking her wrist to churn the wok. As I watched Ngin-Ngin cook, the loud fan above the stove and the sizzling of hot oil created a white noise that comforted the silence. When we ate together at her plastic-covered dining room table, she picked up clumps of rice with her chopsticks, and I watched her chew each bite completely before picking up another. She pushed her tongue around her mouth to clean the rice out from her front teeth, and I would mirror her doing the same.

When I finally asked Ngin-Ngin to teach me how to cook, it had taken me a while to work up the courage, trying to figure out when was the best time to ask her. One afternoon, eating rice and Chinese sausage, she took the rare moment to sit down, resting her hands on the dining room table in front of her. I began pushing around the rice in my bowl, trying to pick the best words to ask her. When I stopped eating, she looked worried. "It's no good?"

"No Ngin-Ngin—it's good…I just want to know how to make it. Can you tell me?" My eyes darted from her back down to the table; I felt myself sinking into my seat.

"No—no, you don't need to learn, I'll make it for you easy," she waved her hand and laughed gently, cleaning a piece of rice off the table.

"But, I want to learn how to make it. Can I watch you cook it?" I asked again, noticing the hesitation on her face. She laughed again, standing up slowly, her elbows creaking.

"No, no, you need to study—keep reading, keep studying. It's good for you!" she said, walking back into the kitchen.

As I watched her through the door, beginning to wash the dishes, I brought the bowl up to my mouth to hide my embarrassed red cheeks. Her distinctive 'no' rung in my ears, again and again. As I finished, I thought about her hands in the kitchen, scrubbing every surface with a metal sponge, simultaneously beginning preparations for the next meal. While I felt the food my grandmother cooked connected me with her and my culture, cooking served a much more straightforward purpose for my grandparents. When I expressed my interest in learning how to cook Chinese recipes, my grandmother always pressed me to focus on my education. Food was her job; studying was mine. When I was 4, she had me follow her around the house, reciting the alphabet A through Z, and numbers one through a hundred. When I was 10, she had me solve multiplication tables before dinner. But as I sat with my workbooks in the dining room, I longed to be in the kitchen, where the sugary-salty alchemy was being prepared. Sizzling smoke would emanate from the doorway, my grandmother poised in the center of clanging and chopping. Yet despite her efforts to push me out of the kitchen, I was always drawn back, searching for the flavors of my childhood and for the culture I never knew.

As I was drawn to cooking, my mother introduced me into the kitchen, allowing me to act as her sous chef. We began with American classics, from burgers to mashed potatoes and gravy. As I grew older, I began to cook with more Cantonese flavors. I started treating my family to dinner, mirroring both my mother and grandmother in the kitchen. Having always served the family dinners, they were the ones who placed large mounds of rice onto our plates or divided out the thick, long egg noodles. Ngin-Ngin would bring out armfuls of traditional Cantonese meals on metal serving bowls with mountains of lobster and black bean sauce and Chinese broccoli in oyster sauce.

It was fulfilling for me to recreate dishes from my childhood, as I felt the act of cooking them allowed me to enter the kitchen with my grandmother in ways I never was able to when she was alive. While I understood she wanted to keep me out of the kitchen so I could focus on my studies, it was through the food I could connect with her and my heritage. I found that while I relate to my culture through the lens of food, I could also use this lens as a window onto people, a way to further understand and appreciate the multiplicity of identities. While I struggled with the mystery of my own identity in the past, I feel as if I have gone full circle as I search to further understand my identity in relation to others.

Kick It

PEGGY LOU PARDO

It was a frosty, shivery day in February on my first day at Junior High 226. I dragged my feet through the streets of South Ozone Park. This was a neighborhood filled mostly with low-income families, once populated by third-generation Italians who had abandoned the vicinity for better places in the New York City boroughs. They had left the Brown people to fend for themselves in the slummy houses they had owned.

I had been kicked out of P.S. 202, a middle school located in a zone on the opposite side of town called Howard Beach. There, the kids wore the latest trends, always clean and crispy new, but I was not cut out to blend into that lifestyle. I had to transfer in the middle of my seventh-grade school year; this filled me with a sense of shame, but fuck it, I moved on.

On Rockaway Boulevard and 121st Street, where P.S. 226 stood, the sun was gleaming off the icy sidewalks, and the kids were rowdy. Anxiety made its way through the thin winter air, right into my lungs; I felt out of breath. I made it through the sea of menacing faces, and gang-signing hands. Once in the hallway I felt safe, but I was foolish to think that I was. As I took a step through the doors into the staircase, my hair was pulled suddenly from behind, dragging me to the floor with a loud thump. I looked up at the three bearish girls hollering at me and scratching at my skin while continuing their ambush. "You ain't shit, bitch!"

"Whose you think you is?"

"Krystal says hi!"

I kicked up at their lumpy shapes with all my might, stretched my abnormally long arms and latched onto their clothes. I used their weight to pull myself up and stand my ground. I felt their punches and scratches from all angles, waves of pain slamming onto my body. I closed my eyes and swung my arms into every direction with all my strength, not knowing where my blows landed or what my hands grabbed. Somehow, my fearless showmanship made the girls scatter away or maybe it was the security guard that showed up soon after. He found me on my knees, breathing hard, with bloody scratches on my skin, and pounds of weave hair in my hands.

At the nurse's office, I muffled a cry. "Stay still; this gonna burn, child." Through my squinty eyes I could see her soft features; she had tender hands and a soothing voice, her body was plush like a fuzzy sheep.

"Who did this to you?"

"I don't know." Tears fell from my eyes. Not necessarily from the physical pain, but more from my bruised ego, and from the fear that the rest of my time at 226 would be a replay of this day.

"The only way we can protect you is if you tell us who it was."

But I had no idea who these girls were; all I knew is that they were friends with Krystal. That Latin Devil had been left with scratches and bruises after we had it out in 202, while I had walked away unscathed. This angered her, and she used her connections to have her friends get back at me, battering my body and peace of mind, but that didn't last long.

The following weeks were quiet for me in school, but the buzz of the hallways whispered that the girls who had jumped me were in liaison with The Bloods. Somehow, I never saw those girls again. I suspected they were not enrolled in 226, but instead a ring of hooligans that had broken into the building. Though my wounds healed with time, my fear did not go away. Naturally, my stance of constant self-defense fueled me to step quickly and kept my eyes darting in all directions, preparing myself for another attack.

One of the first friends I made in 226 was Damaris; she was an Afro-Latina. Since she represented both cultural groups, she crossed borders between the Latin Kings and The Bloods. I bonded with her out of my need for protection; plus, she was very popular with the boys and being seen with her gave me a sense of belonging and empowerment. One day during class she looked at me and said, "I know who those girls are."

"What girls you talking 'bout?" I asked.

"The ones that jumped you." I stared. Her pretty, round face glowing from the reflection of the sunlight coming through the window. She was much taller than me, probably about a foot; she was well developed for a 12-year-old. She wore Cross Colours gear, Air Jordan kicks, and she wore her hair natural. Her ebony curls bounced with buoyancy and framed her head like a halo, but she was no angel.

"We can get those bitches back," she said. "They won't even know what hit 'em. They are Bloods so will have to get the Kings involved." I shuddered at the thought. I was seriously afraid of being involved with any gang member.

"I don't care about those bitches," I lied. "They are so whack! They ain't even worth my time."

"Cool," she answered, as she looked down at me with her eyes, slowly nodding her head. "Yo! We gonna bounce and go smoke this blunt, you down?"

"I'm down," I said, then continued to trail behind her to the outskirts of the building.

Like many of us that attended 226, Damaris came from a broken home. Her mom worked too much to keep an eye on her whereabouts or her school progress. So, she raised herself. Gang life provided structure and definite protection, and though she was not a legitimate member, she was very well involved and knew many of the right people. Later that day I arrived home, stoned. I had used Visine and perfume to hide my shenanigans from grandma.

"Peggy, mijita, como estuvo la escuela?"

"School was good, Mamili, I had a lovely day." I stared straight into my grandmother's eyes and lied with pride.

"There is some food in the kitchen if you're hungry."

"Did you or mom make it?"

She ignored my question. "I made some coconut rice, fried fish and salad."

"Thanks, grandma." Without meaning to, my voice came out deflated, sad, and thin.

"Que pasa?" She took a pause to stroke my hair. "Your mom is at her second job; she went straight there after she finished babysitting the kids. I think it's going to be a late night for her."

"Isn't it always?" I responded with disdain.

"Common, eat your dinner." She was pacing around the kitchen, finding things to clean and organize. "Then we can study the Bible together, you need to prepare for tomorrow's meeting." I dutifully followed her desires.

It was very hard for me to turn down my grandmother's request. Her soft-spoken, loving manner always creeped into my heart and made me gush with sunlight. She was the pious tower that held our family together, illustrating kindness and unconditional love. During the weekends, we would spend quality time spreading the word of God to our neighbors or attending meetings for worship. On the other side of the spectrum, Lila or Lilita, as the family had dubbed my mother, rarely joined us for any activities. Her spiritual faith was missing, and her time was seized by familial responsibilities. That didn't surprise me; after all, she was a single mom who had suffered the razor-sharp side of love and constant male letdowns. My mom was an immigrant in a land of promise who faced hardships to get ahead, difficulties that manifested from her inability to speak the language, or her absence of finances to fit into certain social circles.

Not having a lot of one-on-one time with my mother left me feeling empty. Here I was, finally living in New York City, reunited with her after four years of her absence. Plucked from the comfort of living with my grandparents in Colombia, I was happy as a lamb on a meadow to be by her side, yet I received little of her attention. It felt as though, once again, I had been pawned off to my grandparent's keeping. Without hesitation, I rebelled. Initially, it was a silent storm, one that only rained upon my friends and enemies at school, then it slowly trickled onto innocent bystanders. Finally, it became very apparent to my family that the halo-wearing Peggy, who was often the teacher's pet, who led honor rolls in various subjects, and who could recite Bible verses, was no more. Getting into mischief was a game to me, one in which I excelled. And the more I rolled the dice, the easier it became to be a detached human being—to ignore the pain of others. My choices were the family or the streets, but all I could see was a cloud of weed smoke with my shadow cast in it. Nothing else existed.

Peer Pressure

Embracing Good Influences

WANETT CLYDE

I was the last person in my family born in Cumberland Hospital, a Brooklyn hospital shuttered by the city in 1983 despite community opposition. We lived across the street from the hospital in the Walt Whitman Houses Public Housing Projects, which together with the nearby Ingersoll Houses, was simply called Fort Greene. My parents, still teenagers in high school, were both born and raised in Brooklyn. Like many Brown children of the 1980s with very young parents, I was raised by something of a committee, its chief members being both sets of grandparents; my maternal and parental grands, descended from southern farmers in Sumpter, South Carolina; Caroline County, Virginia; Lee County, Alabama; and Henderson, North Carolina.

My mother's parents were young pre-teens when they arrived in the North, and met and married quite young. My dad's parents were closer to adulthood when they made the move north and were married much later in life. My grandfathers were Army veterans who never talked about their experiences. My grandmothers juggled raising children with work for a time. Three of my four grandparents worked in stable, union-backed positions until retirement and set store by this path. My dad's parents were savvy and managed to take advantage of the shift in housing options to secure ownership of a condo unit a short distance away, still in the Fort Greene area. My mom's parents, perhaps wary of, or unprepared, for homeownership, stayed in their double-sized project apartment, two units that had been combined for large families. Though my mom and I had briefly moved out, I spent the greater bulk of my formative years in this same unit with an array of extended family.

I was a bright student. I learned to read before I started school, beginning early my love affair with books and perhaps foreshadowing my eventual career as a librarian. But the move away from— and then back to—Fort Greene, and the trying circumstances of the return, had interrupted my fourth-grade year. A lack of understanding from my new teacher led to dismal grades for me and a long-lasting negative impact on my confidence in my intelligence. I rallied the next two years under the tutelage of teachers who, perhaps, had skills working with students in transition. These teachers made an effort to support the things I excelled at, for example, writing and reading, in a way that my fourth-grade teacher did not. But issues at home made the transition to junior high, an already dicey period in a child's life, rockier. By this time, I had a longed-for little sister, Krystal, whose safety and happiness exceeded concerns for my own. I was suffering from an exceptionally awkward period, and a shift in the kinds of life circumstances I had to deal with. My grades, and attitude to school, were affected. Again.

My awkwardness, general tendency to worry about everything and new, challenging life realities followed me to high school. I had never really regained my confidence, and I believe that the things I missed while flailing in the fourth and seventh grades left crucial gaps in my education. I was suffering from teenage apathy and dealing with increasingly difficult family issues that I kept secret from everyone except two trusted friends, YaaSmin and Maria, whose support I realize in hindsight was my saving grace.

It wasn't until twelfth grade, with a very real chance of being left back for missing gym class (incredibly stupid of me), that I finally had a class I enjoyed. My English teacher, John LaBonne, an elegant Black man who drank Evian and read the *New York Times*, who we all initially hated for his insistence on quality and tough grading of our minimal efforts, got permission to offer a film class. We read Sapphire's *Push*, Truman Capote's *In Cold Blood* and Mario Puzo's *The Godfather*. A very fast reader, I was often chapters ahead of my classmates and stayed after class to talk with Mr. LaBonne about what I'd read. We watched film versions of the last two books, the beauty of *The Godfather* awakening something in me.

My classmates with better prospects were in and out of the nearby guidance counselor's office. Those who had the grades and attractive extracurricular activities had a choice of future paths. My best friend was applying to Grambling State University, with the help of our physics teacher, an alum. I don't recall much about my meeting with the counselor, or if it even took place, but the teacher who was helping Maria noticed something was up with me and my clear lack of ambition. She managed to do what no other person in the school had accomplished in the years prior: she got me to open up about my issues at home. She was sympathetic and maybe wished she had pushed me sooner. But, it all felt like too little, too late, to me. I still loved *The Godfather*, dreamed of filmmaking, and sometimes reread the kind note Mr. LaBonne put in my yearbook, telling me he couldn't wait to see my work on the big screen. When I graduated in 1997, by the skin of my teeth and with immense joy, I vowed that I was done with school, forever. I'm happy—two years later—that my teenage conviction was all bravado.

As a first-generation college student, like many of our students today, I had to learn how to navigate the higher education landscape without much assistance. The person whose opinion held the most sway over me, my maternal Grandmother, was outwardly and vocally opposed to higher education. A member of the Jehovah's Witness faith, she was mostly motivated by her religious conviction that life was better spent removing yourself from worldly spaces and temptations. She was at least partially suspicious of ambitious, educated people, and very wary of the financial investment and entanglement with loan officers that paying for school would require. She had discouraged my aunts and uncles from attending college, and was now saying the same to me and my cousin Demone, the eldest of her grandchildren. Demone had chosen to enlist in the military, which she also opposed, based on her religious reasoning and suspicions. Meanwhile, if you recall, I, wildly happy to be done with high school, had decided to do nothing. Absolutely nothing.

When the time came for Demone to be deployed, he and I had traveled to his rendezvous point in the city and I cried all the way down Manhattan island after I hugged him goodbye. I spent most of the summer dealing with his absence and bracing myself for my best friend's imminent departure to Grambling State. I was depressed and very, very lazy. This mood persisted for a while until my mother, who I had assumed was prompted by my grandmother, forced a choice: I would do something and I would do it quickly. My mom later confided that a kind, female doctor I had seen when my sadness had started manifesting itself in alarming chest pains, advised her to make me do something to shake myself out of my stupor.

Having graduated from high school, I did not have the benefit of a guidance counselor, or other school staff, to walk me through the college application or financial aid process. And though my mother's ultimatum spurred me to action, she was unable to provide any help. Fumbling alone, I applied to, and was ultimately denied admission to, my first and only choice, Brooklyn College. My high school grades had been abysmal, to say the least. I knew so little about the admission process that this fact had not seemed like a roadblock. It seems so stunningly naïve now. Or perhaps it speaks to the great chasm in my knowledge of the whole admissions process.

Having failed at college, because applying to the one school was all I had planned for, I tried working instead. With the help of my aunt, who worked at an agency placing temporary workers, I got my first job selling AT&T's first cell phones at a table stationed outside of The Wiz electronics store in downtown Brooklyn. Later, after having made a favorable impression on the store manager, Dehomey, a young Black woman of conviction who rubbed some the wrong way with her steadfastness and demand for quality, I was hired at the store as a cashier.

It was at The Wiz where I had my "aha" moment. All of my young, Black, female coworkers were juggling work and school and dating, and even second jobs. I would frequently see them working on homework when the store was slow or overhear conversations about exams or study groups. Even as young women, they were discussing their savings goals. One coworker, Lilah, whose brothers often stopped by, manifested the kind of family dynamic and teamwork that I longed for. Our supervisor Blanca fully supported our educational goals, and scheduled shifts to accommodate our class schedules and family responsibilities. My coworkers were driven and ambitious, but also fun and stylish and interesting. It seemed entirely possible that I could be as driven and ambitious as they were. I reconsidered college.

This time I applied to BMCC, a community college whose role was as an intermediary between high school and four-year institutions. It was exactly what I needed, though I didn't know it at first. I was admitted to the school easily enough, but I still had a lot to learn about the business of officially enrolling and registering for classes. As such, my first semester was something of a comedy of errors. I couldn't locate any of the necessary identifying documents the registrar's office needed. I didn't even know my social security number. I felt deeply unsupported by my grandmother, who should have been keeping these documents safe, and had no ready answer as to why they were missing. There were mad dashes to too many city offices, inevitably with second visits, after I was always missing something. In this time before 9/11, it was relatively easy to recreate my paper identity, a luxury that current students don't have.

After all of that running around, I was told I had missed the deadline for the Free Application for Federal Student Aid (FAFSA). I didn't even know what FAFSA was. I also lost my wallet (containing hundreds of dollars) on my way to pay tuition—a devastating blow for someone determined to do everything on their own after the missing documents' debacle. I rallied, with reluctant financial help from my family, and with the first day of class looming, set about choosing classes from the meager offerings left so late in the process. I signed up for an 8 a.m. class on a Saturday morning and had all my classes on different days of the week. I practically lived on campus. I also spent a fortune on new books because the used copies had sold quickly. Nobody told me you could ask for an over-tally of a closed class. I had no idea students sold used books to each other independently from the bookstore.

Despite these hurdles, I discovered, to my extreme surprise, that I had the ability to do well. Really well. I earned an A in my stats class (a course I would never have taken if not for the lateness of my registration) and performed well enough overall to make the Dean's List. My first semester at BMCC stood out among the happiest times in my life until that point. The realization that college might be an adventure was a revelation. That first semester restored some of my confidence from those early school years when I had been in top classes and getting top grades.

That's not to say that it was all wonderful. I became quite ill at the start of one spring term. I had vomited most of the day and into the night. In the morning, my grandma told my aunt to call me an ambulance to take me to the ER because she was concerned that I was dehydrated; I couldn't even keep water down. After a bumpy ambulance ride, a male nurse in the emergency room suspected that pregnancy was the reason for the vomiting, and several tests were conducted. It turned out that I had appendicitis and required immediate surgery. I had my appendix removed later that day. Defying my family's wishes to stay in bed and recover, I managed to miss only one class that spring, taking cabs over the Brooklyn Bridge until I had healed enough to face the subway steps. There were courses I struggled through—chemistry and biology were never fun for me—and I carried my hatred for homework into my coursework at BMCC. The lack of confidence in my writing, an effect of those long-ago interrupted grammar lessons in fourth grade, made the English courses more challenging.

Above all, it was the loss of a beloved uncle Garey, who was dying of cancer that same spring, that revealed yet another way I was unprepared for the various types of communication necessary in a college setting. That semester I got my first—and only—F. It did not occur to me to share my hardship with my professors. I had a history of keeping my personal problems to myself. This learned secrecy had been necessary in the past and had become second nature. The looming loss consumed me and distracted me from everything. No one close to me had ever died before. I still had all my grandparents, a team of aunts and uncles, and an army of cousins, people I saw all the time. I was devastated for my dad, my grandma, and most especially for Demone, who was away on base and unable to be present as his father rapidly declined. My French professor, the giver of the F, was the only one to notice that something was amiss with me. I had taken a French class with him the prior semester; not only did I enjoy the class immensely, but I also performed quite well (to my surprise, once again). He was baffled and disappointed, I think, that I seemed to be elsewhere. He literally said this to me in class once; he looked at me and said something like, "You're not even here." I left him no choice but to fail me.

Back in those early days of college, I lacked the experience to know that my professors might offer me support and understanding if I shared that I felt myself flailing. Many students now are as clueless as I was then. I viewed sharing my problems as a sign of weakness. I thought they were a private matter, and also dismissed them as negative influences creeping from the recesses of my mind. I hadn't a clue that there were—are—university services to guide you through these difficulties. My French professor was already concerned about me. He had expressed that he would be understanding by acknowledging that he'd recognized that something was wrong. I can remember that class session with perfect clarity. Trying not to cry, as I looked at him, and shaking my head in small, side-to-side jerks that communicated, "Yes, there is a problem, and, no, I will not share it with you."

Later that term, I made, what was for me, an incredibly bold and out-of-character choice. After the unexpected appendectomy, and while my uncle Garey was still in Brooklyn Hospital where I had my surgery, my anthropology professor announced in class the deadline to apply for summer study-abroad programs. She encouraged us all to apply to get a feel for living in a foreign land, especially if we wanted to be anthropologists. I took the handout, and my mind started whirring. My professor, a young woman of color, was super cool, beautiful, and interesting in my view. I was riveted by her depiction of an anthropologists' nomadic life. Thinking back, I was likely imagining escaping my then-life circumstances. I was 20 years old. The loss of my uncle Garey seemed certain. I was possibly in love for the first time (and a little terrified by the idea). Mostly, I still had trouble dealing with and talking about anything that was troubling me.

I looked at the study-abroad options, marveling that they even existed. I had been a student at BMCC for nearly two years, and I had never even heard of the program. Once I decided to go, I knew I wanted to go to Africa, for I had enjoyed my Black Studies coursework. Though my family had lived through segregation, the Great Migration, the fight for civil rights and likely experienced discrimination, they did not talk openly about any of these experiences. And I did not have the wherewithal to ask. My junior high and high school principals, a Black woman and man, respectively, were both deeply invested in teaching their Brown students about their history, but I had too much going on at the time to absorb much of it. Truthfully, at our age and in our generation, many of us ignored or were bored by their efforts. I know now that a history of racism in schools, the overall effect that a lack of opportunities had on my family and my neighbors, the broad and powerful impact of drug abuse in 1980s Brooklyn, all these and more created the conditions for our apathy.

At BMCC, I began to love and celebrate that history that had once bored me. I thought I could get one of the letters of recommendation I needed for the summer program from a professor in whose class I had earned an A. I hurried over to the African American Studies office and ran right into him; I only remember his name as "Professor Clarke." I asked if he would be willing to write the letter. He asked me for my grade in his class. After smilingly double-checking in the official records, he agreed. And from there it was a race to get everything done before the deadline. Quickly, I wrote an essay for a scholarship. I counted my savings. And I dealt with my family. It's safe to say that they were less than enthused about my traveling to another country. Thanks to my aunt Harriet, I had traveled some, mostly up and down the East Coast. There were also a few summer trips to Virginia with my grandparents. Though I enjoyed those journeys, I had never considered traveling abroad. Suddenly, it was all I could think about. Faced with my first great personal loss, the death of my uncle Garey to cancer, life had taken on a "the time is NOW" urgency that I couldn't communicate.

Once I learned that I had been accepted into the program, financing the trip was the next hurdle. This last point of contention was neatly plucked out of my family's hands when I won the maximum scholarship amount, $1000, which was just enough to supplement my financial aid and cover the full cost of the course, airfare, and accommodations. My essay asked this question: could I, with my deep attachment to my family, live abroad as an anthropologist? Or, should I plan to pick up where Mr. LaBonne and my high school English class left off and major in film studies? Whatever the eventual answer would be, I was off to Senegal, whether my family liked it or not. I was excited to meet my cohort, which included a man in his 70s and many young men and women of color. Though some of my family members were eventually excited that I was going, with my paternal grandpa mostly celebrating the bragging rights I afforded him, no one offered me any financial support. I used my modest savings from financial aid reimbursement checks and work earnings to prepare beforehand and to feed myself once there.

Traveling to Senegal became an even bigger milestone than I expected. Some last-minute news almost led to me cancelling the trip. The afternoon I was scheduled to meet my cohort at the passport office, two days before our departure, I instead headed to BMCC. Through tears, I told the department's secretary that I wouldn't be able to go. She remembered my name and that I was the only one to get the maximum scholarship amount. She was sad I wasn't going to make use of it. Though she didn't know exactly what was wrong, she encouraged me to speak with Eleanor Drabo, the professor leading the trip. Professor Drabo, another of the strong women I would meet in my life, was very matter of fact with me. She told me I should go despite my concerns. She told me to complete the passport application to not foreclose the possibility of going and to let her know what I wanted to do after sleeping on it.

These two conversations changed the course of my life. Once again, it was with guidance from women that I eventually made my decision. I did go to Dakar, Senegal. I did see the Door of No Return on Gorée Island. I waded in Pink Lake with my new friends. I visited churches with all Black angels and learned to answer, "*Ça va bien, et tu?*" to locals hailing me. I learned that I was indeed too close to my family to be so far away, and experienced a homesickness so acute it made me short and snappy with many people. I cried when I got to have a short phone conversation with my sister, who I had never been so far from and who had been the hardest to say goodbye. I experienced real panic when all my snacks from home ran out and then sheer joy when we discovered a Chinese restaurant and grocery store near our hotel.

In August 2000, I landed at JFK, 20+ days after my departure, thinner, browner, and with lots of souvenirs. I held onto my sister the entire ride from the airport and wept in the arms of grandma, the skeptic. I slept for hours, and, on waking up, ate pancakes— not crèpes—for the first time in weeks. I shared my pre-trip-almost-cancelled-everything news with my family: I was expecting a baby. I was going to be 21 that October, and at the time, grateful that the timing of her arrival in March allowed me to finish the coursework necessary to earn my Associate's degree at BMCC in December. That child is now 18 years old. She has begun her own life cycle with CUNY as she awaits news about which school she will attend in the fall.

When we discussed her future, I always pushed for her to go away to college. I had, well, have, deep regrets about missing out on this experience. While I was fortunate to brush up against many people who influenced me and shaped my identity as a scholar and career woman, all the time remaining in my hometown, I still wonder how going away to college and separating from my family might have impacted me or enhanced my independence. I still want that opportunity for her, especially the confidence that that independence brings. However, I know that my choices and regrets are not for her to correct; her life is her own. I am grateful that she wants my guidance, but I am careful not to abuse her faith in me. She is very attached to our family, and her three siblings are equally devoted to her. CUNY is the right choice to supply her with a great education and to keep together our tightly knit unit.

I could never have imagined that I would work for CUNY, let alone be a member of its faculty. My journey through academia to my current position as the Collections Management Librarian at

City Tech has been one of continual self-discovery and self-actu-alization. It truly began with seeing my peers modeling behaviors that were not readily available to me. My education continued in that vein as I was fortunate to be surrounded at work with young, ambitious, energetic CUNY students who were always multi-tasking, just like my former Wiz coworkers, juggling school with work, families, and fun. Growing up, I had no near-relations in college, so there was no opportunity to see up close this life path. I was fortunate that my coworkers had been exposed to this journey. By watching them work and study and live, I realized that I could do it, too.

The ability to achieve was always there within me, but my cir-cumstances prevented me from seeing a variety of options.

Some of us need to see a thing up close to make it seem pos-sible, doable. I am grateful to the many women and a few men who inspired me, directly and indirectly. Thank you to my aunt Harriet. And to YaaSmin and Maria and Mr. LaBonne. Thank you to every woman who referred me to a friend, who recognized my name on a job application and decided to give me a chance, who championed me for promotional opportunities, and who gave me a chance to learn on the job with the safety net of knowing that to fall short was not the same as failure. I am grateful you trusted me not to squander a chance that Brown girls from Brooklyn projects with bad grades and tough lives too rarely receive: the chance to reach far beyond their own expectations and to succeed.

Living Conditions

JOSE LOPEZ

Yeah I sold drugs for a living, that's a given
Why is it? Why don't y'all try to visit the neighborhoods, I live in?
My mind been through hell, my neighborhood is crime central
Where cops lock you up more than try to defend you
I push you to the limit when I'm needing the wealth...

— Jay-Z, "Can I Live II"

More than just me living in these conditions that society constructed for people like me. My vision was slightly different than most of us, but artists like Jay-Z paint the picture perfectly. Living in low-income neighborhoods in New York City, you experience what you initially perceived as normal living. The quote clearly depicts the choices we are constantly faced with in our mission to thrive. My early memories of life start off with me, my siblings and my mother standing in the lobby of our Harlem building waiting for our three-foot block of cheese. It was the infamous welfare line, where most of our meals came from.

What was normal to us was sharing food with our neighbors and practicing the "roll off the bed to the floor" method as a maneuver to duck the constant shootouts. Paint peeling off the walls was like the late-night snack of choice, which would later turn into lead poisoning. Roaches were a constant nuisance as we constantly picked them out of the cereal. We could not afford to throw out the food; it was all we had. Random knocks on the door were mostly temporary intense moments. There was a rash of people getting shot in the eyes through the peepholes; you never just look. You had to make sure you opened the peephole first, then ask who it was. Never open the door if you don't see anyone, no matter what.

Our apartments were in constant need of repairs that would almost never happen. We normally didn't have television unless my mother had overtime or a boyfriend that helped. Christmas and Thanksgiving were nonexistent in our homes; we all relied on neighbors to gather up food resources. In my house, we almost never had a Christmas tree or any gifts under the ones we did have. I never even knew what it felt like to have air conditioning until my mid-20s, when I actually had a job.

When I mentioned my mother and her boyfriends, I want to be clear that it wasn't as if she was less of a mom. She was a great mother; she was just trying to find the right person to be with. Things didn't always work out until she actually found the man she is still married to right now. It clearly was not easy for her, raising four kids, with absent fathers, on her own. Also, the public housing system promotes poverty with its 30% of earnings method of payment. If my mother earned overtime, the rent would instantly go up, leaving no room for savings or progression. Hence, people practiced how to stay poor but still make a living.

Living with my mother was tough, but the love was always there and frankly, all that mattered. It was a constant battle with the landlords over heat, hot water issues, and repairs. We found ways to survive as she learned English and put herself through school. My father, a Vietnam veteran, was an absent parent for the most part. He was a smart man (160 IQ) that turned into a pretty boy street hustler battling PTSD. His nickname in the neighborhood was "Rambo" because of his resemblance and violent nature.

My friends and I would run around the neighborhood to find things to do, often turning to sports. We would make up games, like bean shooting wars and manhunt, with the other sections of the projects. The public housing complexes are usually divided into subsections; your friends normally came from your section or schools. The lack of resources forced us to use our imaginations, and we created bean shooters from 25-cent juice bottles with rubber bands and balloons. We would take the hard beans from our homes and play war games in the middle of the complex against the other sections.

As we grew older, we became tired of the made-up games and started venturing six blocks south into the Upper East Side. We could not believe what we were looking at! There were cafés, movie theaters, dog parks, actual parks, doormen, yellow cabs, school kids in uniforms…we had discovered a new world. As a group with no money, we began to steal fruits, cutlery from the sidewalk cafes, even the salt and pepper shakers. When we would go visit this modern park called Asphalt Green—we were in heaven. We got to play with the rich kids and compete in sports. They would leave their valuables on the ground unattended and, quite frankly, we would steal them.

One day the rich kids asked why we were stealing this stuff. "It's free in Asphalt Green for all of us." Once they crossed the border to hang out with us, at that point, they knew why and immediately felt bad for us. They saw the lack of resources and how dilapidated our apartments were and could not believe that this was the situation so close to them. One kid told us, "Mom and Dad told us never to come up here; now I know why, but that is not fair.

Sorry you guys live like this." I explained to them that I even have people in my family that will not allow my cousins to come visit me here because they were told the same thing.

They saw for the first time what a crackhead looked like, what was a drug dealer, an abandoned car, crack buildings, and even violence. They asked, "Where are your parks and why don't your basketball courts have rims?" We showed them how the community put money together to fix our own parks and how we painted the basketball courts ourselves. We showed how the community filled with Blacks and Latinos was forgotten about. No community centers; my elementary school literally fell apart during a snowstorm.

The buildings we lived in were disgusting; we took our Upper East Side friends inside. We showed them the "crackhead staircase" where the fiends would do their drugs and use the bathroom. We told them never to walk over here with slippers because of the loose needles all over the place. We did have the "graffiti staircase," which was filled with amazing art murals that depicted our stories on the walls. They loved the artsy staircases, but that was the only thing my friends liked about our buildings.

Most of us did not get past ninth grade and did not have critical thinking skills or enough mathematical skills. Half the kids in the community could not read. Needless to say, the kids from the Upper East Side were shocked, but also grateful for what they had. Some were actually embarrassed about their "White privilege." The one thing we had in common was sports; that's how we got along, although in the shadows, as they technically were not allowed in East Harlem.

There was a time in my life when my grandparents offered to raise me in their home. It was a large, three-family home that my grandparents bought in the 1960s. It had everything, a three-car garage, seven bedrooms, a basement, four full bathrooms and a backyard. One level of the house was twice the size of my family's modest apartment that was home to six, sometimes seven, people. That was a place far from perfect but full of love, religion, and togetherness: family was everything to my grandparents. My mother's heart sunk when the offer was made because the decision was in my hands. I just couldn't. I felt like I would be abandoning my siblings and, most importantly my mother.

My grandparents went to church often and celebrated all the holidays. On Halloween, the house was turned into a haunted house. Thanksgiving was filled with family and tons of food. Christmas was a spectacular event where my uncle would literally dress as Santa Claus in the middle of the night and place the gifts under the tree. They had huge New Year's parties in the basement and Easter egg hunts in the spring. The family was the perfect reflection of American sitcoms during those times. They would often say to me, "We are not rich; we are just a normal family." What they did not understand was that to me they were rich. I do not think they fully grasped the situation I was living in.

The mornings were always filled with all types of food for breakfast. My grandmother would wake up at 4 a.m. to start the cooking. My grandfather would go to the deli to pick all kinds of cold cuts and fresh bread. The table would be set up with eggs, bacon, deli meats, bread, cereal, coffee and orange juice. It was like a picnic for me every morning in that house. While breakfast was being consumed, my grandparents were already preparing dinner and snacks for later.

This did not exist in my mother's home. Breakfast was often eaten at school at 6 a.m., and we weren't sure where our snacks or dinner would come from. You opened the fridge in my home, and it was almost always empty. My friends would often joke about that, hence my first nickname of "Flaco" (Spanish, for skinny). We would almost always eat corned beef with white rice and french fries. Needless to say, we ate a lot of processed foods, as opposed to the more organic meals served at the home in the Bronx.

Everyone in the Bronx home went to private schools and graduated from college with no less than a bachelor's degree. All my cousins and aunts have gone to college and graduated. They all had decided on careers and set their paths before they even left high school. They attended Pace University, Rutgers University; some joined the military or went to nursing school. My family members are teachers, principals, accountants, corporate business members, military officers, hotel managers, mechanical technicians, and medical professionals.

In the late 1980s and early 1990s, that house had computers to teach the kids how to type and use the new technology of the time. That was the first time in my life I saw the home personal computer. In my neighborhood, the only computers we saw were in the principal's office. We had to operate a sort of trade-and-barter system to get some of that new tech in our homes. In all honesty, that trade-and-barter system existed in the shadows of the illegal trade of drug dealing. The only way my Bronx family knew how to get these things was through work and education. They did not fully understand the disadvantages I was dealing with, living in public housing.

SCHOOLS

Like most people in my public housing complex, me and my sisters did not see college as a full option. Most of us thought college would be a blessing, like adding gravy to the turkey. My sisters and I honestly did well in school, but college was more of a pipe dream. It did not exist in the reality of our thoughts. Our schools lacked the resources to cultivate a successful mindset; it was always about doing the minimum to make sure we got a diploma. Our schools did not prepare us for college. The schools I attended were often under budget. They could not afford to hire a math teacher or supply textbooks.

Our schools were more like prison training, to be honest. There were metal detectors and police officers in the lobbies. Before you could enter, you had to be searched and have your bags scanned. The outside of the school was surrounded by gangs, looking to recruit new members, trying to get us to forget about school. *"There ain't no money in there, little homies, look at my pockets, they phat. We your family, we gotta stick together. Dem white teachers don't give a shit about you, for real. Ask my boy right here how he doing since he joined the family. We run the city. Fuck all that bullshit in there."* The teachers in my school were often intimidated and constantly threatened; many left the school crying and quit. Some teachers did resist and did the best they could to help us succeed with limited resources.

The sad fact was that many of my classmates disappeared over the course of my four years in Monroe High School. We started with a class of 300 students. Over the summer, some were arrested, others were killed over neighborhood beefs, and some just dropped out. Many of my classmates dealt drugs to help support their families. Often times in the open in front of the school staff. Our sports program was the only thing that worked well. Monroe High School has the top public school baseball program in the city. Many of our players went into professional leagues and top collegiate programs.

The sports program is the only thing that kept me in school. If I did not make that baseball team, I do not think I would have graduated. Coach Turo demanded our best in the classroom first; the field was always secondary. He knew the disadvantages we had. Coach always told us, "Baseball is the way out for many of you guys; stay focused. If you do not do well in class you cannot play. If you do well in class and play hard, I will make sure you go to college no matter what."

Towards the end of my high school education, the school was struggling financially. We had no textbooks and were understaffed. We did not have enough math teachers or counselors, but we did have enough security guards. There were no senior trips. Prom was literally at a local bowling alley that the students had to pay for. We paid for yearbooks and photos that we never received. There was no money for books, trips, teachers, computers, or SAT preps. The funny thing was that the baseball program magically received a $30 million donation. It was for equipment, field upgrades, and new buses for traveling.

Fortunately, the coach actually cared about the students, so he made sure to pump some of that money into a new building. It had modern tech installed and afterschool programs to help students graduate. When graduation finally came, out of 300 hundred students from my class, only twelve of us graduated. Only four of the twelve would go to college; all four of us played a sport. When I finally started college, I was lost. I did not have the skills to survive at St. John's University. I was too scared to go away to school, so I eventually ended up in Borough of Manhattan Community College. Still, I was lost and ended up on academic probation. Then 9/11 happened and I decided to leave school for a while.

The lack of resources and education put me and many of my classmates in a difficult situation in college. Going to math class and trying to figure out what a fraction is was depressing. Other students and professors would say, "You should have learned this in high school." I did not have a math teacher for two years, so how could I possibly know about fractions. After a while college was a source of depression. I was lost. I would call my high school classmates, and they had the same issues. At the end of the day, we knew we were set up to fail.

Without college sports to play, we were done. Most just took jobs and quit. Some of us are still friends and are in constant contact. A couple of us are finally in college and are having some kind of success now, but we were robbed of our youths and time. What should have been done years ago, we are now doing in our 30s. The Upper East Side friends already have their careers; some are about to retire. They have families, houses, condos, cars, and a decent work-life balance. They attended schools like U Penn, NYU, Columbia, SUNY, and CUNY. They had the resources and the preparation needed to succeed.

Just like my family members that were raised in the suburbs, they had free SAT prep classes, critical thinking skills classes, afterschool tutors, and volunteer programs that helped further them along in life. Most had pre-calculus math and an intro statistics class in high school. Their schools even taught them how to drive and manage their incomes. Senior trips were free. Yearbooks were given and built to last. Their proms were held in the school, making them free to attend. All their schools had connections to major universities that gave students a pathway to higher education. Before they graduated, they all took aptitude tests to help them find their passions and skills sets. Most of the students knew what they wanted to do and how to do it.

LIFE PATHS

Growing up, I was big on sports. It provided me an outlet to get away from issues I had at home. We always had football, baseball and basketball tournaments against other housing projects. These tournaments were really important to us. It gave us a sense of importance. We were the "hood" celebrities. The people that funded our teams were often the "drug crews" from the area. They would supply uniforms, food, and sometimes transportation to other boroughs. Those were the times when most started to look up to them as our role models. It was almost like a predetermined path that we follow in their footsteps. I credit most of the hustlers for actually trying to push us away from that life, hence the sports teams and leagues. As I entered high school, the influence from the sports pushed me to play in school. I got to play top-level baseball in school and college for a while. It was the best time in my life and the reason why I finished high school and entered college. Then, unfortunately, I was hurt playing football and had to leave school because of the injury.

After I left college, I started to work as a stock worker at P.C. Richard and Son. I was learning how to survive on my own, as my mother had left the apartment to me. Things were ok, but I did not have a college degree or any other meaningful skill sets. I did well enough at work to earn a promotion to sales. That was it for me: my success had finally come. I was going to make a six-figure salary, but then I got injured. I visited the doctor's office and was told that I needed surgery and that I would not be able to work.

That was one of the lowest points in my life. How was I going to be able to pay my rent? Eventually, I would fall behind in all of my bills, not able to pay for rent, cable, credit cards, or phone. Most of my closest friends at that time were hustlers (code for drug dealers). They knew about my issues and wanted to help. Me knowing I had a large family, with some of them doing well enough in life to be able to help out, I asked. Not one offered me help. My grandparents had just passed away; if they were still alive at that time, I would have gotten their help.

My mother had just started a new life and was not financially stable enough to help. My father always was absent and did not offer to help, either. The only people that helped were the neighborhood hustlers, my childhood friends. That said, it's hard for me to say this, but so I began my path in the drug trade (marijuana). I had no choice. I was going to lose everything, my home and my independence; at 25 years old, my life was in jeopardy. So, like many living in situations like mine, I had to learn how to hustle.

> *I had to hustle, my back to the wall, ashy knuckles*
> *Pockets filled with a lotta lint, not a cent*
> *Gotta vent, lotta innocent lives lost on the project bench*
> *What you hollerin'? Gotta pay rent, bring dollars in...*

— Louis Resto, Jay-Z & Eminem, "Renegade"

I struggled every day, living like this; I felt like I was betraying myself and not upholding my values. Over time, I simply got used to it and started to succeed financially. The irony is that hustling taught me a lot about managing people and money. It also was a life full of stress and violence. I never thought in my life I would have to learn how to be tough and be willing to do what was necessary to protect myself. Thank god, I never had to pull a trigger as some of my colleagues had to. I did have to deal with the police department raiding my home and destroying my property. I was not even charged with a crime. They came into my home on someone's word. I couldn't understand why the police were in my home. I was not selling crack cocaine. I could not afford to sue the police department after this incident.

This path I took could have been avoided completely, but I was not given much choice. I kind of chose to walk a thin line, not trying to get caught up in the "game." I chose to keep it simple and work for myself, away from any gangs and organizations. My friends were in similar situations and viewed things much the same way I did. In a way, this raid was a blessing in disguise; it showed the authorities that I was not a gang member or part of any criminal organization.

There was a tradition in my community. If you got your door kicked in, you were officially a part of the community. Many doors in my building have scars from the many break-ins executed by the police department. Often for the most minor of charges, most times on hearsay from the people called informants. Who were frequently criminals themselves trying to stay out of prison. Many of my friends and neighbors would eventually be arrested by the federal government. Most were charged under the federal RICO law targeting organized crime. That was a total lie as the only organization involved was friends and neighbors living in similar circumstances.

I vividly remember the day my aunt asked me to pick her up from work. She had been under a tremendous amount of stress at work and could not handle the culture being cultivated there. My aunt started having health issues from the stress, so she had to make a choice. She consulted with my family members at home and they all agreed to band together to help her financially. They convinced her to quit and take as much time as she needed to get right. They gave her everything she needed—food, shelter, a vehicle, and much more.

I looked at this situation and said to myself, "What happened when I got hurt at work? I didn't get this help." I never spoke about it to them, but it hurt me deeply. I was forced to choose another life to survive until I was healthy enough to work. I did not have the luxury of recovering under the familial umbrella; they left me to figure it out on my own. Until this day, a few years later, they are still supporting her.

My affluent side of the family would often do this for others as well. They would help their colleagues from work, letting them live rent-free until they could recover. Even my sister, who grew up in their home, would be allowed to finish college without work; they would take care of her children and their needs while she earned her degree. The choice I made to live with my mother and not them was the turning point in my life. It's not fair because I am still a Lopez, the last Lopez carrying the name.

I would never regret living with my mother because she did the best with what she had. I could not help but wonder, was this some kind of I-told-you-so thing where they wanted to show the benefits of me living there. Within my own family, you can see this trend where those with more resources will always help. When I was talking with one of my family members who had lived in the house, she brought up how better I would have been if my mother or I had chosen to leave me there. She said I would have had access to better schools, the best clothes, religion, and connections within the family.

I wanted to ask her, "Why did you choose not to help me, anyway? It was like you were waiting for grandma and grandpa to die, just to prove some point." It was hard hearing that from a family member considered a part of my nuclear family. She even acknowledged that we have family that takes full advantage of their "White privileges," actually marrying into white families to further distance themselves from their heritage. Even the more upper-class family members, deliberately keeping my cousins away from the city, that was done to create a wedge between the lower-class part of the family and the upper-class side. The perception was that we were a bad influence.

The friends I have grown up with from the Upper East Side were experiencing the same ideologies from their family as well. The creation of this idea that we were a bad influence. Not once did people think that maybe they would be the influence that we needed—giving us an example or a better path to success. As they continued into college, our friendships would fade away. The opportunities they had created that separation. We were not afforded those opportunities. Our reality was vastly different from theirs.

People would never understand that no one wants to actually sell drugs or commit crimes. We all wanted to be like *The Fresh Prince of Bel-Air* and find our Uncle Phil. We had dreams of college and success beyond our neighborhoods. We just did not have the support from family, friends or the community. The paths we chose were not predetermined; they were chosen out of necessity. Like many authors and musicians would say, "We want to do more than just survive; we want to thrive." The problem is we needed to find ways to survive first, so we could then begin to thrive.

This is true for all people in America; we all want to thrive. The significant difference is the resources we are given. If we all had the proper support systems in place, believe me, no one would choose to commit crimes. It sounds funny but look at the movie *Trading Places* with Eddie Murphy and Dan Aykroyd. The premise was to prove that any person can succeed if given the opportunity. The plot had some other issues, but the point was proven that your environment is often the reason behind your decisions.

Like many of my friends, I ended choosing a path that was available to me in my environment. We had to play the cards we were dealt. Those who did make it out would forget about us left behind. Our environment was a constant competition with everyone trying to outdo the next one. My friends from the Upper East Side lived in an environment where one person would help lift the next person, and so on. If you had a good job with a company, you would always say, "Hey bro, we are hiring. I'll put in a word for you, I got you." When you needed help in my neighborhood, the famous quote was, "Yo, I got you bro. I'll get you a pack. You know, get this dude to put on the clock, get that money" (code for "sell these drugs, it's your way out").

Like my affluent family members, my friends from the Upper East Side would go on to college prepared. They got their careers, their marriages, their homes, cars, and kids. Most of us are either in prison, just out of prison, working some dead-end job or just going back to college. These are real-life examples of what advantages and disadvantages look like.

References

JAY-Z. (1996). *Can I Live II.* Reasonable Doubt. Priority Records & Roc-A-Fella Records. D&D Studios, NYC.

RESTO, Luis, JAY-Z & Eminem. *Renegade.* (2001). The Blueprint. Def Jam Recordings & Roc-A-Fella Records. Baseline Studios, NYC.

Dogana

SAMRAH SHOAIB

"I need to talk to you."

"Okay?" I responded. "What is it?"

She was sitting at the kitchen table, staring at me. Normally, she would be chopping up onions or boiling the rice, or doing one of the million things she did in a day. I hardly ever saw her sit still. She looked...hesitant. I could feel her question coming.

"You...and that girl. Your friend. What's going on between the two of you?"

"What do you mean?" I said, knowing exactly what she meant.

"Something doesn't seem normal about your relationship with her. It seems...unnatural."

"There's nothing going on between us," I said. "Stop asking me weird questions."

"This is so fucking good," she said, with a mouthful of daal.

"Oh yeah?" I was surprised. I had spent the larger portion of my life avoiding my mom's home-cooked daal and roti. "I'm just glad we could figure out how to feed your vegan ass in this house."

She looked at me and giggled. Her eyes sparkled as she did.

They were brown, slightly lighter than my own, but still dark enough to be called brown. I knew that laugh; it only came out of her when she was her happiest…more specifically when she was eating.

"Ro-thi" she said, emphasizing the second half of the word way more than needed.

"No, it's roti," I said.

"Rodi," she repeated, while scrunching up her face as if that was going to help. She was wrong, she was even eating it wrong. She took the spoon, scooped up some daal, and gently placed it on a piece of roti.

"Are you lesbian?" This time around I didn't see the question coming, mainly because I didn't even know that my mother knew the word lesbian.

"What's wrong with you? Why would you ask me that again?" I could feel myself getting defensive. "I already told you that I'm not. She's just a really good friend, okay?" I stormed out of the kitchen.

I wasn't angry, just afraid that the truth would spill from my mouth.

My mother is the most resilient person I know. She spent her whole life giving and getting nothing in return. She spent scorching Sunday afternoons in Liberty Bazaar bargaining with angry men. She spent weeks campaigning for my father's election. For both his elections. She once drove all the way across town to give a man medicine who came knocking on our door, asking for help to save his father because he couldn't afford the medication on his own.

She told my father that she would do anything and go anywhere to educate her daughters, that she would leave the city on her own if he wouldn't leave with her. Her kindness was her resistance, but she was often just reduced to being a really, really good cook.

I once heard this tale of these indigenous women from Rajasthan, India. Around 1973, the government had ordered that all the trees surrounding their villages be taken down. These women refused to give up the only home they knew. They refused to, yet again, let the land get harmed for colonial reasons. So, when the men arrived with their bulldozers to take down the trees, these women prepared a feast for them. They told them that they should eat before they took up such a hefty load of work. The men happily agreed. While they were indulging in the feast, the women started to slip away, one by one. Without drawing any attention, they started hugging the trees and, when it finally came time to bulldoze them, they were being hugged by every woman in the region. The men couldn't get themselves to do it. They couldn't bring themselves to hurt the women who had just fed them, and so they left.

I still laugh at the pettiness of it all. I'm still amused that only Brown women would use guilt-tripping to start an entire movement. These women resisted through their kindness and food. The Chipko movement was not only a conservation movement but also a feminist uprising that allowed these women to keep their communal land since Western ideas of privatized land ownership didn't allow many women to own property. It was also a gentle reminder that no one can truly own this land.

"Sooo, I wanted to talk to you about the conversation I had with my parents," she said. "Okay?" I replied.

"I was talking to my dad, and it came up that your parents don't know about your sexuality. That really surprised him. He assumed that your parents knew because I'm always sleeping over. He also asked me why they didn't know, and I told him that it's because your parents are religious. He got kind of concerned about that."

"Why's that?"

"You know…things you always see on the news and stuff about what religious parents do when they find out that their kids are gay. They're just concerned about both of our safeties."

I looked at her. I could feel the emotions coming, but I couldn't quite figure out if I was just angry or sad or both.

"You think my parents are going to hurt us because they're Muslim?"

"NO. I didn't say that. Neither of us did. They're just worried, and they would've been regardless of what religion your parents are. It's not really about your religion; it's about how religious they are."

"That logic doesn't make any sense." I could feel myself getting louder, "Your dad is a fucking pastor."

"You're taking this the wrong way. This conversation wouldn't even be happening if your parents, whether they are religious or not, knew. The fact that they don't, red flags for my parents," she responded.

"You think my mother doesn't know? Do you think she's stupid? Just because I haven't come out to her doesn't mean shit. She is very aware of what's happening in her house. Do you think that my mother would be making you food every time you came over if she wanted to hurt us? Because you best believe that she's known about our relationship. It's a shame. You have your liberal-ass parents who have their PhDs, and they still think my parents are savages. And then you have my father who is driving a cab every day to make ends meet. You think he came here to be looked at this way? You come over every day to such a welcoming environment and you have the nerve to say that my parents would hurt us? And I get it. Your parents might be concerned, and your safety is all that they can think of right now. But what the fuck is your excuse? How dare you not evaluate your own Islamophobia?" I was sobbing at this point.

"I don't think you realize what you're saying right now," she said softly.

"You're not going out."

"What? Since when do you tell me not to go out?"

"I have been asking you for a month. A MONTH to clean out your room so we can move all your furniture to the other room. You know I don't have any time before your dad, and I move to Pakistan, and you're not helping at all." She started getting louder, "I am so sick of it. You're badtameez. You don't listen to me, and you think I'm a maid who's only good for cooking. I don't know what your relationship with that girl is, but I'm sick of you putting her before your own family. I am your mother."

"JUST LEAVE ME ALONE. I'm so sick of you saying the same thing over and over again. There's nothing going on between us!"

"It's so obvious. You spend all your time with her. And you... if you keep this going, you're going to Jahannam. You hear me?"

We were sitting in a Chinese food restaurant just a few blocks from school.

"You seem down," Muntaha said, while fixing her hijab. She

had recently started wearing it again. She stopped after that guy threw hot coffee on her last summer.

"I feel like a bad Muslim. I feel like I'm going to hell. I love being gay, but I don't think God will love me for being gay," I said.

"Don't say that. You're a good person, and God doesn't hate you. He has no reason to," she replied.

"I just don't know what it means to be Desi, Muslim, and queer. I don't know if any of it is worth it. I can lose my entire family and community over this…and for what? Some college relationship?"

"I know, it's hard being Muslim and queer, and it's not fair that all these annoying ass white kids get to walk around with accepting ass families, while we can't even come out to the people we love the most. When in fact, they're the assholes who colonized us and instilled homophobia in our communities. Besides, you're technically doing the Lord's work by avoiding men. They're all trash."

The anxiety is getting to me, but I don't let it show. I hand her the matching duppata with her outfit. She is dressed in a burgundy salwar kameez with gold trimmings and dark green stones. She looks beautiful.

Today is Eid-ul-fitr, marking the end of Ramadan. All my relatives are coming over soon, and I have invited my girlfriend over to celebrate with us. It only seemed fair after I spent Christmas with her family. My nerves are getting to me. What if they find out that we're together? What if I slip up and call her "babe"?

My mother comes into the room and tells me that my dad is asking for us. She then tells my partner that there are some vegan-friendly things to eat in the kitchen. We leave the room and my dad hands me money as my Eiddie. I smile and give him a hug. He turns to my girlfriend and hands her money as well. He then proceeds to pat her head. She looks at me with confusion, wondering why he is touching her head.

"It's cultural," I whisper. "He's giving you his blessings."

The gathering is slowing down, and we both manage to escape. Today is also Pride, a day we had been looking forward to and we are now planning to go to a party in the Lower East Side. We are wearing shorts and crop tops and no longer in Desi attire.

We walk into the party, and I see my friends. I begin walking towards them while taking in my surroundings. I see my mentor dancing with his friends. There's a moment of awkwardness after we see each other, and then we smile. I wave at him. He's unapologetically queer, Black, and beautiful. I look at people sitting in the corner, and I realize that my professor is sitting there with her wife. She catches my eye and waves me over. I begin walking towards her. Suddenly, Palestinian music starts blasting and the men in front of me start doing Dabke. A Desi woman approaches me and hands me a sticker that says Hot Queer Asian. I look at my girlfriend and laugh.

She gently holds my hand. "Eid Mubarak," she says.

I smile. "Happy Pride."

My Mask

JAVIER RIVEROS

Myself, might I ask…
Why would I wear such a mask?

In hopes of playing the part
before reality spotlights the start.
As I am numb on command
and laugh for display,
personality be betrayed,
My mind projects its fictions at hand.

However, the sincerest always floats,
even when the sun is diminished,
and the warm, summer day is finished
as I scratch and scribble these notes.

Herein lies the truth
within the wrinkles of this book, I decree:
We are who they want us to be.

And that is the story of my youth.

Tears leave me, soothed.

ORGANIZING AND ACTIVISM

Systematic Seesaw

LISA DAZZELL

Race in America is one word:
A seesaw
In order to keep you up
We must be down
No alternating positions.
No

        balance.

The

        working

                order.

(In)Visible Freedom

THE THEATER FOR SOCIAL CHANGE

The Theater for Social Change is a project of the College and Community Fellowship. The performance text of *(In)Visible Freedom* was written by Teronia Campbell, Selina Fulford, Katherine Sweetness Jennings, Yolanda Johnson-Peterkin, Denise McFarland, and Edna, in collaboration with director Nina Angela Mercer. The play was performed at the Martin E. Segal Theater, The Graduate Center, on Thursday, October 25, 2018.

Note on the Production of *(In)Visible Freedom*

GRACE M. CHO AND ROSE M. KIM

(In)Visible Freedom is an original theater piece collaboratively produced by the College and Community Fellowship's Theater for Social Change and Autoethnographies of Public Education and Racial (In)Justice research team, which we led as part of the 2017-2019 Andrew W. Mellon Seminar on Public Engagement and Collaborative Research at the Center for the Humanities at The Graduate Center, CUNY. The interdisciplinary seminar sought to promote the public humanities by bringing together academic and wider communities around topics of pressing social importance.

To help create this original work of autoethnographic reflections on public education and racial justice/injustice, the research team enlisted Nina Angela Mercer, a doctoral fellow of theater and performance at The Graduate Center, to work with the theater ensemble composed of CCF alumnae. The women met regularly over a year to create this piece which debuted at The Graduate Center's Martin E. Segal Theatre on October 25, 2018. Robin McGinty, a doctoral student in earth and environmental sciences at The Graduate Center, served as documentarian for the project.

In a sense, this project was a long time in the making, dating back to our days as sociology students at The Graduate Center in the 1990s and 2000s. CCF was then a fledgling organization housed in the office of the Center for the Study of Women and Society. One of us (Grace) had the privilege of working as a graduate student fellow with CCF from 2000 to 2002. When considering potential partners for our research projects, we remembered the important social justice work being done by CCF and its roots in

The Graduate Center.

Back then, the Center for the Study of Women and Society was under the leadership of Patricia Clough, one of our professors. She did something methodologically and pedagogically radical in sociology at the time, which was to encourage students to write autoethnography. In Patricia's words, autoethnography's "aim is to give a personal accounting of the observer, which is typically disavowed in traditional social science writing... It does this by making the ethnographer the subject-object of observation, exploring experience from the inside of the ethnographer's life" (2000, p. 16).

While not all uses of autoethnography are radical, she taught us to engage with it as a practice of decolonizing knowledge production, and simultaneously of giving legitimacy to our own lived experiences. This idea resonates with one of the central questions posed in *(In)Visible Freedom*: "Who's telling my story and are they telling it right?"

We hope that this project not only adds depth and nuance to the kind of data that are typically collected in studies of race, public education, and incarceration, but also privileges these women's telling of their own stories as the most valuable form of knowledge production.

References

Clough, Patricia. 2000. *Autoaffection: Unconscious thought in the age of teletechnology*. University of Minnesota Press.

Preface

ROBIN MCGINTY

Words like Freedom

There are words like Freedom
sweet and wonderful to say.
On my heartstrings freedom sings
All day everyday.

There are words like Liberty
That almost make me cry.
If you had known what I know
you would know why.

— Langston Hughes ("The Panther and the Lash," 1967)

Recalling the blues sensibility of the poet Langston Hughes's "Words like Freedom" as an articulation of the dialectic of freedom and unfreedom, *(In)Visible Freedom* is a project birthed from the intimacy of pain and joy, of loss and struggle, of mourning and salvation embedded in the aesthetics of radical hope and aspiration. Hughes's poem invokes a sharp distinction between freedom and liberty as a nuanced riff on the tensions and contradictions inherent to both freedom and liberty in the guise of a mournful sorrow song. As a performance, *(In)Visible Freedom* foregrounds the stories of formerly incarcerated Black women that are in part, shaped by the prison and its afterlife as the peculiar arrangements of freedom and liberty. The lived experiences of the College and Community Fellowship (CCF) women who make up the Theater for Social Change (TSC) are grounded in a vernacular that expresses the ways of knowing and attending to the world. In much the same way as Hughes does, *(In)Visible Freedom* summons us to contemplate our own conceptualizations of freedom and liberty.

Traversing the spaces of the historically marginalized, traditionally bound up somewhere between omission and erasure, *(In)Visible Freedom* offers compelling autoethnographies that unsettles the discourse of mass incarceration, its genealogy and processes. At its core, *(In)Visible Freedom* are the narratives of memory and meaning-making that contextualizes a *humanness* steeped in the familiarity of a space said to exist between "a rock and a hard place."

In offering the interconnectivity of these relations as intimate, violent and complex, the narratives of the women also do the work of disrupting dominant understandings of knowledge production. Thus, in reproducing memory as the repositories of specialized knowledges, *(In)Visible Freedom* stands in testimony of the intersectionality of prison and its afterlife, race and gender, systemic punishment and structural dispossession. Simultaneously, the narratives deriving from *(In)Visible Freedom* reflect struggle and resistance in negotiating the carceral conditions of the prison's afterlife in the face of what is held and remembered. In centering the narratives of formerly incarcerated women, *(In)Visible Freedom* provides an intervention that contests the utility and mechanisms of omission and erasure.

COLLEGE AND COMMUNITY FELLOWSHIP

Struggle has been a part of my life and my community since the beginning. I am never far from struggle, never far from applauding it, from talking about it, and making sure we never forget that struggle has been a part of humanity.

— Nikki Finney ("So I Became a Witness: An Interview with Nikki Finney," 2012)

Since its inception at the CUNY Graduate Center in 2000, the overarching mission of CCF has been to provide supports for formerly incarcerated women pursuing higher education. As it stands, it is the only organization in New York City exclusively devoted to women returning home from prison, as well as those women who are currently justice-involved in prioritizing the attainment of a college degree. To date, CCF reports "students have earned 327 degrees (including a PhD and a JD), achieving cohort graduation rates up to 93% and a 16-year recidivism rate of .06% (compared to 40% for New York State overall)."

As a reflection of the historical desire of newly freed people to be educated, CCF enjoins a timeless yearning with the urgency of now. Long committed to the idea that engaging in higher education is one of the most effective means of reducing recidivism, CCF women are also leaders in a growing network of advocates for criminal justice reform. This ever-expanding network includes grassroots activists who seek to privilege the voices, knowledges and experiences of formerly incarcerated persons in the nation's public discourse vis-à-vis the phenomena of 'mass incarceration' and its myriad of related issues.

THEATER FOR SOCIAL CHANGE

"The blues is an impulse to keep the painful details and episodes of a brutal experience alive in one's aching consciousness, to finger its jagged grain, and to transcend it, not by the consolation of philosophy but by squeezing from it a near-tragic, near-comic lyricism. As a form, the blues is an autobiographical chronicle of personal catastrophe expressed lyrically."

— Ralph Ellison (*Living with Music: Jazz Writings,* 2001)

As one of CCF's earliest initiatives, the Theater for Social Change performers are an ensemble of CCF students and alumnae who write and perform for a wide range of audiences across the nation in venues that include prisons, college campuses, and churches; they have also collaborated with other community-based organizations to create work that provokes a re-thinking of the life experiences of formerly incarcerated women, community and meaning, aspiration and struggle. TSC uses performance as a medium to make visible the chronicles of catastrophic policies that have disproportionately impacted poor and working-class African-American and Latino communities. It is no secret these same communities have borne the brunt of the devastating impact of nearly a half-century of mass incarceration, which has resulted in a pernicious form of socio-economic disenfranchisement and discrimination as a marker of what many deem a form of "second-class citizenship."

Thus, the blues lyricism of the TSC ensemble resides in the telling of the stories which function in such a way as to negate and transcend erasure by omission, fostering a departure from the trope of despair—and instead, positing the personal narratives of radical hope and aspirations we as the formerly incarcerated hold for ourselves, our families and our communities. In the same manner of what scholar Alexis Pauline Gumbs describes as the "shapeshifters and survivors," TSC's *(In)Visible Freedom* can be imagined as the testimonies which acknowledge and honor our memories—and our truths.

they ask me to remember
but they want me to remember
their memories
and i keep on remembering
mine.

— Lucille Clifton *("why some people be mad at me sometimes." The Collected Poems of Lucille Clifton 1965-2010)*

Director's Note

NINA ANGELA MERCER

Theater for Social Change: (In)Visible Freedom is a collective meditation on strategies for greater justice, and the never-ending work of getting more free. In this collectively devised performance piece, TSC shares experiential knowledge and critical analyses specific to the cultures of incarceration, violence, and social control that challenge our positionality in relation to freedom. We encourage our audience to nod, shout a praise, or word of agreement, as TSC shares stories of kinship, struggle, and celebration. This is for all of us.

At the beginning of the process of creating this theatrical performance, TSC decided to read *When They Call You A Terrorist: A Black Lives Matter Memoir* by Patrisse Khan-Cullors and asha bandele as a way to deepen critical analyses of systems of social control that impact our lives on an intimate and broad scale within a racialized, gendered, economic, and historical context. The book gave us a solid jumping-off place to consider qualitative research and self-reflection as tools for telling multiple autobiographical stories indelibly impacted by incarceration, re-entry, and the role of various experiential knowledges of freedom. We rooted our writing processes in autoethnographic prose and poetry while also centering various theater-devising techniques to create the actual performance.

Central to our creative exploration was the practice of "courageous conversation." Each time we met, we sat at a table as a sisterhood, often over a meal. At this table, conversations flourished. These courageous table conversations were steeped in the blues and its "call and response" aesthetic. So, it felt organic to bring that same raw honesty into the actual performance. We also wanted to maintain the political urgency of our current contemporary moment and found ways to highlight the external factors challenging individual lives, despite the progress inherent in re-entry and education, as well as significant personal and communal advances. Furthermore, we wanted to be sure to incorporate a "call to action" into the piece to encourage hope, continued work, and personal accountability in the struggle toward more fully actualized freedom.

Still, this is a work-in-process. We are still uncovering layers and learning, allowing the work to lead us into its next iteration. And we are excited to share this current version of *(In)Visible Freedom* with you all. We hope that your experience of these stories will lead us into a rich conversation that sparks new possibilities.

(In)Visible Freedom

By Theater for Social Change

Though the stage is dark, we hear a recording of "I Am My Sister's Keeper." The lights rise, and we see the women from **Theater for Social Change** *sitting scattered about the stage in chairs, looking at the audience.* **EDNA** *and* **YOLANDA** *rise from their seats and take positions center stage.*

The music fades down. **EDNA** *and* **YOLANDA** *are speaking to each other and the audience.*

Edna:

Freedom.

Yolanda:

It's more complicated than just getting out.

Edna:

It is a political act.

Yolanda:

It means taking up space.

Edna:

Daring to create, resist, and speak truth to power.

Yolanda:

But what does freedom look like?

Edna:

And how do you hold onto it once you get it?

Yolanda:

It's not so simple. Sometimes it seems invisible.

Edna:

Like a figment of our imagination, just slipping through our fingers.

Yolanda:

But I know it's mine.

Edna:

A state of mind, just like bars can be sometimes.

*The lights rise to illuminate the entire performance space, revealing all of the **women from TSC** sitting in chairs. As each **woman** speaks, she stands until all are standing together.*

Selina:

It's a constant struggle we can't give up.

Teronia:

Always pushing us to take up space, own our truth.

Denise:

Telling our own stories.

Katherine:

Telling our own lives.

All of the women take a seat on the stage, except *Edna*, who stands center stage.

Edna:

Can I / Dare I, speak this out loud?

Teronia:

Go on! Speak it.

Edna:

It was so long ago, but…I believe it all impacts the trajectory of my life / OUR LIVES!! Or maybe not. I don't know.

Will I ever know? Will we ever know? Shit, is it now necessary to know as it's done!?

I never really ever spoke it out loud. We never did.

All women:

Now's the time!

Edna:

When I was a child, I always thought there were too many restrictions placed on me, always felt I was not allowed to be free to be me…

As I grew older and became a teen, I not only thought there were too many restrictions, I thought there was an actual conspiracy against me that would not allow me to be free to be me…

As a young adult, I was quite clear that the conspiracy to stagnate my ability to be me was nothing but my mother, the woman who birth me. I was sure that she did not love me or care that I just wanted to be free to be me…

So I did everything I could to get away from the force that I felt stagnated my ability to be free to be me…

Running away, I had the unfortunate opportunity to be free to be me before I was fully prepared…

I did not realize her need to protect her child. I certainly didn't understand her desire to safeguard her teen. And as a young adult, quite frankly, I didn't need her opinion or approval!

Years passed and I grew older. I was fortunate enough to survive the world, unprepared for its response to me being free to be me…

Somehow, some way, I returned back to the mother, the conspiracy, the woman who gave me life, and found that she was waiting there with open arms. A loving force that only wanted the best for me, always…

I was blessed to return to that same opportunity that I ran away from so many years ago. This time, I felt as she watched me grow emotionally and spiritually. She continued to be protective, however, it no longer felt restrictive. At times, I still believed there was a conspiracy; however, I knew the depths of it to be derived from a love like no other. It was at those times that I truly appreciated her.

She now protects and watches over me from above. Before leaving this world, she had found that I had earned the right to be free to be me…

Yolanda:

But freedom still ain't free…

Katherine:

We are still seeking a better life, still seeking that elusive freedom. But now, the restrictions are social controls in a country carrying the same underlying, subliminal messages, which include hatred, segregation, and exclusion just because we're different from the traditional source of "power" in this country. These forces create a defamation of so many Black women's lives.

Edna:

It's undeniable. Everything is uncloaked to the point that we can fully see them—there are no blinders, no way to avoid the truth!

The only way to make things change is to be the change—commit to the process of change.

Let's BE CLEAR! 45 has led a chaotic and uncompromising climate for all of America; but especially those of us who are not white, straight, and male!

And his election was NOT an accident; it certainly wasn't happenstance that he was elected to the position of Commander-in-Chief, after the service of one of the greatest leaders this country has known.

We all know that Mr. Obama was a slap in the face to the establishment— NOT ONCE BUT TWICE, HAHA!! And some felt the need to get us back at the risk of losing a nation!! That's some scary shit, right y'all!

I mean, look at what has been done—A reality TV star has become the leader of the free world—*(sarcastically!)* yeah, free world!

Katherine:

We as a movement MUST continue to work to change the narrative somehow!! We must remember that the society continues to be shocked at our resiliency. We have withstood all that they have thrown at us!

Yolanda:

Heroin in the 60's/70's.

Denise:

Crack in the 80's/90's.

Katherine:

Removing Pell grants from prison to keeping us binded, keeping us blinded, and keeping us shackled.

Edna:

YET HERE WE ARE!! HERE WE WILL BE...TOGETHER, SISTERS GETTING MORE FREE EVERY DAY.

Edna takes a seat, and Yolanda stands center stage.

Yolanda:

I used to sing a beautiful song...
Once education is obtained, we find it hard to get a up from poverty job
You dangle education and make it hard
You mangle information to keep me confused
Was it you that stifled migration to make everyone lose?
Oh, let's not forget that you pay me much less
Your real goal is to keep me in debt
You hate me—yet—if it looks like I'm winning—you stand by my side.

Yolanda sings Stanza 1 of Abby's song.

Yolanda:

Don't you care that I already live in sorrow and pain
I am constantly riddled with my own heartache and shame
I had no idea of the lifetime of pain—that I had caused
It's an open wound with no healing or gauge

The pain never goes away it's just sometimes placed on pause
I try to relieve it every chance that I get
I am clear that I'm somewhat to blame
Oh, but not for it all
You charted this course so I would take the fall

I used to sing a beautiful song.

Yolanda/Edna sings second stanza of Abby's song.

Yolanda:

Was it you that stifled my voice?

Yes—you did it not even bothering to give me a choice

I certainly did not walk down this alley by choice!

Do you want to come and walk in my shoes?

Don't look at me like that,

Believe me, I tried really hard to fight back—

Three college degrees later I got educated

My voice is now tailored—it's spirituality that keeps me fighting this war!

Yet you make sure to remind and condemn me wherever I go

Hey, I want you to know that your treatment of me is a continuous sin +++

We see you clearly perpetrators of pain, lurking and twisting all for your gain!

**She said it was rape, since he was a Black man he went to prison

But when the white man was accused those in power made a different decision!

They said if I hum…

Yolanda/Edna sing 3rd stanza of Abby's song.

Yolanda:

They-they—who? Oh, yea, that's right! They is YOU.

I know you think that I don't have a clue

Although it's been years since I've done something wrong

You press that button of oppression every chance you get

To watch me suffer again and again,

You did it

You targeted generations

You took my grandfather

Took my father too

Then 1 of my brothers

You skipped my mother

Then you got me

But oh—oh you were not done yet you took my prize possession

You encaged my son

Yeah…I guess you think you've won!

Denise *makes her way to center stage.*

Denise:

I am an African-American woman who grew up in the sixties. I am the fourth oldest and the first girl of 10 siblings. When reading this memoir, *When They Call You a Terrorist*, a lot of uncomfortable memories and feelings came rushing back to me. It was like reliving my life again. I mean, there were moments on the bus when tears would start flooding down my face uncontrollably. It was really me reliving each and every second again and again. So, I can identify with Patrisse. Is she telling my story and is she telling it right? When Patrisse referred to her father being on drugs and being a three-time loser, I thought of me and my son. We both picked up four felonies while selling and using drugs. Who's telling my story and are they telling it right?

Katherine:

Talk about it.

Denise:

If my son or I ever return to crime and get convicted, they would sentence us to five years to life. I am so grateful that he is living a crime-free life after all those years of dealing with the prison system. You know, I remember having a conversation with him pertaining to people close to you dying when he is locked up, too. A prime example is his father passing away while he was completing a six-year sentence, and three years in. My son was denied the opportunity to get closure and say his goodbye. Although he pretended that it didn't bother him, I knew it did. My son and his father had a close relationship when he was younger. He spent plenty of nights at his great-grandmother house where they bonded together. However, as my son got older, he wanted to follow behind his mother—Oh yeah, that's me.

Teronia:

Tell your story.

Denise:

I was very young when I had my son—pregnant at the age of sixteen, and gave birth at the age of seventeen. You know I thought I was grown, being the oldest girl and babysitting my siblings. I felt I would be able to raise my own child, which really wasn't true. I wasn't ready at all. Only if I would have lived my life differently by staying in school and getting my GED and asking for help when needed. It took me going upstate twice before I said enough and it took me 33 years later before I obtained my GED/AS 2006 then in 2008 BS.

That's my story, my road to freedom. And I'm still on it.

*Denise sits, and **Teronia** stands.*

Teronia:

I'm telling my STORY,

And I'm worthy of my dreams

I thought I was unique

I was abandoned at the door

Where is my biological father?

He didn't look back and where did he go

He didn't take me to the park nor did he push me in the swing

My little sibling's father was there

   "Sometimes"

I was jealous and I didn't care

But he insisted, so I started to try

He bought me a cute little teddy-bear

   BUT

Then the touching and fondling came

 I wasn't the same

I couldn't tell Mama, I thought she thought he was chocolate cake

Mama worked hard

Dressed and fed four kids

Always working and going to school

She took care of us and showed us love

   BUT

A part was still missing

I felt disregarded by helpless father

I was left alone, I didn't feel whole

Although Mamma love did her part

I felt my father betrayal, uncared and unloved

So I branched out

Looking for love in all the wrong places

I found drugs in the beginning it took away the pain

At the end, it was dark, cold, wicked and was a vicious cycle without my permission

What a shame?

Who's the blame

Jail became an option

I went there several times and then I was offered a program

Best thing that ever happened,

I was institutionalized for 25 months and was being rehabilitated

During that treatment, I got a chance to share, there were a lot of me-too moments

I wasn't alone and I accepted the fact that my father wasn't there

I talk and talk and went to therapy

I began to Heal.

Denise:

We can heal.

Teronia:

I came home and was introduced to education through CCF.

We all returned to school, so I followed the path.

I found a sister circle of inspiring women—

Theater for Social Change.

AND WE All drop THE PAIN

AND finally that moment came

It was like a dream come true

I WALKED ACROSS THAT STAGE TO RECEIVE MY BACHELOR'S

and MASTER'S DEGREE. It felt like heaven.

BUT

PAIN still remains,

People suffering from mental illness

Doing time because they weren't medicated!

So they lock them up and throw away the key.

This system is upsetting

As I continue to stand tall and try to help all

I will continue to teach and preach, encouraging everyone to talk about their feelings,

Tell your story, your truth,

Because, guess what? YOU will find out that you not alone.

Learn to heal so you can deal and help someone who's on that wheel.

Katherine *stands and hugs* **Teronia**. **Teronia** *takes a seat.*

Katherine:

Short story, long story—everybody has a story.

But who's telling my story? And are they telling it right?

Today I am telling my story.

I have had a full life. Full of laughter and pain.

I want to say you don't know my story. I wish I could say you don't know my story.

However, the truth of the matter is my story has been told for years by both men and women, free and incarcerated. And now, most recently, you can hear echoes of my story inside a book that declares Black Lives do Matter.

Am I implying the absence of a father figure in my life caused me to make poor decisions? And, can I live a productive life with a void in my soul??

Am I implying the lack of education of my parents being viewed as a deficit left me without a role model, making it more convenient for me not to be a college graduate?

I think I am implying those things.

Having a baby before I graduated from high school, leaving home before I had a job; I was not able to obtain or maintain employment. Had no one noticed how broken and neglected this little girl was?

Let me tell you about one defining moment—November 1991, I arrived at my destination and was intercepted by the police.

"Oh God!!! How shall I survive this ordeal?" was my thought?

1991—I was arrested in a courtroom outside of the United States, sentenced to four years of prison, to work for pennies, and be subjugated by others who look like me, while perceiving me as a threat to their existence.

Has this atmosphere been designed to correct or punish?? Can anyone survive or thrive in this atmosphere? Would college mend the hurt of this broken little girl waiting for her father to return to her to make everything ok?

My mind spoke loudly—higher education is the key to your freedom.

And I stand before you strong and confident. I managed to find strength in the trauma of giving birth at the age of 15, before I could successfully take care of myself. The healing has begun.

No more seeking the approval of a father in a society that views me as an object, not designed for greatness, but a pawn to be used, abused and disposed of.

Don't sleep on me beloved!!

I have used my energy to defy the odds by enrolling in college, to keep a promise I made to myself several years ago back in third grade before my dreams became an inconvenience to others. I attended college to be an example to my two college-educated sons. I stayed there until I completed it in spite of my ignorance of living in a country with citizens who have to be told our lives matter.

Those barbed wires and cement walls you erected for me, could not hold me, nor shall the other devices you have constructed be a prison for me. I have come from broken to blessed, from trauma to teachable.

It has been said, "When the student is ready, the teacher will appear." This access to education has shown me liberation and Freedom.

In spite of your negative labeling, and oppressive constructs stemming from fear and arrogance, I rise.

Those boxes you put on a housing or employment application, can't stop and won't stop me. I shall check the box that allows me to identify myself as courageous, resilient, sensitive, informed, capable and intentional. Don't sleep on me!!

And don't waste any audacity to forget or even deliberately not invite me to a table where injustice/equality issues are being discussed **for I decree there is no table, or discussion to be had about us without Us.**

Katherine takes a seat, and *Selina* rises and walks to center stage.

Selina:

Black Lives Matter! An old story for a new generation. A generational story. It's Patrisse's story, and it's Asha's story. It's Harriet Tubman's story. It's Angela Davis's story. It's Cynthia, Carole, Addie Mae and Denise's story—The four little Black girls killed in a church bombing years ago in Birmingham, Alabama.

It's even Viola's story, the only white woman killed by the Klan because she felt that Black Lives Matter. Then, and now today, it's Heather's story—another young white woman killed at a white supremacist rally in Charlottesville, Virginia.

That same old story.

Well, it's my story now. It's our story. The same old story.

I think it's time for us to rewrite our story. We must change the narrative, the language, and the authors of this story. We will rewrite our story, and its new title will be a human story, a story of love, compassion, and understanding. Justice for all of humanity.

Let's take the wheel people, and stop being passengers in a vehicle of hate. Let's drive our vehicle with love as our guide. Let's right these wrongs. We are all in this together. So, let's not be divided. Let's join our hearts in love. Let us rise as a band of people, inviting all that is good and just. Let's speak words of kindness and justice.

I know, I know…I know what you are thinking! Rewriting our story is not going to be an easy task. But guess what? We can do it. I believe we can uproot the roots of hatred deeply rooted in our society, and start planting new seeds that will grow new roots, roots of love and compassion for one another. We can do it one person, one family, one community, one nation at a time.

A human story—that's our story. And we are sticking to it.

Tonight, I am inviting you to stand with us.

Stand up for the good inside of us all, stand up for change, stand up for Humanity.

TSC continues the call to action for the audience until all are standing together.

SOUND: "I Am My Sister's Keeper" reprise.

= The End =

AFTERWORD

Singing My Story, Singing My Truth: Coming to Voice through Song

ABBY DOBSON

Singing is like breathing and music is like medicine in times of turmoil and war. Singing is at the root of how I choose to be of service as an artist and global citizen. While I love to sing alone, it is a privilege to do so with and for community. In October 2018, I had the pleasure and privilege to share an abbreviated version of a workshop series I created with a group of fierce Black women participants in the Theater for Social Change. A voice-based empowerment workshop, "*Singing My Story, Singing My Truth: Coming to Voice through Song*" was created for Black women and girls. It is a workshop that seeks to help facilitate the revelations, healing and joy that owning and sharing one's story through creative expression and song can bring.

The workshop recognizes that creating music based on one's own story is a form of self-care. It hopes to help create brave spaces with participants through singing, storytelling and active listening to discover and recover our authentic voices powered by our own stories, knowledge, and dreams. It is my hope and intention that each woman in this sister circle uses it to create and perfect some of the tools she needs to be restored and empowered, starting with her voice, her breath, her experiences, her intentions and her dreams for a better world beyond and without all forms of violence against women, including poverty, sexual trauma, racism and mass incarceration, to name just a few.

Last October we sang "I'm Worthy" together. The melody and words were created to soothe, inspire and heal. It was written to encourage us to have empathy for ourselves as Black women and girls. "I'm Worthy" is a song of affirmation and a tool for empowerment through song. It was created to remind each one of us just how valuable and valued we are.

"I'm Worthy"

I am beautiful
One of a kind
A special someone
A treasure to find
I am holy
A gift to this world
I am worthy of all my dreams

The world can test me
My spirit won't die
Try to hurt me
But I will survive
Some tried to break me
But I'm still alive
And I'm worthy of all my dreams
Yes, I'm worthy of all my dreams

I will fight
For what I believe
You are not alone
you can count on me
I'm my sister's keeper
I know her pain
No matter the cost
I'll say her name

"This Isn't Going to Work"

Barriers to Higher Education for Welfare Recipients in NYC

CYNTHIA TOBAR

INTRODUCTION

"Case closed." Seeing that stamp on my file at the Human Resources Administration office sent a chill down my spine. I had just disclosed to my caseworker that I was accepted as an undergrad at Hunter College. While normally this would be cause for celebration, my caseworker informed me that by choosing to accept a seat at Hunter I would no longer qualify for the welfare benefits that were sheltering me and my son. As a single mother looking for a better future for my family, the alternative of accepting benefits, along with a workfare assignment of scraping gum off subway platforms, was unacceptable. Instead, I chose to rack up student debt and rely on part-time jobs and food stamps to make ends meet while in school.

College students on welfare face stark choices. They are coerced to choose low-skilled work with no long-term economic benefits over a college education which can propel them and their families out of cyclical poverty. This substantially undermines fair and equitable access to higher education, chipping away at the promise of college for students receiving welfare. People enduring hard economic times should not have to choose between their everyday survival and their hopes for a better future. Too many are stuck in no-win situations that compromise honest attempts to improve their life chances. This chapter explains the history of the current situation and highlights how student activism at CUNY has pushed back against these punitive measures while also arguing that more needs to be done by policymakers to make an effective case for correcting a train of exclusions, prejudices, and hierarchies that adversely affect college students in the welfare system.

Today's dire situation is rooted in the rise of punitive welfare reform policy in the 1990s at the federal, state and city levels that had a direct effect on access to higher education for welfare recipient students attending the City University of New York (CUNY). This policy was enacted in 1995 when the city instituted the Work Experience Program (WEP), which required welfare recipients to perform unpaid labor for the city. WEP was created in tandem with the 1996 Personal Responsibility Work Opportunity Reconciliation Act (PRWOR), the federal welfare reform legislation turning welfare funds and jurisdiction primarily over to individual states, which President Bill Clinton signed into law, making good on his 1992 campaign promise to "end welfare as we know it." The law's aim was to discourage illegitimacy and teen pregnancy by denying benefits to mothers who had additional children while on welfare and mandating work requirements within two years of receiving benefits to promote individual responsibility. Hundreds of thousands of people were removed from the welfare rolls with no guarantee of employment training or education. At CUNY, enrollment of welfare recipients fell from 28,000 in 1996 to 7000 in 2000 (Weikart, 2005, p.421) as students dropped out to fulfill workfare obligations.

POLITICAL ORIGINS AND THE RISE OF PUNITIVE WELFARE REFORM

The political changes in the decades since the 1960s have led to increasingly unfavorable policies for poor students. Gary Berg (2016) indicates this is due to two public misconceptions about poor students: (1) that "their position in society is a result of a combination of inadequate talent and flawed values"; and (2) "that individuals are primarily responsible for changing their condition" (p.119). These incorrect assumptions open the door to value-based arguments where some will speak about college as a place that is not appropriate for everyone, while diverting attention away from the immediate source of concern which is that poor students are not given the same level of access to higher education. These two beliefs limit social mobility and maintain deep class divisions within higher education, fulfilling a "self-maintenance tendency," which ensures those who are elite will continue to enjoy privilege (Berg, 2016, p.143).

In the 1980s, as a backlash to liberal social policies of the 1960s, conservative rhetoric surrounding race, gender, sexual deviance, fraud, family breakup, and community disintegration came to dominate discussions of welfare and Black poverty (Gilder, 1987; Murray, 1984). This fueled stereotypes and images of Black women as "welfare queens," a term infamously coined by President Ronald Reagan, which dominated public and political discourse that pushed for legislative changes to social welfare policy, beginning in the late 1970s and coming to fruition in the 1990s (Nadasen, 2005). This socially conservative discourse shifted blame onto the victims of systemic, historic oppression and racism, claiming that by focusing on structural explanations for poverty, liberals had steered social policy off course, causing the state to distribute economic opportunities and rewards outside the marketplace (Gilder, 1987; Murray, 1984).

In 1988, drawing on socially conservative views of the minority poor as cultural outsiders who avoided work and had children out of wedlock (Gilder, 1987; Murray, 1984), Reagan began to make a case for paternalistic social programs designed to regulate the behavior of the poor with the Family Support Act (FSA). This was the first time a welfare policy demanded that mothers with young children work, yet it made allowances for welfare recipients to attend four-year colleges (Weikart, 2005, p.420). However, the 1988 FSA mandated job training for every state and shifted the emphasis to work (Weikart, 2005, p. 420).

In 1996, Clinton, under pressure from an empowered Republican Congress, eliminated these programs and instituted Temporary Aid to Needy Families (TANF), that set a five-year, lifetime limit for recipients receiving federal welfare benefits and requiring states to value "work first" without accommodating those who wished to go to college. The emphasis of TANF was to reduce caseloads by ensuring that poor recipients did not turn welfare into a "way of life"; there was no mention of pulling them out of poverty or helping them to achieve a higher quality of life (Bok and Simmons, 2002, pp. 218-219). This was bolstered by a significant policy shift to the right that deemphasized the importance of education to skills-building training and towards prioritizing a strong work ethic as a "cultural value" amongst the poor (Shaw, 2006, p. 35). In effect, TANF limited higher education to one year of vocational education, yet it allowed states the option of offering limited access to college and gave them free reign to interpret what that type of access could look like (Weikart, 2005, p. 420).

This welfare backlash in antipoverty public discourse amongst policymakers began to target social policy focused on children and family, unfairly stigmatizing single, female-headed households.

Kenneth Neubeck and Noel Cazenave (2001) indicate that even the semantic rewording surrounding welfare policy, from Aid for Dependent Children (ADC) to Aid for Families with Dependent Children (AFDC) demonstrates the emphasis was on the provision of a "suitable home," despite an applicant's economic need. In fact, ADC provisions during the 1960s were contingent on the recipient's marital status to qualify for aid, as K.J. Neubeck and N.A. Cazenave (2001) explain:

> One of these rules denied aid to children in situations where "the mother associates with a man in a relationship similar to that of husband and wife, and the mother, her children, and the man live in a family setting regardless of whether the man is the father of the children." The second rule forbade aid to children when the "mother maintains a 'husband-wife relationship' and the man continues a relationship with the children similar to that of father and child, even though the man claims to be living at an address different from the mother's address. (p. 101)

In short, these two rules outlawed any type of out-of-wedlock "husband-wife relationship," which reflected "a preoccupation with controlling the alleged sexual immorality and supposed preference for welfare over work of one group: African-American females" (Neubeck and Cazenave, 2001, p. 4). Bok and Simmons also point out that one of TANF's main directives was to "end the dependence of needy parents by promoting job preparation, work and marriage...prevent and reduce out-of-wedlock pregnancies; and encourage the formation and maintenance of two-parent families" (2002, p. 218). Even though the critique focuses on the implicit racism of welfare policy, it is also evident these rules were implicitly sexist and heterosexist, unfairly stigmatizing single female-headed households.

UNEQUAL ACCESS TO PUBLIC HIGHER EDUCATION

Many people have strong opinions on the issue of welfare, either demonstrating their full support of or opposition to social programs aimed at reducing poverty, hardship, and inequality. Given contentious debates of who is deserving of a higher education within our society, it has been difficult to develop opportunities that promote open dialog between supporters and opponents of welfare reform. This section will consider how this has had a detrimental effect on welfare recipients' access to higher education in New York City, especially for CUNY students.

After PRWOR was enacted in 1996, many states curtailed support of higher education and instead emphasized workfare programs due to mandates that permitted no more than 20% of their clients to fulfill work requirements through educational activities that included pursuing postsecondary degrees (Pearson, 2007; Weikart, 2005). This was the result of TANF, which was implemented in tandem with PRWOR, and limited benefits to a lifetime total of five years (Weikart, 2005, p. 416). Under TANF regulations, only one year of postsecondary education was allowed; vocational education was prioritized; and, states were ordered to have 50% of welfare recipients working by 2002 (Weikart, 2005, p. 417). In this high-pressure environment to fulfill workfare quotas, offering the four-year time investment of higher education fell by the wayside.

Race was also a critical factor when examining trends on how this policy was applied nationally. This is an especially conspicuous factor because African-Americans never comprised a majority of those who received welfare to begin with, constituting only 35% to 46% of TANF recipients between 1969 to 2001 (Edelman, 2004, p. 392). Not all states responded favorably to welfare recipients who wanted to attend college, but the states that did also established additional strict mandates, such as not allowing classroom hours to count toward satisfying the workfare requirements, enacting brief time limits for completion, demanding that recipients maintain certain grade point averages, and/or requiring students to pursue a prescribed list of occupations and college programs that theoretically would lead to immediate employment (Weikart, 2005; Abramovitz, 2003; Bok, 2003). The statistical results of such punitive social policy was staggering: by 1998, college enrollment among welfare recipients declined 20% nationally and at some four-year colleges decreases for this group culminated as high as 77% (Duquaine-Watson, 2007, p. 230).

While 49 states and the District of Columbia chose to continue to permit postsecondary education as part of their approved job training activities, access to such programs was also limited in a more insidious way. Since procedures, which varied state by state, were put in place so that welfare recipients who wished to pursue a college education had to fulfill specific mandates, a large amount of power was placed with individual caseworkers who would interface with recipients. Caseworkers determined who could be allowed to enroll in degree programs, determined which of those programs had a likelihood of leading to employment, and decided what counted as "satisfactory progress" as defined by federal and state guidelines (Pearson, 2007, p. 724). A. F. Pearson (2007) detected that case managers were choosing to enforce workfare versus assisting students to pursue the college education they desired because the latter would entail a longer investment of time; case managers, who viewed immediate employment as mandatory, widely considered a college education a "luxury" (p. 743).

This perspective was compounded by the fact that case managers themselves were low-paid clerical workers with conflicting beliefs around who was deserving of an opportunity to pursue a college education. This frequently resulted in case managers resenting welfare recipients who applied for cash assistance, benefits and housing since they themselves were struggling in high-stress social service jobs that lacked the same benefits (Pearson, 2007, p. 743). All this serves to highlight the contentious power dynamics between caseworkers, who have a wide latitude of discretion in the implementation of workfare requirements, and welfare recipients, who are in a more vulnerable position. Michael Lipsky (1980) proposed that the very nature of how caseworkers interact with their clients translates to how policy is interpreted and enacted at the ground level, which is sanctioned within governance structures that oversee social policy. As such, policy implementation is shaped by "street-level bureaucrats," which include caseworkers who have a degree of discretion in how they carry out their functions.

Such policy-shaping activities have been described by K.B. Smith and C.W. Larimer (2017) as using a "bottom-up" approach that puts an emphasis on the behavior and choices of implementers" (p. 176). From the "bottom-up" vantage point, real policy implementation occurs only when those on the periphery, the caseworkers, are actively involved in its execution (Smith and Larimer, 2017, p. 176). These tensions play out while case managers negotiate cultural definitions of "work"—promoting jobs over education, discouraging welfare recipients from pursuing higher education and unwittingly perpetuating gender, race, and class inequalities (Pearson, 2007, p. 724).

This pushback by caseworkers was prevalent despite the benefits a college degree can provide poor, working-class students, a student population that CUNY has long sought to serve. CUNY has long been influenced by a strong commitment to public access to higher education, a spirit that is prevalent among its faculty and student body and emblematic of dramatic demographic, social, economic, technological, and political shifts in New York City (Fabricant and Brier, 2016). In the 1990s, 26,000 CUNY students relied on public benefits; 90% were women (Price, 2003). A 2003 study by the Howard Samuels Policy Institute of CUNY surveyed 158 single-mother college students who were on welfare in New York. Their findings reported that one hundred percent of these former welfare recipients who earned four-year degrees stopped relying on public-benefit programs, compared to 81% of those who got two-year degrees (Price, 2003). More than ever, given the current demands of the job market, recipients who live in poverty can move off welfare and secure meaningful employment with a livable wage once they attain the skills and credentials of a college degree. These findings support the strong correlation between access to education and a family's economic stability.

In 1995, under Mayor Rudolph Giuliani's administration, New York City instituted the Work Experience Program (WEP), which required welfare recipients to perform unpaid labor for the city. WEP was created in tandem with PRWOR legislation turning welfare funds and their jurisdiction primarily over to individual states. In a 1999 study for the city's Parks Department, over 20 current and past Parks employees and outside experts agreed to be interviewed and provided much of the information included here. According to the respondents, the city gave welfare recipients menial work assignments, with no guarantee of employment training or education, and at worksites far from their schools, which made it difficult for many to continue their education (Weikart, 2005; Cohen, 1999).

The situation became worse for welfare recipient students in 1997, when in response to the passage of TANF, New York State

Governor George Pataki proposed the Welfare Reform Act, which divided welfare recipients into two camps: (1) Family Assistance, which provided public assistance to families with children; and (2) Safety Net Assistance, which was established for needy persons who were not caring for children. This legislation was typical of the hostility demonstrated by the city to any form of education for welfare recipients under the notion that "more emphasis on education would mean less emphasis on work" (Weikart, 2005, p. 425). Other examples of this hostility by the Giuliani administration in the 1990s included the city conducting sham assessments and automatically assigning all persons to workfare; its refusal to allow workfare sites to take place on college campuses, which was in violation of New York State Law; and ignoring proposed plans by CUNY officials to incorporate workfare for welfare recipient students (Weikart, 2005, p. 425). The city had even gone as far as to impose workfare assignments on 19-year-old welfare recipients in lieu of them attending high school (Bodack, 2000).

The hostility towards supporting higher education for welfare recipients as enacted in this social policy took its toll at CUNY, where enrollment of welfare recipients fell from 28,000 in 1996 to 7000 in 2000 as students dropped out to fulfill their workfare obligations (Weikart, 2005, p. 421). According to Melinda Lackey, who then was an intern researcher at the Howard Samuels Policy Institute, "these students were targeted as the most able-bodied population that if put into a workfare program might give the workfare program good numbers and have it look successful" (Tobar, 2012). In exchange for giving up their studies, these students were offered workfare positions which consisted of working for the Parks Department or the Sanitation Department. This training was deemed work in the real world, but students were typically given menial assignments such as cleaning bathrooms (Keiser,

2004; Tobar, 2012). For these former college students, the work experience was not propelling them out of poverty, but instead pushing them into a dead-end workfare assignment that came at the expense of their education (Weikart, 2005, pp. 422-423).

As captured by Vanessa Lyles' experience as a student welfare recipient, compliance with WEP threatened to end her pursuit of a four-year degree at CUNY. Born and raised in the Bronx, her father was a musician who worked maintenance jobs to help support the family. Her parents nurtured Vanessa and her siblings in their love of the arts. She had a happy upbringing before her parents split up when she began high school, with her mother simultaneously going back to college. She followed her passion for art and music throughout high school but did not go to college right away. She became a single mother and could only pursue her two-year degree when a few years later, she got a job at the New York Technical College, which offered her tuition reimbursement. Vanessa pursued her studies there and excelled before she got married. Later, she had her second child and subsequently divorced. At that point, she decided to go back to school to pursue her bachelor's degree at Hunter College while on public assistance. As Vanessa, then 47, explained:

> When I was on public assistance, they were like, "What do you want to do?" I said, "Well, I'm going to go back to school." And they looked at me and they were like, "Oh, okay, so you're going to go get a two-year degree." I'm like, No, I'm going to get a four-year degree." And they said, "You can't get a four-year degree on public assistance." "Can't? Why not?" You know, what is that about?
>
> And, I started to read. And, like, I'm entitled to go to school, and I'm going to go to school, and I'm not going to go to a two-year school, I'm going to go to a four-year school. And, I think at that time—yeah, I did, I had my associate degree already from New York Technical College, and

I was going to go to a four-year school now. So they were like, "Well, no, you can go and be a home health aide, or you can go and get a clerical position. These are the things that you can do." And they had a list of positions that I could have, like, kind of on a sheet. I'm like, "Well, this isn't going to work." (Tobar, 2011a)

In this excerpt, Vanessa depicted the message communicated by her caseworker, which was contextualized as discouraging her from pursuing a four-year degree. As noted earlier, caseworkers have been identified as playing critical roles in how minorities have historically been marginalized in welfare programs before the 1970s (Katz 1989; Lieberman 1998; Piven and Cloward 1977; Pearson, 2007). During the 1990s, state and local governments gained more discretion in the implementation of welfare policies with waivers granted by the federal government along with the passage of PRWOR in 1996. Keiser (2004) points out that the race of an individual client may affect the interaction the client has with "street-level bureaucrat" caseworkers who have a tendency to favor clients who resemble themselves and discriminate against those from different class or racial backgrounds (p. 316). Race influences and structures public policy to such an extent that Black welfare recipients report lower levels of caseworker support for formal education than do White welfare recipients (Keiser, 2004, p. 316). This, in comparison to WEP, highlights the impact institutional policies and caseworker practices had in excluding thousands of welfare recipient students from college in New York City. Next, I will present how the Welfare Rights Initiative was able to achieve two of the policy recommendations listed above in New York City, by establishing itself as an on-campus advocacy center and expanding the work activity definition, effectively increasing access to higher education for welfare recipient students.

STUDENT ACTIVISM AND ADVOCACY AT CUNY

It is essential to note the impact that the student activist organization Welfare Rights Initiative (WRI) had through a tireless lobbying and coalition-building campaign to change punitive New York State welfare policy (Weikart, 2005, p. 426). I was introduced to WRI towards my senior year at Hunter and was an active student-participant in their advocacy efforts. In 2011, I decided to return to WRI and collect interviews with the founders and participants in order to document their role in advocating for equity in higher education. Formed in 1995 at Hunter College, WRI's mission was to help CUNY students on public assistance remain in college; it served mainly as an information and advocacy hub for students to become aware of how social policy choices were affecting their chances at higher education (Tobar, 2012). WRI evolved from its beginnings as an awareness-building course to an overall community leadership program. Dillonna Lewis, co-executive director of WRI, witnessed much of this change:

> I think in the early years of WRI, it was about training students to be more involved. Not so much that students started off being involved. With the students, it was a first-time experience. One of the things that I realized is that when someone comes to you, before you say, 'Here is the ticket, get on that bus and go to Albany and advocate for your rights,' you have to make sure that students feel confident and prepared to self-advocate. If someone can't feed their kids, and I don't feel empowered, they won't feel eager to jump on a bus to Albany […] I always tell students, 'We don't give you strength. You don't come to WRI and we give you a voice. You always had a voice, but it's just that now you can see different ways to make your voice more effective. (Tobar, 2011a)

WRI leadership soon realized, however, that educational out-reach alone would not be enough to address the struggles students were facing. "These students were targeted as the most able-bod-ied population that if put into a workfare program might give the workfare program good numbers and have it look successful," according to Melinda Lackey, founding director of WRI (Tobar, 2012a). For these former college students, this type of "work" ex-perience was not going to propel them out of poverty.

WRI began to hold strategizing meetings during their annual retreats and soon realized that the key to affecting real change re-quired an active lobbying campaign aimed at the New York State Legislature to expand the definition of work activity to include work-study and internships (Weikart, 2005, p. 426). They were determined to build bipartisan support for a work-study internship bill in New York City and New York State that would convince legislators, particularly upstate Republicans, that work and edu-cation were not conflicting values and that education was the key towards social mobility for students. WRI joined the advocacy coalition Welfare Rights Network (WRN), which was a collabo-ration among the Welfare Law Center (WLC), The Urban Justice Center, and was sponsored by the Federation of Protestant Welfare Agencies. WRN consisted of hundreds of organizations that met and established strategies to garner legislative support through a lobbying campaign (Weikart, 2005, p. 428). In 2000, they received bipartisan sponsorship of the bill from Democratic Senator Rober-to Ramirez and Republican Senator Raymond Meier and passed the Work-Study and Internship Law, which allowed 15-20 work-study and internship hours per week to count toward a college stu-dent's public assistance work requirement and prohibited welfare officials from unreasonably interfering with the student's ability to attend classes (Weikart, 2005, p. 428).

Mayzabeth Lopez, a WRI student organizer who wanted to break free from an early life of poverty and family struggles, recalled her first meeting with Meir and her initial hesitancy towards collaboration with the conservative state senator:

> …we brought him over to Hunter so he could see how hard students were working to graduate from school. He said a lot of things like, "When I was in school, I worked two jobs. I used to scrub toilets. I did this. I used to bag groceries." In essence he was saying, "Why can't you all do the same thing? If I worked two jobs, why can't you work two jobs?" And so at first I would think why would I even consider having a dialogue with someone who does not come from my world or understand my issues?" (Tobar, 2012b).

However, once Meier arrived at Hunter and witnessed firsthand how students were experiencing hurdles around work-study activities and continuing their education, and how WRI's services were, in fact, essential in helping students, he experienced a change of heart. Lopez was impressed by Meier's ability to be open to constructive conversations after that, culminating in his full support for the bill. The public forums, meetings, and outreach efforts paid off: in 2010, New York Governor David Paterson signed the Work Study Internship Law (HRA P.D #02-07-EMP), which made it permanent (Lane, 2010). As I hope this example illustrates, successful legislative advocacy can help affect public policy change that focuses on changing social structures of unjust systems and institutions.

CONCLUSION

More can and should be done to provide equitable educational resources to all students aspiring to higher education. There is an inherent value created when marginalized students are given the opportunity to become involved in legal advocacy to create and enforce social policy that directly affects their access to higher education. These stories can help bolster evidence in social research as well as better inform activism and advocacy. We can help create new spaces for policy that will ensure equitable access to higher education for these students, while amplifying the voices of those who have traditionally been left out of policymaking. This, not politics as usual, is what sparks dialog and empowers us to co-create solutions.

References

Abramovitz, M. (1988). *Regulating the lives of women: Social welfare policy from colonial times to the present*. South End Press.

Abramovitz, M. (1996). *Under attack, fighting back: Women and welfare in the United States*. Monthly Review Press.

Acevedo-Gil, N., & Zerquera, D. D. (2016). Community college first-year experience programs: Examining student access, experience, and success from the student perspective. *New Directions for Community Colleges*, (175), 71–82.

Austin, S. A., & McDermott, K. A. (2003). College persistence among single mothers after welfare reform: An exploratory study. *Journal of College Student Retention: Research, Theory & Practice*, 5(2), 93–113.

Baum, S., Ma, J., & Payea, K. (2013). Education pays: The benefits of higher education for individuals and society. College Board. p. 16.

Berg, G. A. (2016). *Low income students and the perpetuation of inequality: Higher education in America*. Routledge Press.

Bodack, S. F. (2000). Can New York City prevent welfare recipients from finishing high school. *Columbia Journal of Law and Social. Problems*, (34), 203.

Bok, M. (2003, April). Education and training for low-income women: An elusive goal. Paper presented at the 2003 annual conference of the Urban Affairs Association, Cleveland, OH.

Bok, M., & Simmons, L. (2002). Post-welfare reform, low-income families and the dissolution of the safety net. *Journal of Family and Economic Issues*, 23(3), 217–238.

Bowen, W.G., Kurzweil, M.A., & Tobin, E.M. (2005). *Equity and excellence in American higher education*. University of Virginia Press.

Cohen, S. (1999). Managing workfare: The case of the work experience program in the New York City Parks Department. PricewaterhouseCoopers Endowment for the Business of Government.

Duquaine-Watson, J. M. (2007). "Pretty darned cold": Single mother students and the community college climate in post-welfare reform America. *Equity & Excellence in Education*, 40(3), 229-240.

Edelman, P. (1997). The worst thing Bill Clinton has done. *The Atlantic*. Retrieved from https://www. theatlantic.com/magazine/archive/1997/03/the-worst-thing-bill-clinton-has-done/376797/. Accessed on June 1, 2021.

Edelman, P. (2004). Welfare and the politics of race: Same tune, new lyrics. *Georgetown Journal on Poverty Law & Policy*, (11), 389.

Fabricant, M., & Brier, S. (2016). *Austerity blues: Fighting for the soul of public higher education*. JHU Press.

Flanders, S. (2001, June 13) When a day's work still doesn't count. *New York Times*. Retrieved from http:// www.nytimes.com/2001/06/13/nyregion/when-a-day-s-work-still-doesn-t-count.html. Accessed on June 1, 2021.

Gilder, G. (1981). *Wealth and Poverty*. Basic Books.

Jacobs, J. A., & Winslow, S. (2003). Welfare reform and enrollment in postsecondary education. *The Annals of the American Academy of Political and Social Science*, 586(1), 194–217.

Katz, M. B. (1990). *The undeserving poor: From the war on poverty to the war on welfare*. Pantheon Books.

Keiser, L. R., Mueser, P. R., & Choi, S. W. (2004). Race, bureaucratic discretion, and the implementation of welfare reform. *American Journal of Political Science*, 48(2), 314–327.

Ladson-Billings, G., "Race still matters: Critical race theory in education," Apple, Au, & Gandin (Eds.), *The Routledge International Handbook of Critical Education* (2009), 110–122.

Lane, M. (2010, July 10). A Modest Law with Great Potential [Blog post]. Retrieved from http://drumma-jorinst.tumblr.com/post/10285860295/a-modest-law-with-great-potential.

Levitan, S.A. and Johnson, J.M. (1984). Beyond the safety net: Reviving the promise. Ballinger Publishing.

Lipsky, M. (1971). Street-level bureaucracy and the analysis of urban reform. *Urban Affairs Quarterly*, 6(4), 391–409.

Lopez [Interview transcript]. Retrieved from Welfare Rights Initiative Oral History Project website: http:// wri-voices.org/interview/mayzabeth-lopez-interview. Accessed on June 1, 2021.

Mead, L. M. (1986). *Beyond entitlement: The social obligation of citizenship*. Free Press.

Murray, C. (1984). *Losing ground: American social policy, 1950–1980*. Basic Books.

Murray, C. (1993). Welfare and the family: The U.S. experience. *Journal of Labor Economics*, 11(1, Part 2), S224-S262.

Nadasen, P. (2005). *Welfare warriors: The welfare rights movement in the United States*. Routledge.

Neubeck, K. J., & Cazenave, N. A. (2001). *Welfare racism: Playing the race card against America's poor*. Routledge.

Page, S. B., & Larner, M. B. (1997). Introduction to the AFDC Program. The future of children, 20-27.

Pearson, A. F. (2007). The new welfare trap: Case managers, college education, and TANF policy. *Gender & Society*, 21(5), 723–748.

Piven, F. F. (1998). Welfare reform and the economic and cultural reconstruction of low wage labor markets. *City & Society*, 10(1), 21-36.

Price, Charles, Tracy, Steffy, Tracy McFarlane. (2003). Continuing a Commitment to the Higher Education Option: Model State Legislation, College Programs, and Advocacy Organizations that Support Access to Post-Secondary Education for Public Assistance Recipients. Howard Samuels State Management and Policy Center of the City University of New York.

Rector, R. (1993). Welfare reform, dependency reduction, and labor market entry. *Journal of Labor Research*, 14(3), 283–297.

Schram, S. F., Soss, J., Fording, R. C., & Houser, L. (2009). Deciding to discipline: Race, choice, and punishment at the frontlines of welfare reform. *American Sociological Review*, 74(3), 398–422.

Shaw, K. M. (2004). Using feminist critical policy analysis in the realm of higher education: The case of welfare reform as gendered educational policy. *The Journal of Higher Education*, 75(1), 56–79.

Shaw, K. M., Goldrick-Rab, S., Mazzeo, C., & Jacobs, J. A. (2006). Putting poor people to work: How the work-first idea eroded college access for the poor. Russell Sage Foundation.

Smith, K. B., & Larimer, C. W. (2017). *The public policy theory primer*. Routledge.

Solórzano D., Yosso T. (2002). Critical race methodology: Counterstorytelling as an analytical framework for education research. *Qualitative Inquiry*, (8), 23–44.

Tobar, C. (Interviewer) & Lewis, D. (Interviewee). (2011a). Interview with Dillonna Lewis [Interview transcript]. Retrieved from Welfare Rights Initiative Oral History Project website: http://wri-voices.org/interview/dillonna-lewis-interview.

Tobar, C. (Interviewer) & Lyles, V. (Interviewee). (2011b). Interview with Vanessa Lyles [Interview transcript]. Retrieved from Welfare Rights Initiative Oral History Project website: http://wri-voices.org/interview/vanessa-lyles-interview.

Tobar, C. (Interviewer) & Lackey, M. (Interviewee). (2012a). Interview with Melinda Lackey [Interview transcript]. Retrieved from Welfare Rights Initiative Oral History Project website: http://wri-voices.org/interview/melinda-lackey-interview.

Tobar, C. (Interviewer) & Lopez, M. (Interviewee). (2012b). Interview with Mayzabeth "Ginger".

Weikart, L. (2005). The era of meanness: Welfare reform and barriers to a college degree. *Affilia* 20(4), 416–433.

When to Step Up, Step Back

How to Advocate for Students by Letting *Them* Speak

MARIA VERA, AA AND SHIRLEY LEYRO, PhD

INTRODUCTION: MARIA VERA

When you tell someone that you are undocumented, it changes their perception of you. Whenever I have disclosed my status, people automatically shut down and give me a pitying look while moving their hand to their heart and solemnly saying, "I'm so sorry." Although this may come from a place of good intentions—to me, it's more about pacifying guilt rather than voicing genuine concern. I have seen this reaction so many times I find it comical, for it assumes that being undocumented is something to be ashamed of. I feel unheard and unseen when people change how they interact with me once they know that I am undocumented. They no longer see me as "Maria Vera," but as someone who needs to be "helped" or "saved." Let me be clear: my status does not define who I am.

For example, in high school, while my guidance counselor was "helping" me prepare my college applications, she cried when she found out I was undocumented. At that moment, our roles changed, and instead of her counseling me, I was forced to counsel her. Instead of her supporting me through the process, the burden was on me to console her. This weight extended beyond that one occasion because afterwards, every time we saw each other in the hallways and made eye contact, she just sadly smiled at me. To me, being an ally does not mean simply asking me how I am doing or asking how you can help. It requires acknowledging the continuous struggle of undocumented citizens. It is not about "you."

A LESSON IN HUMILITY: SHIRLEY LEYRO

Maria is a former student at Borough of Manhattan Community College (BMCC) where I work. She was president of the BMCC DREAM Team, the undocumented students' club. For over a year, I worked closely with Maria as the faculty advisor to the club, and still work closely with her now on other endeavors. When I read her words, they struck me deeply—I found them to be so incredibly raw and honest, and they made me rethink my entire approach to this article. I realized that while many of us have been doing what we believe to be "good work" on behalf of our students, we still have much more work to do. Too often, help is geared toward the advocate's social location, creating a protective and paternalistic form of advocacy.

Although initially meant to be a short essay on "best practices" of active support and advocacy for students, writing this article has become autoethnographic as I found myself forced to find a critical distance and to evaluate my own behavior. I found myself thinking about the concept of "stepping up, stepping back," which refers to the notion of advocating for groups by yielding them the stage. As educators, we can "step up" by supporting students as they take the lead in demanding action and recognition from their colleges. I am reminded of the time right after the 2016 presidential election when the prospect of navigating an administration openly hostile to the noncitizen community—and in particular against the undocumented community—became a reality.

Faculty and staff on campuses across CUNY were grappling

to find ways to help students who were in a state of uncertainty and insecurity. The students were worried for themselves and their families as the newly elected president promised to rescind DACA protections and other forms of protected status, and to begin an aggressive deportation campaign against all undocumented individuals (Gomez, 2017). The administration also engaged in rhetoric that threatened several groups, including the LGBTQ and the Muslim communities, and passed sweeping policy changes to take away their rights (Brennan Center, 2018; Hilal, 2017). Many students were related to individuals, or were themselves, members of the very groups being targeted. A campus-wide coalition was formed to share information on how best to serve the students' needs. The coalition did a great job and is still actively addressing students' needs in a still tumultuous and hostile political climate.

As we were figuring out how to "step up" for them, the students were giving us lessons on how to "step back," as they took the initiative to advocate for themselves. I witnessed this when the BMCC DREAM Team wrote a letter to the university president requesting—*demanding*—a statement of support. This letter was conceptualized and produced by the students alone. It was a bold move, for campus leadership across CUNY had issued tepid responses against the government's plans; however, the silence from the BMCC administration was particularly noteworthy since our campus had the largest student population at the community and senior levels, including that of undocumented students. A few days after receiving the communication, then-President Antonio Perez released a statement of support on the school's website. Whether his statement was a direct result of the students' letter or purely coincidental, it can be assumed that the students' actions had an impact on his words. The students' campaign taught me a valuable lesson regarding their resiliency, their capacity to speak for themselves, and their competence in leadership: the "kids" will be alright.

It was this courageous act of self-advocacy that showed me that the students could take care of themselves and that the most effective way to help them was to amplify their voices by giving them the space and resources they needed to make that happen. Part of the problem is that many of us, while acknowledging the paternalistic nature of traditional teaching, perpetuate it ourselves without even realizing it. We can be adherents to the tenets of the "pedagogy of the oppressed," while still engaging in practices that are colonial in nature (Freire, 1970).

This is a struggle I know well. In my research, I look at the traumatizing impact of immigration enforcement and its toll on the mental well-being of immigrants, their families, and their communities. As a result, I understand the importance of protecting and advocating for the noncitizen population in my job as an educator in the university system and the consequences when society does not. This is the reality for most of us who advocate for any group we seek to protect and fight for: our desire to support and fight for the rights of vulnerable groups often stems from personal or professional experiences. This can create a blind spot, and as a result, we fail to see the power differential that professors hold over students. Our preoccupation with our own experiences creates a situation where we marginalize the students' knowledge, experiences, and needs.

While our intentions may seem well-meaning and altruistic, we must be cognizant that our responsibilities and roles as advocates are not to take the lead but rather to stand in support of and buttress the students' efforts. How can we balance our good intentions and motivations to help our students without falling into the old paternalistic tendencies? Maria provides us with some guidance when she tells us to seek ways to *share* our resources with students and to always include them at the table when making plans. Continue to learn from students about the best way to support their causes.

STEPPING UP BY STEPPING BACK

Here are some suggestions to be effective advocates:

Do not tokenize. Our students are not just storytellers or sources of quotations. They should be treated as leaders in these movements, as well as experts and decision-makers. Maria's recommendation is directly from the New York State Youth Leadership Council's advice on how to *Be An Accomplice.* Founded in 2007, NYSYLC was the first undocumented youth-led organization in New York to empower young undocumented people in their journey of advocacy and self-expression (https://www.nysylc.org). They have created a list of actions for those who want to support and serve as advocates for the undocumented or for any other group. To be an accomplice means to build a relationship that results in more than the singular, isolated efforts that have come to define allyship. Other suggestions are on the group's website.

Join an organization that already exists. Many who are interested in helping vulnerable groups do so by rallying their considerable cultural and social capital to create organizations. But starting an organization from scratch is unnecessary and may conflict with the objectives of those you want to help since you may be taking away resources from or competing for attention with already-established grassroots organizations. The most practical way to find an organization meeting the students' needs is to ask them directly.

Give up the mic. It is important for all decisions to be made not on behalf of our students, but in conjunction with them. Whether it be an interview, conference, speaking engagement, or writing project, our responsibility as advocates should be to center our students and to bring them with us as we participate in these endeavors. Our students deserve to be in the room *where it happens when it's happening*.

CONCLUSION: SHIRLEY

As one of the first advisors to the undocumented students' club at John Jay College, to my current tenure as advisor to the BMCC DREAM Team, I have witnessed first-hand how the political climate has impacted the daily lives of our students. The harmful consequences of anti-immigrant sentiments are not limited to our undocumented students. With a large percentage of immigrant families being of mixed status, there is trauma being experienced by many of our students, undocumented or not. Undocumented students, however, occupy an extremely vulnerable position, with their immigration status compounding the already stressful obligations of being a college student. From supporting students when coming out of the shadows to backing them as they navigate a governmental administration that is openly hostile to their very existence, I have tried to be an advocate, protector, guardian, and proud witness to the growth and maturity of this extremely vulnerable but incredibly resilient group. My experiences have shown me that the students do not need anyone to speak *for* them, but rather, someone to stand by—indeed, behind them—as they fight to be heard.

CONCLUSION: MARIA

The only way to have true allyship is if we all work together. This article is a great example of how we can collaborate. In this case, having someone who holds a PhD in criminal justice and a history of working with undocumented students creates a well-rounded perspective and gives validation to the article. Based on my experiences, being an ally does not mean simply asking me how I am doing or how you can help. It involves acknowledging our continuous struggle as undocumented citizens. It is not about "you." Understand that there are limited resources and that we often lack a network of other educators and organizations that have valuable resources.

References

Brennan Center: New Analysis: Trump Administration Targets Muslim, LGBTQ, Black Lives Matter Communities with Countering Violent Extremism Programs. Retrieved from: https://www.brennancenter. org/press-release/new-analysis-trump-administration-targets-muslim-lgbtq-black-lives-matter-communities.

Freire, Paolo (1970). *Pedagogy of the oppressed.* Bloomsbury Publishing.

Gomez, A. (2017, Feb. 21). "Homeland security unveils sweeping plan to deport undocumented immigrants." *USA Today*

Hilal, M. (2017). Trump's year in Islamaphobia. Institute for Policy Studies. Retrieved from: https://ips-dc. org/trumps-year-islamophobia/.

On Strike

Student Activism, CUNY, and Engaged Anthropology

KATHERINE T. MCCAFFREY, CHRISTINE KOVIC, AND
CHARLES R. MENZIES

We huddled on the marble steps of the New York Public Library shortly before sunrise. It was April 16, 1991, with one month left in the semester, and we planned to shut down our school. Days earlier, we had joined hundreds of students, faculty, and labor leaders at a City College rally in Harlem denouncing a $92 million budget cut to the City University of New York (CUNY) and a dramatic tuition increase proposed by Governor Mario Cuomo.

Figure 1: CUNY March in Harlem. Photo courtesy of Katherine McCaffrey.

By April 10, undergraduates had shut down six CUNY campuses, partially or completely. We planned to occupy The Graduate Center (GC) in solidarity with the undergraduate mobilization. As we gathered at 42nd Street, across from the eighteen-story office tower where we studied, we discussed strategy and assigned tasks. One group prepared to enter the building to barricade the connection to the adjacent Grace Building. Another group planned to secure the exterior doors of The Graduate Center with bicycle locks. We recorded our names and emergency contact information with a representative from the National Lawyers Guild.

The takeover involved several surprises. We hadn't anticipated finding security guards in the building controlling the doors; we "invited" them to leave. We also found the metal gates to the "mall"—a walkway connecting 42nd to 43rd Streets—lowered and locked. Nonetheless, we managed to barricade the only street entrance to the building. Once inside, we recorded a message on the switchboard declaring the campus "liberated," and organized groups to address security, outreach, and communication. We strategized on how to broaden support. What we had planned as a one-day strike in solidarity with students at other CUNY campuses instead became a ten-day occupation as scores of students joined activities, discussions, and a giant camp-out at the liberated Graduate Center.[1]

This essay is a collective effort of three GC anthropology alumni to recover a relatively unnoticed and undertheorized chapter of the ongoing struggle for a just city that emerged from the City University of New York. The largest urban university in the United States, CUNY embodied an optimistic democratic sentiment, an ideal of equal educational opportunity and access. We reflect here on one chapter of the fight to defend public education at CUNY, which has long been at the epicenter of national efforts to define higher education and, ultimately, the nature of democracy in the United States.[2]

The CUNY strikes in 1991 were part of a larger story of austerity imposed upon New York City after the fiscal crisis of 1976, and community efforts to resist it. While much has been written about the mass movements, strikes and radical politics that shaped New York City, very little has been written about CUNY's connection to these often overlapping and intersecting mobilizations.[3] Student mobilizations that emerged from the CUNY system from the mid-1970s to the mid-1990s were not narrowly framed to oppose tuition hikes, but were more broadly conceptualized as resistance against austerity measures and the expanding war economy. As such, our essay here contributes to an overlooked and important dimension of New York City's working-class history and political movements.

The 1991 strike at The Graduate Center was born in the anthropology department and reflected the progressive education we received in a program rooted not only in Marxist theory, but practice. As we will discuss, our CUNY anthropology training recognized the interconnected and unequal world that we inhabited and encouraged us to use the tools of anthropology to change it. A key element of our department's identity and dynamism emerged from the public nature of the City University system and neoliberal threats to the material basis of this education. Austerity ultimately had the effect of unifying students and faculty alike in this assault against such a crucial public good. We explore here the strike as a manifestation of this struggle, and the crucible from which a publicly engaged anthropology with the potential to transform society emerged.

BACKGROUND: CUNY AS A CONTESTED MODEL OF DEMOCRATIC EDUCATION

CUNY has its origins in the Free Academy for males established by public referendum in New York in 1847, a place where "the children of the rich and poor [could] take their seats together and know of no distinctions save that of industry, good conduct and intellect."[4] The Free Academy was the first free public institution of higher learning in the United States. In his opening address, its first president Dr. Horace Webster declared that the new school would test:

> [...] whether the highest education can be given to the masses, whether the children of the whole people can be educated; and whether an insti-tution of learning of the highest grade can be successfully controlled by the popular will, not by the privileged few, but by the privileged many.
> (Women's City Club, 1975, p. 14)

With its notion of higher education as a right, Kim Phillips-Fein notes, CUNY "articulated a conception of citizenship that was much more expansive than any to be found at the national level" (2017, p. 243).

The Free Academy, renamed the City College of New York (CCNY) in 1929, became the Harlem-based flagship of a system of city-supported colleges. Hunter was established as a women's college in 1870, and later expanded into the Bronx as Lehman College. Brooklyn College was founded in 1930 and Queens in 1937. Eventually, during the administration of New York State Governor Nelson Rockefeller in 1961, the multiple campuses were consoli-dated into a single City University of New York system. The Grad-uate School was established at this time.

Even when it fell short of its lofty goals, the CUNY system did demonstrate remarkable success as an avenue for advancement, educating generations of working-class New Yorkers, particularly Jewish immigrants from Eastern Europe who swelled its ranks at the turn of the twentieth century.[5] Its alumni include thirteen Nobel Laureates, the highest of any public university. CUNY maintained its position as a free academy in the face of the financial pressures of the Great Depression when New York's acting Mayor Joseph McKee proposed closing down the municipal college system entirely. In an early foreshadowing of struggles to come, the CCNY alumni association issued a scathing attack on those who would try to dismantle their alma mater:

> Now when the government of the city is profoundly disturbed by municipal problems of the gravest nature, all the tribe of detractors, whining over the shrinkage of their bloated money bags, jealous of a life and purpose they cannot understand, and dissembling under the cloak of civic welfare their hatred of races and creeds not their own, rise up in ignorance and hypocrisy to call the college a luxury, and by their blatancy in troubled times, to disturb the calm minds of those who desire to do well. (Neumann, 1984, p. 119)

CUNY struggled throughout its history to expand its mission of access while fending off efforts to dismantle the school entirely. Battles over access peaked in the late 1960s and CUNY adopted an "open admissions" policy that transformed the demographics of the school to reflect the rapidly changing multicultural landscape of New York City. During the fiscal turmoil of the mid-1970s—a concerted power grab by the city's elites to reshape New York's priorities—CUNY became a central target of fiscal austerity. Long an irritant to its private rivals, Columbia and New York University, CUNY now fell into the crosshairs of President Gerald Ford's aim, who made "disciplining" New York City a central goal of his administration.[6] In October 1975, the *New York Daily News* ran the headline "Ford to City: Drop Dead." Phillips-Fein notes that "CUNY was a particular bête noire of the Ford administration: it seemed the ultimate symbol of municipal largesse, the embodiment of its most utopian promises" (2017, 100).

When New York's Mayor Beame was forced by the MAC board to impose tuition on CUNY, he balked, noting that the money raised by tuition would be only a fraction of what the city needed, while the poor and working-class students would find the fees a real burden.[7] He noted that he himself was a beneficiary of a free CUNY education (Phillips-Fein, 2017, pp. 139, 142). But the point was not practical, but ideological. "[MAC trustee] Rohatyn told him that he didn't get it: it wasn't the money that mattered but the symbolism of it, the evidence that the city was changing its lifestyle for good" (Phillips-Fein, 2017, p. 139). In the summer of 1976, CUNY's Board relented to ongoing political pressure and imposed tuition for the first time in the university's 130-year history.

CUNY students have a history of militancy and the strategic and successful use of collective action.[8] For example, a 1969 City College student strike demanding increased enrollment of African American and Puerto Rican students forced the university to adopt the "open admissions" policy granting access to any NYC high school graduate. CUNY student activism carried over into the fiscal crisis. When Mayor Abraham Beame proposed slashing the CUNY budget by $70 million, students occupied the dean's office at Hunter College, the administration building at City College, and organized a protest at Gracie Mansion attended by over a thousand, mostly African-American student protesters (Phillips-Fein, 2017, p. 91).

The cuts to the CUNY budget in 1976 left the university in turmoil. The brief, bold experiment of "open admissions" was crushed. Between 1977–1980, CUNY saw 50% fewer Black and Latina/o first-year students among its entering class, with students of color increasingly relegated to the community colleges, a foreshadowing of increasing racial disparities in higher education. The CUNY student body shrank by 25%.

THE CUNY GRADUATE CENTER: UNIVERSITY FLAGSHIP AND REARGUARD OF THE STRIKE

We are a public university that has always made a huge difference to the way we function. We're not just a pale imitation of Columbia where many of us [faculty] got our own training. We are grounded in the outside world. We're grounded in New York City. We believe in activism. And we know how to make do with not very much. We've always been on the verge of one budget crisis or another.

— Sydel Silverman

The Graduate School was born during one of the most optimistic periods of CUNY's history, at a time when both higher education expanded dramatically in the United States and New York State significantly augmented its educational resources. In 1961, Governor Nelson Rockefeller signed legislation creating the City University of New York, and at the same time, gave the new institution the authority to grant doctoral and postgraduate professional degrees. Mina Rees, a mathematician who was honored for her leadership of the Office of Naval Research during WWII, was the Graduate School's first dean, and assumed the task of creating a new school from the ground up. Drawing on a British paradigm, she organized doctoral education in a consortial model, where faculty from the undergraduate campuses would maintain primary lines at the colleges, but contribute to graduate education in a separate, stand-alone graduate school. Rees found support for the plan in Albert Bowker, an ambitious, competitive chancellor who came to CUNY from Stanford and once told the president of Columbia University, "We're going to overwhelm you. We're going to build the strongest graduate school in the city" (Anderson, 2011, p. 19). By 1971 CUNY's administration, recognizing the school's success under Rees's stewardship, accorded the graduate school status as its own college with Rees as president. Other university-wide, non-doctoral research and education programs were transferred under its umbrella to establish The CUNY Graduate School and University Center.

At the outset, Rees's vision of this new public graduate school was ambitious and intellectual. She wrote:

> Education is not designed to prepare people to do whatever work flows from the blind and predestined imperative of technology; rather, it is intended to educate people of vision and sensitivity, who will be motivated to direct technology into humanly constructive channels. (cited in Anderson, 2011, pp. 6–7)

The academic success of the school, however, soon became mired in New York's fiscal implosion. Amidst a climate of ruthless austerity, graduate education itself came under attack, as Sydel Silverman,[9] the executive officer of the anthropology department from 1975 to 1986 remembered:

> The sentiment was, "Who needs graduate study when times are tough?" A lot of the politicians and the public felt that CUNY should not have doctoral studies, that it as a luxury we could not afford. NYU and Columbia chimed in with the position that CUNY is a good place to train the working class for the labor market of the City. The intellectual work of doctoral study could best be done by the privates. And we fought that for several years. The University actually closed down for several weeks during that period. We all went on unemployment.[10]

A consequence of the backlash against CUNY graduate education in the mid-1970s was that it unified the faculty. "One thing that we had in common was that no one was going to tell us we were unessential. We developed a battle plan," recalled Silverman. The Graduate Center, she noted, which depended on the good will of the colleges to release its faculty to teach, assumed a central role in bringing everyone together: "That created goodwill all around."

ANTHROPOLOGY AT THE GRADUATE CENTER

The CUNY anthropology program that we joined was an expression of a model of education that was public and accessible, a reflection of New York's political culture that was shaped by working-class movements. It was also born out of the discipline's internal struggles over the colonial legacies and ethics of anthropology which came to a head during the Vietnam War. In 1970, Eric Wolf and Joseph Jorgensen, both then at the University of Michigan, clashed with Margaret Mead in highly publicized hearings over the use of anthropological data in counterinsurgency efforts in Thailand. Wolf subsequently arrived at CUNY (Lehman College) where he joined Delmos Jones, another anthropologist ensnared in the Thailand controversy.[11] Jones, who had been working with hill tribes in northern Thailand, terminated and refused to publish his research when he understood the CIA's interest in using his findings to develop counterinsurgency plans in Thailand. An African American born to sharecroppers on a farm in Alabama, Jones researched inequality and subordination in several regions, and became the lone anthropologist who refused to cooperate with the CIA on the project (Susser, 2000). The CUNY anthropology program was thus infused with this sensibility, critical of positivist notions of anthropology as objective data collection, and mindful instead of its entanglement with colonialism and violence. As Jorgensen and Wolf (1970) wrote in their landmark essay in *The New York Review of Books*:

> Anthropology is not a dispassionate science like astronomy, which springs from the contemplation of things at a distance. It is the outcome of a historical process, which has made the larger part of mankind [*sic*] subservient to the other, and during which millions of innocent human beings have had their resources plundered, their institutions and beliefs destroyed while they themselves were ruthlessly killed, thrown into bondage, and contaminated by diseases they were unable to resist.

We entered The Graduate Center shortly after Wolf had published the acclaimed *Europe and the People Without History* (1982) and took seminars with a scholar whose lifework embodied the intersection of politics, scholarship and activism. In the late 1980s and early 1990s, when we arrived, there was a continued push to decolonize the discipline, following earlier scholarship such as Dell Hymes's 1969 edited volume *Reinventing Anthropology,* which increasingly clashed with a postmodern turn in anthropology, or what was then called the *cultural critique*. The Graduate Center aligned in the first camp, and was known as a center for a materialist, often Marxist, approach centered especially in political economy. The same year of the strike, Faye Harrison's edited book *Decolonizing Anthropology: Moving Further toward an Anthropology for Liberation* (1991) was published by the Association for Black Anthropologists. In the introduction, Harrison describes an activist anthropology "committed to and engaged in struggles against racist oppression, gender inequality, class disparities, and international patterns of exploitation and 'difference' rooted largely in capitalist world development" (p. 2). She challenged the relative lack of attention to race in anthropology before 1990, calling for more ethnographic examination of racism and white supremacy.

At CUNY, we were reading critiques of capitalism and co-lonialism by major Third World theorists including Walter Rod-ney's *How Europe Underdeveloped Africa* (1974), Frantz Fanon's *The Wretched of the Earth* (1963), C.L.R. James' *Black Jacobins* (1938) and Eric Williams's *Capitalism and Slavery* (1944). We read books by our professors such as June Nash's *We Eat the Mines and the Mines Eat Us* (1979) that documented exploita-tion and the extraction of wealth in Bolivian tin mines and Gerald Sider's *Culture and Class in Anthropology and History: A New-foundland Illustration* (1986) that brought class analysis into the concept of culture. In courses addressing gender, urban anthropol-ogy, and the global factory, we focused on understanding multiple inequalities (especially based on class, race, and gender) and the ways in which people organized to resist them. Ida Susser's *Nor-man Street* (1982), which documented community organizing in Brooklyn's Greenpoint/Williamsburg neighborhood following the fiscal austerity of the 1970s, and Leith Mullings's edited volume *Cities of the United States* (1987) informed our understanding of the struggles that shaped the urban environment we inhabited while studying in New York City.

Faye Harrison called on anthropologists to collaborate with "studied populations." In our experience, there was no "ivory tow-er" at The Graduate Center; faculty and students were actively engaged with multiple communities and social justice struggles in New York and other sites. To name a few: graduate student Al-fredo Gonzalez joined the militant, direct action Latino Caucus of ACT/UP to fight the AIDS crisis (see Gonzalez 2008); our class-mate Rosamel Millaman was a leader of the Mapuche nation in Chile;[12] Professor Leith Mullings examined racial disparities in health in the Harlem Birth Right project through qualitative and community participatory methods (Mullings and Wali, 2001); Professor Gerald Sider was a civil rights organizer in the Carolinas; and Professor Ida Susser collaborated with local populations to prevent AIDS among the homeless in New York City and later in South Africa. Our professors supported and encouraged our activism in New York and beyond, and research that could impact public policy.

Indeed, Leith Mullings's chapter in *Gender and Anthropology* (1989) explored the ways "gender constructs have direct consequences for policy decisions and rationalizations" in the United States (p. 31). In short, our experiences were in stark contrast to those of Philippe Bourgois (1991), who was threatened with expulsion from his graduate program at Stanford University for going to the media and Capitol Hill to denounce brutal state violence in El Salvador. Our professors encouraged critical examination of social movements and public policy, and an engaged anthropology that could impact social change.

THE STRIKE

We were all graduate students in the CUNY anthropology department in the early 1990s and helped to organize the 1991 strike and to occupy our graduate school building for ten days. The world was rapidly changing after the collapse of the Soviet Union, but our hope for the growth of freedom and democracy seemed dispelled by the U.S. invasion of Iraq. There would be no peace dividend but a continued erosion of the public sector and an expansion of military spending.

Conditions continued to worsen, and we entered The Graduate Center as Governor Mario Cuomo and CUNY's Board of Trustees proposed a series of tuition hikes; budget cuts in the university's operating budget; and reductions of student aid. Student mobilization in 1989 succeeded in fighting a proposed $200 tuition increase. In 1991, however, the proposed cuts were starker: Cuomo demanded a $53 million cut in the university's operating budget, a $500 tuition increase, and a sharp reduction in state tuition assistance.

We each brought particular experiences of student activism. Menzies originated from British Columbia, Canada, noted for one of the most militant sections of Canada's working class at the time (Menzies, 2010). Kovic and McCaffrey had been involved in mobilizations for women's rights as undergraduates. During the Fall 1990 semester, we had protested a potential U.S. invasion of Iraq. We'd set up a table with signs on The Graduate Center Mall, handed out flyers to passersby, and asked people to sign an anti-war petition. In the winter of 1990, together with our colleagues, some of us created a poster featuring pictures of Mario Cuomo, then Governor of New York, W. Ann Reynolds, then Chancellor of CUNY, and Saddam Hussein, then president of Iraq.

Under their pictures, our caption read: "Who is the real enemy?" We were facing a massive increase in tuition fees and a nearly debilitating budget cut. From this perspective, the representatives of political elites in the United States seemed far more of a threat than any distant political leader. The flyer made it clear that tax cuts for the wealthy in New York had led to a decrease in revenue and a budget deficit. The final line read: "Now we have a $6 billion deficit that Mr. Cuomo wants to come from our pockets."

The CUNY strike was system-wide. Spurred into action by student activists at the City College of New York (CCNY), groups of students began taking over their campuses throughout the system. By the end of the occupation more than two-thirds of CUNY was under student occupation. At The Graduate Center, we organized an action in support of the colleges. Our core group, a dozen or so people, was comprised primarily of anthropology students. We shared a common socialist political orientation that informed our approach to organization.

Who's the real enemy?

□   □   □

"Tuition hikes are inevitable."   "The cuts will leave the strength   "This will be the mother
                                   of the state intact."   of all battles."

Or all of the above?

What do these three have in common? They are willing to sacrifice their people for the power of a few....

Mr. Cuomo calls for:

• A $92 million cut in state aid to CUNY
• A $500 a year tuition hike in addition to an already authorized $200 increase.
• Massive cuts in financial aid, including a $400 annual reduction in TAP affecting approximately 50,000 students, the elimination of Regents, Empire State, nursing and other state funded scholarships.

What does this mean for CUNY?

• Students will be priced out of higher education.
• Already overworked students will face longer hours on the job.
• Administration and faculty cuts, overburdened teachers and staff, furloughs and paylags for workers.
• Massive reductions in course offerings, overcrowding of classrooms.
• Deterioration of the physical plant.
• Reduction in library hours, books purchased, computer services, countless other crucial student services.

Why is all of this happening?

• Mr. Cuomo has spent 10 years cutting taxes for the rich.
   1) Cuomo has cut the top income tax rates more than 50% in the last 10 years.
   2) While the wealthiest 1% in the USA increase their incomes by 86%

Figure 2: Anti-War Poster. Poster image courtesy of Katherine McCaffrey.

Several of us had established contacts with fellow students at CCNY. There they had organized themselves on a tight, cadre-style organization. Their decision-making was based upon group membership as defined from the start of the occupation. In contrast, we argued for an open political structure in which membership would expand according to participation. If you join, you have a voice. Our model even extended to letting anyone who wished to participate in our open-air daily forums (more below). For our CCNY colleagues, their organization made sense as they faced a multi-building campus. For us, with one office tower in midtown and a socialism-from-below approach, it made more sense to organize through a participatory democratic fashion.

PARTICIPATORY DEMOCRACY INSIDE AND OUT-SIDE THE UNIVERSITY

As the GC strike unfolded, a form of participatory democracy developed outside and inside the occupied building in which we engaged in long conversations to define the roots of the problems we faced and debated actions to create change. We saw the attacks on higher education as part of the neoliberal assault on the city. Our involvement in the strike, and even the framing of the protest as a challenge of austerity, connected to our training in engaged, activist anthropology at The Graduate Center.

In discussions inside the building, in plebiscites on the mall, at meetings on other campuses, at teach-ins and public protests, we created a space for discussion among ourselves as students and with key interlocutors. Solidary with the undergraduate CUNY campuses, which had been the initial motivation for the GC strike, remained a key motivation. During the afternoon of the first day of the occupation, we held an open forum on the 42nd Street Mall. With the metal gates blocking the entrance to the mall, the forum spilled into the sidewalk, making it visible to passersby. At the forum, people came together to discuss the occupation as well as the broader issue of budget cuts to the CUNY system and other state services. We had a microphone and selected one of the strikers to facilitate discussion. On the first day, GC students, faculty, and community members spoke about the importance of CUNY colleges in opening the possibility for themselves and their family members to go to college. Some shared concerns that the dramatic budget cuts would mean fewer faculty and fewer courses, delaying graduation for students; and that with higher tuition and less financial aid and scholarships, many would be unable to complete their studies or even go to college in the first place. Leith Mullings, one of our professors, recalled how she, her parents, and her siblings were able to go to college because CUNY had been tuition-free.[13] Since The Graduate Center was located in an area of high pedestrian traffic, people from the streets stopped to listen and speak at these forums. The graduate students were in a unique position—many taught as part-time (adjunct) instructors at the undergraduate colleges and had heard student concerns about the impact of the cuts.

At the end of the first day, those attending the forum proposed a vote on whether to keep the building occupied for the next day.[14] The vote created a shared sense of the occupation, since the strike affected all students. It was also an attempt to involve more students in the decision-making process and the strike itself. The first vote was overwhelmingly in favor of continued occupation; we made plans to stay overnight in the building. Every day of the strike, we held a public forum in the afternoon, followed by a vote on whether to keep the building closed.[15]

Beyond the daily forums on the mall, those of us within the occupied Graduate Center engaged in heated discussions about public education and our strategies for change. Early in the occupation, we found a directory of all GC students with their contact information. We organized a team to call them, breaking up the list alphabetically, informing them of the building's occupation, and inviting them to the daily forums and to participate in the protests. We worked together to craft documents of demands. On April 18, just two days into the strike, a document titled "Graduate Center Student Strike Update" included sixteen demands. Some of our demands were tied directly to the building occupation—we demanded that police or security forces would not be brought to campus and that disciplinary action would not be taken against the striking students. Some demands were tied to the budget cuts—we demanded that the CUNY Administration and Chancellor Reynolds present a plan to immediately escalate pressure on state legislators to stop the cuts. Additional demands targeted inequalities with The Graduate Center itself. Students insisted that graduate programs recruit students and faculty "particularly from the CUNY system to reflect the racial and ethnic diversity of the City of New York...affirmatively in support of those of the working class and to disallow discrimination of gender and sexual orientation."[16]

We spent hours, days, and nights in the building, creating friendships and relationships, and debating strategies. We debated the possibility of free tuition.[17] We talked about what "liberated pedagogy" looked like within and beyond the classroom. We opened the building to a teach-in for one day. Early in the occupation, some strikers organized a training on non-violent protest so that all strikers would be prepared to respond should police enter the building. The training served much more broadly for those who would later be involved in protests. One day, some of us linked arms and shut down 42nd Street to draw attention to the budget cuts.

Outside The Graduate Center, CUNY students organized strategy sessions at some of the occupied campuses, allowing a space for people to create a shared vision. We joined meetings at BMCC, Hunter College, and CCNY, among other campuses, gathering with students to plan actions. These meetings continued after the strike had ended, with students joining SER–Students for Educational Rights, initially founded in 1989 at CCNY.

In making connections to other campuses and students and other struggles against austerity measures, the strike reflected a form of *commoning*, a grassroots effort to create horizontal connections to build a new vision of society. Ida Susser (2017), a professor of anthropology at Hunter College and The Graduate Center, has used the term commoning to describe grassroots movements in Europe and the United States that "reorient discourse and practice in terms of a public good and the redistribution of shared resources toward a more equal world" in response to right-wing regimes (p. 1). At the time of the strike, we discussed the value of public education, as well as other public services, in contrast to austerity measures and militarization. Susser (2016) and other scholars note that as commoning movements build consensus across difference, protestors live "the alternative futures in the process of mobilization" (p. 189).

In the strike, we sought to create a space for participatory democracy where students, and to some extent, faculty, alumni, and other New Yorkers, engaged in conversations and debates about how to challenge austerity measures and the future of public education. Indeed, the meetings within The Graduate Center often went on for hours and hours.

These conversations and debates are similar to what anthropologist Averill Leslie describes as "collaborative democracy" where participants worked together to create an agenda. In his research on the Occupy Wall Street Movement and local town-meeting-style democracies in a small town in Vermont, Leslie (2013) observed that a collaborative democracy developed decisions motivated by "care" in contrast to an adversarial democracy of "allies and enemies" where each side fights to defend their position (p. 39). In the space of The Graduate Center, a community of students who had much in common, the possibility of engaging in debates is not surprising. Unlike Occupy Wall Street, we crafted clear demands—demands that grew and changed as we interacted in the occupied building. What was unique for the student strikers is that we argued about the merits of continuing the shutdown, of moving to other targets such as the state's capitol, Albany, of taking to the streets, or of engaging in other acts of protest at the same time as we debated ways to make the classroom, the university, and college more equitable.

One point of ongoing debate was how to act to stop the budget cuts facing the university and the city. We were well aware that the targets of our protest were far from the occupied Graduate Center. We started our occupation as a consciously symbolic act and worked to make our demands visible and connect the CUNY building occupations to anti-austerity activism. We realized that simply taking over a piece of real estate had no independent value or meaning outside of the wider context of struggle.

As a doctoral-granting institution, The Graduate Center had prestige within the CUNY system but was not a center of power. The power of the action was the possibility of creating solidarity with the tens of thousands of New York students at colleges like Bronx, CCNY, Hostos, Hunter, Lehman, Queens, and York. Our targets included Governor Cuomo in Albany and CUNY Chancellor W. Ann Reynolds, who supported what she called the "inevitable" tuition hikes and who had called for stricter admission requirements. We knew that decisions were made at the chancellor's and governor's offices; in addition, we wanted to challenge the broader national context in which war, police, and prisons were prioritized over education. We observed that policymakers were cutting social spending while investing more for militarization, particularly for the invasion of Iraq at the federal level, and cutting income tax rates for the wealthiest New Yorkers at the state level.

Just weeks before the Occupation, a group of students had participated in Albany protests against state budget cuts and tuition hikes. The *New York Times* reported:

> The rally, called 'Operation Budget Storm,' [a play on the US invasion of Iraq called Operation Desert Storm] drew an estimated 20,000 people to Albany to urge the state legislature to soften Mr. Cuomo's proposed cuts by imposing higher taxes on the wealthy and on corporations. Organized by the [Black and Puerto Rican Legislative] caucus and many of the state's largest trade unions, the demonstration was one of the largest in state history.[18]

Figure 3: March in Albany. Photo courtesy of Katherine McCaffrey.

During the strike, the daily discussions and plebiscites sought, in a limited fashion, to connect to New Yorkers and to publicize the strike. The GC flyer "Who's the real enemy?" ended with a call to join the Albany protesters in their demands for money for "education, healthcare, housing, and social services." On April 17, some of us left the building to join striking homecare workers at a rally in lower Manhattan.[19] In these actions, as well as protests against austerity that followed the strike, graduate students connected their struggles to others that sought a redistribution of resources for the common good in New York City and the nation.

THE END OF THE STRIKE

In part because of the strong community created inside The Graduate Center and the intensity of the discussions taking place, many of the striking students became attached to the occupied space. Those of us who had organized the occupation argued that our only power lay in our ability to extend our struggle beyond the building and to forge real political linkages with local trade unions and community movements such as we saw represented in the college-based struggles. We rejected the idea that a group of elite outsiders (many of us graduate students were out-of-state students) could build a progressive movement in one office tower. Eventually, a compromise was reached that allowed us to hand over the building to the administration while holding onto some modest political gains.[20] We released the campus at noon on April 25, after ten days of occupation, following negotiations on a series of demands with the GC administration. We emphasized that opening The Graduate Center allowed us to take struggles beyond the building. The conditions for leaving the building included (1) a statement of support from administrators for student struggles against the budget cuts; (2) establishment of an emergency ad-hoc committee to plan a long-range strategy to resist cuts; (3) creation of a committee to address issues within GC; (4) agreement that no disciplinary action be taken against the students; and (5) creation of a resource center for CUNY-wide coalition against cuts.[21]

What was the outcome of the building occupation? The strike at The Graduate Center and the other CUNY campuses did not stop the tuition increase or the budget cuts, although the increase in tuition was phased in over a period of years and some of the funds were restored. In contrast to 1989, as noted earlier, Governor Cuomo vetoed a proposed CUNY tuition hike following significant student protest; students took over a City College administrative building, protested at most campuses, and held a major rally at Federal Hall in downtown Manhattan.[22] In 1991, the protests failed to stop the cuts, and news reports were dismissive of the strike. The press criticized the building takeovers, chastising students for interrupting classes. Stephen Cahn, then GC's acting president, expressed a similar sentiment in a letter to the striking students stating, "As long-planned conferences are cancelled, publication deadlines are missed, admission applications go unanswered, and dissertations cannot be completed in time for commencement, you are jeopardizing the life of the institution you seek to defend."[23]

Today, 28 years later, a neoliberal model is even more prevalent at U.S. universities, including CUNY. In the 1990s, Chancellor Ann Reynolds sought to remove remedial courses from the senior colleges, and in 1998, the Board of Trustees voted to do so, effectively ending open admissions (Picciano and Jordan, 2018). Indeed, a $300 annual tuition increase for CUNY students was planned for each year from 2011 to 2015. In 2016, CUNY's faculty union, the Professional Staff Congress, voted resoundingly to authorize a strike if a fair contract could not be reached, protesting six years without a raise, and five without a contract. They also protested the meager pay of adjunct professors at $3000 a course. Even with the increases in tuition, CUNY remains woefully underfunded.

The neoliberal restructuring of the university reproduces and exacerbates existing inequalities based on race and class as programs to support underrepresented students are cut or underfunded. In February 1992, more than 250 students and professors filed a lawsuit challenging racial discrimination based on funding disparities between CUNY and the State University of New York (SUNY). While state funding per student at CUNY was $6,927, where 64% of the students were people of color, it was $7,653 per student at SUNY, where 87% of the students were White.[24] The Court of Appeals eventually dismissed the case, ruling that the state had not engaged in intentional discrimination. However, the court did not deny the disparate funding between the two systems. The disparities between CUNY and SUNY continue. In September 2019, a University Faculty Senate study found inequities in the faculty-student ratios between the systems, with 45 full-time faculty per 1000 full-time students at SUNY in 2017 and only 35 per 1000 students at CUNY.[25]

The strike did not succeed in obtaining more state funding for CUNY or in lessening inequalities. We understand the impact of the strike, however, to extend beyond the short-term concessions and consequences that unfolded in the weeks, months, and even years following the occupation. As participants, our occupation of The Graduate Center did have profound effects that carried forward in our lives as academics and members of civil society. For those of us who participated in the occupation, the strike was a core aspect of our CUNY anthropology education. It strengthened our commitment to public education. It provided us with the tools to document and challenge exploitation in multiple forms.

In the CUNY anthropology program, we learned that there was no separation between research and the so-called "real world." Anthropology was always relevant as it sought to decipher systems of power and amplify the voices of people whose experiences were too often obscured and discounted. Indeed, Kovic notes that years later, when she was collaborating with the Fray Bartolome de Las Casas Human Rights Center in Chiapas, Mexico, the work of documenting human rights abuses was familiar to her as an anthropologist:

> Recording and transcribing testimonies of violations, systematizing the cases, and above all, locating the patterns of abuses as tied to state practices involved precisely the research skills I had learned as a graduate student. My advisors never pushed me to be an "objective" or "neutral" observer but instead asked how I could stand in solidarity with Indigenous peoples in southern Mexico. Indeed, when I learned about the Zapatista uprising of 1994, I was in the United States preparing for my comprehensive exams. When I called June Nash she said, "You left at the wrong time."

Our professors nurtured and supported scholarship that interrogated systems of power and validated indigenous and subaltern peoples' experiences and struggles. Ida Susser, for example, encouraged McCaffrey to investigate the history of CUNY for Susser's urban anthropology seminar, a version of which McCaffrey published in the GC student newspaper the *Advocate*, and supervised McCaffrey's research on anti-military protest in Puerto Rico. McCaffrey remembers,

> The student strike, coupled with the Gulf War, which unfolded several months earlier, shaped the course of my research and my identity as a scholar and anthropologist. The first Gulf War was so disheartening: the

end of the Cold War spawned hope in a meaningful "peace dividend." Instead, the United States mobilized troops to intervene in the tangled conflict of two Gulf oil states to ensure its access to petroleum. I resolved to orient my research to consider some aspect of the powerful and pernicious role the US military played on the global stage. When I learned about a grassroots social movement against the US military presence in Vieques, Puerto Rico, I was inspired to conduct fieldwork about the consequences of the military occupation of that island.[26]

Today, all three of us teach at public universities. Our CUNY experience reinforced for us the importance of high-quality public education. Although it didn't always realize its status as a great equalizer, CUNY demonstrated that a public institution could provide hope, opportunity, and encouragement to a diverse and vibrant student body. It could accomplish this not by erasing, but by reflecting and validating students' cultural, racial and class experiences. It could foment research that challenged relations of power and social inequality. "Teaching anthropology at a public university in Texas," Kovic notes, "connects to my experiences as a graduate student at CUNY":

Scholars now refer to the neoliberal model of higher education—with reduced public spending and a view of education as a commodity that serves capitalism. In this context, the lessons of the strike stay with me, especially of being able to work together with a group of students to connect the fight for higher education to broader struggles against austerity measures in maintaining an alternative vision of what is possible.

Menzies, likewise, reflects that:

Ideas like radical direct democracy, socialism from below, and the capacity of the exploited and the oppressed to self-organize drove my engagement in the CUNY occupation. My experiences of the occupation reaffirmed these ideas and provided illumination in terms of how one might do better next time. I took these experiences forward into my professional and community life. Today I teach at one of Canada's largest public universities. The issues that informed the political struggles of my student years are still with us today. If anything, a pessimist would say the situation is more dire now than ever before. But as a good friend once said when asked, "Why persist?" Because we must, we are in the age of barbarism that Luxemburg worried about over a century ago and the only way out is through collective emancipation Situated in a mainstream center of neoliberalism, university faculty have a role to play in providing the details of the past in such a manner as to be able to deploy that knowledge to shape a better future. Watching the growth of real democratic practice emerge in the microcosm that was the CUNY occupation gives me hope that social change is possible.

Together we learned that collective, open, participatory democracy can transform individuals. We learned that there are moments, places, and times wherein we can turn against the current of privilege and power. Looking back from our vantage point today, we are glad that we had the courage of our convictions, that we took action, and that for a brief moment, we lived in a liberated world.

Acknowledgements

Each of us has a set of people who made our journey as students, and then faculty, possible. At CUNY, we particularly acknowledge the faculty, past and present, who created such a powerful learning place. For each of us in different ways, we thank Jane Schneider (executive office of the PhD program when we were graduate students), Marc Edelman, Delmos Jones, Leith Mullings, June Nash, Gerald Sider, Ida Susser and Eric Wolf. We also thank and acknowledge our comrades in the CUNY anthropology program whose activism inspires and without whom our worlds would be immeasurably impoverished: Betsy Andrews, Leon Arredondo, Helio Belik, Alcira Forero-Peña, Alfredo Gonzalez, Jonathan Hearn, Yvonne Lassalle, Anthony Marcus, Eric McGuckin, Maureen O'Dougherty, Sabyiha Prince, Guita Ranjbaran, Martha Rodriguez, Youngmin Seo, JoAnn Vrilakas, and Amy White. Special thanks to Ida Susser and to the reviewers at *Transforming Anthropology* who provided valuable feedback on the manuscript. We each have important people in our personal lives beyond school who have been there for us through the years; to them, we are earnestly thankful.

References

Anderson, Michael. (2011). "Fifty years at the Center: A history of the Graduate School and University Center of the City University of New York from 1961 to 2011." The Graduate Center.

Bourgois, Philippe. (1991). "Confronting the ethics of ethnography: Lessons from fieldwork in Central America." In *Decolonizing anthropology: Moving further toward an anthropology for liberation*, edited by Faye V. Harrison, pp. 110-26. American Anthropological Association.

Fanon, Frantz. (1963). *The wretched of the earth.* Translated by Constance Farrington. Grove Press.

Gonzalez, Alfredo. (2008). "Latinos ACT UP: Transnational AIDS activism in the 1990s." *NACLA Report on the Americas* 41(4): 35–39.

Gorelick, Sherry. (1980). "City College: The rise and fall of the Free Academy." *Radical America,* 14(5): 21–35.

Harrison, Faye V., Ed. (1991). *Decolonizing anthropology: Moving further toward an anthropology for liberation.* American Anthropological Association.

Hymes, Dell, Ed. (1969). *Reinventing anthropology.* Vintage Books.

James, C.L.R. (1938). *Black Jacobins: Toussaint L'Ouverture and the San Domingo revolution.* Secker and Warburg Ltd.

Jorgensen, Joseph G. and Eric R. Wolf. (1970). "Anthropology on a warpath in Thailand." A special supplement. *The New York Review of Books,* 15(9), November 19.

Leslie, Averill. (2013). "Collaborative democracy: From New England town hall meeting to Occupy Wall Street." *Anthropology Now,* 5(1): 36–45.

Menzies, Charles R. (2010). Reflections on work and activism in the "University of Excellence." *New Proposals,* Vol. 3(2):40–55.

Moody, Kim. (2007). *From welfare state to real estate: Regime change in New York City, 1974 to the present.* The New Press.

Mullings, Leith, Ed. (1987). *Cities of the United States: Studies in urban anthropology.* Columbia University Press.

Mullings, Leith. (1989). "Gender and the application of anthropological knowledge to public policy in the United States." In *Gender and Anthropology: Critical Reviews for Research and Teaching,* edited by Sandra Morgen, pp. 360–81. American Anthropological Association.

Mullings, Leith. (1996). *On our own terms: Race, class and gender in the lives of African-American Women.* Routledge.

Mullings, Leith and Alaka Wali. (2001). *Stress and resilience: The social context of reproduction in central Harlem.* Kluwer Academic/Plenum Publishers.

Nash, June. (1979). *We eat the mines and the mines eat us: Dependency and exploitation in Bolivian tin mines.* Columbia University Press.

Neumann, Florence. (1984). "Access to free public higher education in New York City, 1847–1961." PhD dissertation, CUNY.

Philips-Fein, Kim. (2017). *Fear city: New York City's fiscal crisis and the rise of austerity politics.* Metropolitan Books.

Picciano, Anthony G. and Chet Jordan. (2018). *CUNY's first fifty years: Triumphs and ordeals of a people's university.* Routledge.

Rodney, Walter. (1974). *How Europe underdeveloped Africa.* Howard University Press.

Sider, Gerald M. (1986). *Culture and class in anthropology and history: A Newfoundland illustration.* Cambridge University Press.

Susser, Ida. (1982). *Norman Street, poverty and politics in an urban neighborhood.* Oxford University Press.

Susser, Ida. (2000). "Delmos Jones (1936–1999)." Obituary. *American Anthropologist,* 102(3): 581.

Susser, Ida. (2010). "The anthropologist as social critic: Working toward a more engaged anthropology." *Current Anthropology,* 51(2): 227–33.

Susser, Ida. (2016). "Considering the urban commons: Anthropological approaches to social movements." *Dialectical Anthropology,* 40(3): 183–98.

Susser, Ida. (2017). "Introduction: For or against commoning?" *Focaal: Journal of Global and Historical Anthropology,* 79: 1–5.

Wechsler, Harold S. (1977). *The qualified student: A history of selective college admission in America.* John Wiley and Sons.

Williams, Eric. (1944). *Capitalism and slavery.* University of North Carolina Press.

Wolf, Eric. (1982). *Europe and the people without history.* University of California Press.

Women's City Club. (1975). "The privileged many: A study of the City University's open admissions policy 1970–1975." Women's City Club of New York.

Notes

1   The *New York Times* article "CUNY Students Face Court; Tuition Protest Hits SUNY" (Dennis Hevesi, April 17, 1991) includes a brief description of the closing of The Graduate Center: "The takeover at the City University Graduate Center, on 42nd Street near Avenue of the Americas, started at 7 a.m., when about fifteen students told guards that they were shutting down the building. They barricaded the front doors with a heavy plank and shut off a second entrance on the 12th floor from the adjacent Grace Building."

2   We want to recognize a 1989 student strike that preceded our arrival at The Graduate School. A number of our classmates participated in that strike, and no doubt the mobilization contributed to the understanding of student politics in New York and what was possible. It is beyond the scope of this paper to analyze the 1989 strike, and there remains much work ahead in describing, analyzing and fully appreciating the numerous student demonstrations, rallies, occupations and protests that have shaped the City University of New York in its long history. We hope this paper will inspire more contributions, including others about the 1991 strike.

3   For example, an extensive exhibit at the City Museum of New York, "Activist New York" chronicles "the drama of social activism in New York City from the seventeenth century to the present," including battles over civil rights, wages, sexual orientation, and religious freedom. There is no mention of student struggle. https://www.mcny.org/exhibition/activist-new-york

4   "After Tuition." Editorial. *The New York Times.* June 3, 1976, p. 36.

5   So great was the influx of Jewish students to City College (as the Free Academy was renamed in 1877) that by 1903, 75% of the student body was Eastern European Jews. The relative underrepresentation of Italian and Irish immigrants seems related to the Catholic system of parochial education. Up until 1880, Catholic participation in private schools effectively barred them from entry to City College, which required a diploma from a New York City public high school for admission. The removal of that requirement expanded the number of Catholics who attended City College, but still many more Catholics were encouraged to attend Fordham University, which was conceived as the pinnacle of the Catholic educational system (Wechsler 1977, p. 134).

6   Columbia and New York University, both powerful private competitors, established themselves as antagonists from the earliest days of the Free Academy's founding. At the turn of the century, Columbia University President Nicholas Murray Butler expended a great effort shaping the state education department to serve Columbia's interests. He was instrumental in consolidating control of public education under a single New York State Board of Regents and installing his allies as top officials (Wechsler, 1977, pp. 189–90). Historically, the New York State Board of Regents would be dominated by Columbia trustees and thus decisions about City College would often be at the hands of private and antagonistic interests (Gorelick, 1980, p. 24).

7   The Municipal Assistance Corporation was an entity formed on the state level that assumed power over New York City's finances and operated outside of democratic oversight.

8   For a comprehensive discussion of CUNY student activism, see Gunderson, Christopher. "The Struggle for CUNY: A History of the CUNY Student Movement, 1969-1999." Accessed January 14, 2020. https://eportfolios.macaulay.cuny.edu/hainline2014/files/2014/02/Gunderson_The-Struggle-for-CUNY.pdf.

9   We are very grateful to Jeff Maskovsky for convening an event at The Graduate Center in May 2018 entitled "Hidden Histories of the PhD Program in Anthropology," which captured some of Sydel Silverman's rich knowledge of CUNY history before she passed away on March 25, 2019. All of Silverman's comments in this paper are excerpts from that conversation with Silverman, Leith Mullings, Jane Schneider, Louise Lennihan and Gerald Creed.

10 Not only did graduate education come under attack in CUNY's retrenchment plan in the 1970s, Chancellor Robert J. Kibbee proposed eliminating anthropology, labeled "non-essential," as a major at several campuses to cut costs. Silverman noted that although the CUNY colleges had some 600 anthropology majors, the smallest of the social sciences, a remarkable 25,000 to 30,000 students were enrolled in anthropology courses across the CUNY campuses. The faculty of the different campuses offering anthropology came together to resist this change, although the proposal returned under Chancellor Reynolds in the 1990s.

11 While Jones's central appointment was to The Graduate Center, Wolf was assigned to Lehman College

and taught additional courses at The Graduate Center. Sydel Silverman, Wolf's widow, noted that her husband was committed to teaching undergraduates. A distinguished professor and McArthur "genius award" recipient, Wolf eschewed a more privileged position in midtown, maintaining his main office at Lehman College in the Bronx where he taught undergraduate anthropology in English and Spanish.

12 Millaman, Rosamel. 2007. "Chile's Mapuches organize against NAFTA." NACLA. September 25. Accessed December 30, 2019. https://nacla.org/article/chile%27s-mapuches-organize-against-nafta.

13 In the "Preface" to *On Our Own Terms*, Leith Mullings states: "Because the City University of New York was at that time tuition-free, my father, mother, and all five children were eventually able to attend college" (1996, xiii).

14 According to an interview with striking graduate student Steven Duncombe, the vote on the first day and every day after was unanimously in favor of keeping the building closed ("Graduate Student Support for CUNY-Wide Student Actions." CUNY Digital History Archive. April 25, 1991. Accessed December 30, 2019. http://cdha.cuny.edu/items/show/221.) Our recollection is that there was in fact opposition to continuing the strike. A few people spoke out against our action and voted to end the occupation on the very first day. However, we carried the vote. Menzies recalls it being more difficult to win the vote to end the occupation. We faced two core groups. One was those who insisted we remain until we achieved a total victory. The other was those who had initially voted to end the occupation, but had realized they could disrupt the process by voting to continue the action.

15 We did not see ourselves in a vanguard role. In fact, we remember joking that we were the "rearguard." We had followed the lead of the undergraduate students who had first taken over their buildings.

16 Graduate Center Student Strike Update, April 18, 1991. *The Graduate Student Advocate*, May 1991, page 10.

17 While free education was controversial in 1991, it was a key platform issue for the Democratic party in the 2016 elections. Twenty-six years after the strike, Governor Andrew Cuomo (son of Mario Cuomo) announced that more than half of SUNY and CUNY in-state students would not pay college tuition.

18 Sack, Kevin, "Rally protests cuts in Cuomo budget," *New York Times*, March 20, 1991, B4.

19 A flyer announcing CUNY-wide rally, sponsored by CUNY strikers.

20 We acknowledge the key role Professors Jane Schneider and Leith Mullings played in meeting with students and negotiating actionable demands from the GC administration that allowed us to end the occupation without disciplinary action.

21 See note 16.

22 Nieves, Evelyn. "Students protest new tuition-rise shut 2 CUNY colleges." *New York Times*, April 11, 1991, B1.

23 Letter from Steven M. Cahn, Acting President, April 18, 1991.

24 Verhovek, Sam Howe, "250 at CUNY sue New York, citing racial bias in budget," *New York Times*, February 27, 1992. See also Center for Constitutional Rights (CCR), "Weinbaum v. Cuomo Historic Case," October 9, 2007. Accessed December 19, 2019. https://ccrjustice.org/home/what-we-do/our-cases/weinbaum-v-cuomo.

25 Paul, Ari, 2019. "FT faculty disparity between CUNY, SUNY," *PSC CUNY*, Accessed December 19, 2019. https://psc-cuny.org/clarion/september-2019/ft-faculty-disparity-between-cuny-suny.

26 This activist research agenda was supported by the Intercambio Program at the Center for Puerto Rican Studies, Hunter College, a now defunct academic interchange program between CUNY and the University of Puerto Rico (UPR). The Intercambio program was another example of the unique, vibrant education that was nurtured by a public institution that served a working-class student body of color.

Queens College, Freedom Summer, and Me

Self-Discovery in Archives

VALLAIRE WALLACE

What freedom means to me: Freedom means opportunities—an opportunity for a better education, better jobs, a chance to make more of ourselves.

Freedom means: justice + justice means equality. Freedom means to be equal + to be able to do anything, go anywhere at any time that pleases you.

Freedom means: to be able to speak out, to defend yourself + not get hurt or killed because you spoke out etc."

— Debra Fogg, a student in the Meridian Freedom School

Something about holding a piece of paper that had been in the world longer than I'd been alive really changed me. An activist since high school, I was inspired by my mother, who protested and boycotted whatever she felt was unjust. After I enrolled at Queens College, I continued my activism. After the shooting of Trayvon Martin in 2012, I joined marches and financially supported the Black Lives Matter Movement. I've also joined walkouts to end gun violence, prompted by my fear and disgust that mass shootings are now a regular occurrence. However, it wasn't until I took an English class on researching historical texts and examining original sources in the Queens College Civil Rights Archive that I realized my activist roots and desire for total equality was nothing new. As I read archival letters and details about the QC alumni that participated in the Civil Rights Movement, I realized I was joining generations of students who had attended my college and fought for a more just and equal world.

One of those students, Mark Levy, taught at a Mississippi Freedom School, and submitted writings from his time in Mississippi to the archive. I grew very attached to a letter from one of his students, Debra Fogg. Debra was a young Black girl in his class. Her exact age is unknown because Freedom Schools had a mix of students, ranging from toddlers to teenagers. I cried when I read what she wrote about what Freedom meant to her. She wrote about how a lot of things she considers as "freedom" had yet to be and that people were still trying to find their own freedom. Her letter was written decades ago, the paper she wrote on, older than me, and yet the issues she describes are as relevant today. Many Black kids still cannot "go anywhere at any time that pleases [them]" because of racism; that is partly why the Black Lives Matter Movement exists today. I was touched by how relevant such an old assignment could be.

MARK LEVY AND FREEDOM SCHOOLS

Launched in 1964, Freedom Summer was a political organizing movement whose purpose was to focus "attention on Mississippi" as "the most segregated state in the nation" (Ayers, 381). Among its organizers was the Student Nonviolent Organizing Committee (SNCC), a committee dedicated to desegregation and equality for African Americans during the Civil Rights era. Freedom Schools were an important part of Freedom Summer. The schools sought to give Black students the "academic freedom" their white peers were allowed (Ayers, 381). Run by volunteer college students, the schools covered Black history and Constitutional rights, and encouraged free thinking and critical thought. Levy was among the more than 1000 student volunteers who came from outside the state that summer.

At the time of his journey to Mississippi, Levy had recently graduated with a bachelor's degree in sociology. He was a "co-coordinator and teacher at the Meridian Freedom School in Lauderdale County" ("Mark Levy Finding Aid," 3). His archive is composed primarily of his lessons, lesson plans, and the students' work at the Meridian Freedom School. One of his assignment prompts, in accordance with "encourag[ing] free thinking," was "What does freedom mean to you?" Levy often mixed his historical lessons with essay assignments asking his students personal questions; I think this was an effective teaching strategy. The students, especially Debra, reflected on the reality of their own conditions as they considered world and American history. Their stories were incredible to read.

Debra had a multilayered view of freedom, in the same way as the nation's Founding Fathers. For them, freedom meant liberty for all White colonists, while maintaining the oppressive, demeaning system of slavery; for Debra, freedom meant "opportunities, justice and to defend yourself" without violent repercussions. Such "freedom" has yet to be achieved. Many Black kids still cannot "go anywhere at any time that pleases [them]" because of racism. Too many Black people have been killed with impunity for "doing anything, going anywhere," not allowing us to be considered free. Eric Garner, 43, was standing in front of a store. Trayvon Martin, 17, was walking home. Twelve-year-old Tamir Rice was playing in a park. Death still meets Black people trying to be free; it just comes in the color blue. As long as people are still getting "hurt or killed," then there is no freedom.

Many people wrote letters to Levy during his time in Mississippi. He was quite the popular figure in Queens and Student Association President; I could imagine why! All his writings express leadership and dedication, qualities which made him both strongly loved by activists in the North and South, and strongly hated by the status quo. In his edit of Debra's letter, he comments that her ideas about freedom were "very true." The archive included a "Declaration of Independence" that he gave students; the document detailed the rights that African-Americans deserved to have, such as "equal opportunity, more public libraries and integration in colleges and schools." Levy also received hate mail, and was profiled by the FBI for his activist efforts at the Meridian Freedom School ("Mark Levy Finding Aid").

The more I studied Levy and the movement, I began to truly understand the very real dangers of his activism in Mississippi, a very segregated state. The campus clock tower, named after Andrew Goodman and Michael Schwerner, two Queens College alumni murdered by white supremacists that summer, along with fellow activist James Earl Chaney, is a testament to the dangers the student activists faced. The three men were arrested on false charges by the local police and eventually murdered by members of the White Knights, a chapter of the KKK (Klu Klux Klan). To jump into a fearful situation and do the work, no matter what, is admirable. Activism is dangerous work: the law is often against you, and people in positions of power, too, so your livelihood can be threatened. Many powerful activist leaders, such as Malcolm X, Fred Hampton, and Martin Luther King, Jr., were killed for standing up and "speak[ing] out," or they were exiled, like Assata Shakur.

The activism I do here in New York City is nowhere near the

level of intensity of Levy's activism, but I am all the more appreciative for everything he has done. As a Black New York City native, born and bred, I love having opportunities to learn more about the generations before me. I chose to attend Queens College because my mother attended the college while pregnant with me and excelled. The adventure of digging into my college's archives deepened my connections. I was inspired by Levy, and excited to learn more about him. It was a huge deal, finding heroes who had stepped foot on my campus and were a part of my college's history. I will forever be grateful to Levy for saving these letters and giving them to the archive.

Levy inspired me to further develop my activism and dedication to Queens College, and is one of many reasons I chose to work on the Queens College's newspaper, *The Knight News*. I'm actually Editor-in-Chief now! I have the power to choose what stories are told, and who tells them. I always make sure we have pieces that are critical of societal functions (such as a December 2018 piece I edited that criticized Amazon's proposed move to Long Island City). As a staff writer, I also had the opportunity a few years ago to expose wrongs, such as the underrepresentation of Blacks at Queens College.

Change does not come unless you create it. We all can change our world and reality, but it takes more than one person. It takes more than me, more than Levy, more than Debra. Levy taught me that change has been fought for longer than I've been alive and inspired me to continue to create and fight for better. Freed people are not free—not by Debra's standards, and certainly not by mine. What does freedom mean, and how do we seek our own definition of freedom? It's a question I seek to find the answer to every day. Debra Fogg knew the answer. For now, working to make her answer come true is the best anyone can do.

References

Ayers, William C. "Freedom Schools." *Encyclopedia of curriculum studies*, edited by Craig Kridel, Vol. 1, SAGE Reference, 2010, pp. 381-382.*Gale Virtual Reference Library*. Accessed May 18, 2018. (http://link.galegroup.com.queens.ezproxy.cuny.edu/apps/doc/CX3021500218/GVRL?u=cuny_queens&sid=GVRL&xid=d68e372f)

Freedom School Letter (1964), Box 4, Folder 8, *Mark Levy Collection*, Department of Special Collections and Archives, Queens College, CUNY.

Resistance Everywhere We Went

The Fight for Asian American Studies at CUNY

LINDA LUU

The Asian American Studies Program (AASP) at Hunter College is housed in two small windowless rooms tucked away at the end of a hallway in the West Building. The floor is shared by the Department of Romance Languages and the Department of Classical and Oriental Studies (which, to my knowledge, is the only academic program in the United States that still uses the term "oriental"). The position of the AASP within this spatial configuration, such that visitors to the program are frequently actually looking for the Chinese language program or study abroad opportunities, does not strike me as an accident. Rather, it reflects the fungibility of Asian American studies in the Western orientalist imaginary, that slides over the integrity of Asian American studies as a critical ethnic studies project and likens it to foreign language curricula and study abroad programs.

I was a student at Hunter College from 2013 to 2017 and was involved with student organizing to turn the existing AASP into a full-fledged Asian American Studies Department offering an academic major. Fellow student organizers and I frequently stated the AASP was an intellectual home for students. In truth, the two small offices we were given to build a program were hardly a home. Among students and faculty in the program, it was somewhat of a joke how much we cried in those offices. Sometimes alone, sometimes together. Sometimes after a long day of interfacing with administration, or before a long day of classes, or teaching after coming from another job. I share this to say that if there ever was a space on campus that felt like home, it was forged by us in community under the auspices of institutional neglect and racism, and not handed to us by the institution.

In this chapter, I provide a brief history of the fight for Asian American studies at the City University of New York (CUNY), an overlooked site of student struggles and particularly of student struggles for ethnic studies. I focus on the Hunter AASP, sharing personal reflections from my student organizing experiences. Tracing this history reveals a fraught relationship between students of color and the university, challenging CUNY's public embrace of diversity that has defined its marketing strategy in recent years. It is a relationship that is defined by students of color repeatedly being the ones to initiate the changes they want to see in their educations, demands which the university chooses to interpret and punish as threats to the neoliberal imperial "order" of the university. Finally, I suggest that the radical potential of and need for Asian American studies and ethnic studies lies precisely in their potential to be threats to the university by producing subversive knowledges and actions in line with movements for collective liberation.

THE FIGHT FOR ASIAN AMERICAN STUDIES AT CUNY

The history of CUNY is the history of student struggle. This statement is likely obvious to some and a provocation to others, being that the history of student activism at CUNY is often buried. This institutional memory is difficult to pass on in a university system where a significant portion of students work and attend school part-time, and with campuses dispersed throughout the city's five boroughs. However, revisiting CUNY history challenges the notion that commuter students ever idly passed through the institution. Rather, it demands we recognize students' repeated struggles over power within the largest urban public university system in the country.

The year 1969 figures as an important date in CUNY history. It marks a series of student strikes and building takeovers at the City College of New York (CCNY) and throughout the CUNY system, which led to the establishment of Open Admissions. In response to state budget cuts to SEEK, a program that provides a variety of supports to underrepresented students, and a 20% reduction in admissions, Black and Puerto Rican students at City College took over seventeen buildings, shut down South Campus, and re-named it Malcolm X-Che Guevara University and, later, the University of Harlem.

Amongst other demands, the students called for CUNY's racial composition to reflect that of New York City high schools, which ultimately prompted the Board of Higher Education to institute the policy of Open Admissions, as well as a separate school for Third World (Black, Puerto Rican, and Asian) Studies, reminding us that CUNY was a contemporary in nationwide movements for ethnic studies, despite the attention concentrated on the West Coast in histories of ethnic studies given the Third World Liberation Front. In May 1969, a proposal for such a school was put together by Dr. Wilfred Cartey, a Trinidadian professor of comparative literature and Black studies who, along with students and faculty, was in charge of expanding the existing Department of Urban and Ethnic Studies (Reed, 2013). But perhaps the reason our history pales is because the proposal was shot down. That summer, the college rejected it, fired Cartey, and replaced him with a former Army chaplain who, before this appointment to organize ethnic studies at the college, had only instructed U.S. military personnel (Biondi, 2011).

Protests at City College for ethnic studies continued in the following years and here I want to focus on the Asian Studies department. By 1972, the Department of Urban and Ethnic Studies was split to form four separate ethnic studies departments, including the Department of Asian Studies. However, there were tensions as to whether the department should concentrate on Asian area studies or Asian American studies. With the exception of Professor Betty Lee Sung, who taught the department's first Asian American studies courses in 1970, the department was largely Asia-focused.

In March 1972, a group called Concerned Asian Students staged a three-day takeover of Goethals Hall, which housed the Asian Studies Department. The takeover was prompted by demands for a curriculum that was more Asian-American centered and which spoke to the struggles of local Asian-American communities, as well as for greater student power and representation in departmental policy-making decisions, and the hiring of a new chair and bilingual staff (Kleinman & Arena, 1972). Some 50 to 60 people participated in the takeover, including members of I Wor Kuen, a national Asian American revolutionary organization that drew inspiration from the Black Panther Party and the Young Lords (Liu, Geron & Lai, 2008). Hundreds of Asian, Black, and Puerto Rican students also rallied in front of Cohen Library. Community members from Asian Americans for Action (AAA), the first pan-Asian community organization in New York, provided food and supplies. Yuri Kochiyama, the prominent civil rights activist and AAA member, spoke at the rally, saying the eyes of the community were on the development of Asian Studies at CCNY (Fujino,

2005). The students ended up winning a new department chair, four new faculty positions, a counselor, and a community liaison.

It is important to note the coalitional dimensions of this action, both between students of color on campus, but also between students and community activists. Both I Wor Kuen and AAA membership included CCNY students, many of whom were former college dropouts who went back to school to reconnect with campus struggles (Liu, Geron & Lai, 2008). The Asian Studies program at City College functioned as an academic space and as a space for radical Asians to meet and connect; it grew the Asian American movement in New York. Ethnic studies programs, therefore, are not only borne out of movement struggle, but crucial to maintaining the lifeline of that struggle. Asian American studies also contributed to the formation of other kinds of less grassroots—and even political establishment—formations in terms of social services and advocacy for Asian Americans. New York City Councilwoman Margaret Chin founded the non-profit organization Asian Americans For Equality while attending CCNY in 1974 and cited a course taught by Sung as the turning point for her understanding of the history and struggles of Chinese Americans (Hong, 2017).

In 1975, however, due to the New York City fiscal crisis, concessions won by students were largely reversed and the department suffered serious losses. Because of the "last hired, first fired" policy, by 1978, Betty Lee Sung remained the sole surviving faculty member teaching Asian American studies at CCNY (Wei, 1993). In an interview reflecting on her time at City College, Sung said that from the start, she faced "insurmountable opposition" from faculty, deans, and executive committees who were against her coming into the institution. With Sung's retirement in 1992, any Asian American studies presence within the departmental curriculum effectively ended. Sung said she felt that CCNY was "very happy to get rid of Asian American Studies" (2017, p. 54).

More than a decade after the Goethals Hall takeover, buzz about Asian American studies was picking up at another CUNY campus—Hunter College. Though the first Asian American studies course at Hunter ran in 1972, it was not until 1989 that a confluence of activity by students and faculty would lead to the first full-time tenure-track hire (Hune, 2016).[1] That year, Asian American students brought the annual East Coast Asian American Student Union (ECAASU) conference to Hunter while Assistant Provost Shirley Hune, then-President of the Association for Asian American Studies (AAAS), convened the annual AAAS conference. It was the organization's first conference on the East Coast, and marked the moment that the association, and thereby the field, became national.

Around the same time, CUNY-wide tuition increases prompted another wave of student protests. Strikes and building occupations took place in at least thirteen of CUNY's twenty campuses. The strikes acted as a platform upon which Hunter students made their demands for an Asian American Studies program. It was an opportune time given the presence of Hune as Assistant Provost, and Paul LeClerc as Hunter President, who had a parallel agenda to increase multicultural aspects of the curriculum. Student demands were met and the Asian American Studies Program, offering an Asian American studies minor, was launched in the fall of 1993 with Peter Kwong as its inaugural director.

From its inception, the AASP was conceived to be closely aligned with the struggles of the Asian American community beyond the university. Kwong was clear that the program had obligations and allegiances to serve the people. He immediately convened a Community Advisory Board that included representatives from prominent Asian American organizations and individuals in the city, including the Asian American Legal Defense and Education Fund, *A. Magazine,* Asian American Writers' Workshop, Asian American Arts Centre, Asian Cinevision, Committee Against Anti-Asian Violence, Chinese Staff and Workers Association, and New York Asian Women's Center. In his correspondence with these groups, Kwong wrote, "Mindful of its debts to the community, the program intends to service it" and that the program's students needed to "keep a finger on the pulse of the community."[2]

Documents and meeting minutes from the program's early days show that the program's faculty and students were thinking strategically about using the program's resources to uplift community efforts regarding labor, migration, and women's rights. I read this to mean that the spirit of the program has always been akin to Fred Moten and Stefano Harney's (2013) notion of the undercommons—that of sneaking into the university and stealing what one can in the service of projects for social justice. It is precisely this close collaboration between academic study and activism that defines Asian American studies.

In the following years, the program continued to grow through the labor of faculty and students. With Kwong directing the program at Hunter, and Jack Tchen directing the Asian/American Center at Queens College, CUNY was becoming a leader, alongside counterparts at Columbia University, Cornell University, and the University of Massachusetts Boston, in developing what was a burgeoning model of the discipline: East-of-California Asian American studies.

However, this progress was not met with administrative support. Despite the qualitative growth of the program, faculty and staff spent a great deal of time and labor appealing to administration through data and metrics about the program's deservingness of resources and further investment. The extent of administrative neglect came to a head in 2007, at which point the program no longer had a director because it was given a $0 budget. The program became essentially defunct, unable to carry out its most basic function of granting minors to students.

In the spring of 2007, Hunter College student Olivia Lin knew even before deciding her major that she wanted to minor in Asian American Studies after having taken a course. She was told that she could not declare because the program had no acting head, but to come back after a semester. When Lin went back to the program a semester later and found that nothing had changed, she got together with a group of students to form the Coalition for the Revitalization of Asian American Studies at Hunter (CRAASH). Through a public media campaign that included circulating a petition with over 1000 signatures, writing to public officials, and holding a conference on Asian American studies, CRAASH managed to revive the AASP in one year, and a new director, Jennifer Hayashida, was hired.

Under Hayashida's direction, the program flourished, eventually offering the most Asian American studies courses of any academic program in New York City, and bringing in grants, including a $104,000 National Endowment for the Humanities award for an Asian American literature and film seminar for K-12 teachers. But in terms of administrative support, by the time I arrived at Hunter in 2013, little had changed. The program began with only one full-time tenure-track faculty member and, twenty years later, still had only one full-time instructor, Hayashida, who was not even tenured; all other faculty were adjuncts.

ACTIVISM AS CARE AND THE ADMINISTRATIVE WILL TO MISRECOGNIZE

In March of 2016, CRAASH launched a campaign exposing the state of Asian American studies at Hunter and CUNY. We understood the lack of administrative support for the AASP to be endemic of CUNY's larger institutional failure to support students of color. We held a town hall where we linked our program's struggles to the closures of ethnic studies departments and the tightening of admissions criteria across CUNY that was leading to decreases in Black and Latinx student enrollment (Pérez-Peña, 2012). The town hall took place in the midst of—and was inspired by—a wave of student protests at Yale University and the University of Missouri concerning issues of racial justice and campus climate that made clear to us the stakes of ethnic studies.

We announced five demands: the implementation of an Asian American Studies Department and major; the creation of hiring lines for five full-time Asian American studies faculty; increased funding for the newly created Asian American Studies Department; disaggregation of data on Asian/Asian American students to properly assess needs; and the creation of financial scholarships for Asian/Asian American students with critical needs, especially undocumented, low-income, and LGBTQIA students. For many of us in CRAASH, this town hall and pursuing these demands would permanently change our relationship to the university—how we understood its inner workings and how it saw us.

I want to paint a picture of the textures of engaging in student activism, what it looks like and what it feels like. You are lied to by administrators who do so while making you feel like they are being honest. Each one tries to convince you that *they* are the one you should *really* trust above anyone else. They are playing a game, which you did not ask to be included in, trying to one-up each other as being the most committed to students. The Dean of Arts and Sciences says the school is facing severe budget cuts and that they cannot hire anyone that year, but later the President brags at a public event about how savvy they were with locating funds, hiring a total of thirteen people.

The token administrator-of-color is sent repeatedly to deal with you and tells you that there are "lanes" for students, faculty, and administration and that you, as students, ought to "stay in your lane." Meanwhile, you wonder why this person is spending so much time keeping tabs on you even though they are the school's Title IX coordinator, and the school has just been found to have violated the federal civil rights law barring sexual discrimination.

Campus security cites a fake rule to disband your protest and calls the cops on you. Administrators who have no business directing student clubs and no expertise in Asian American studies continuously tell you what they think is best. Other students tell you that being oppositional to the administration is not the most strategic way to get what you want. They dismissively call you a "rabble-rouser." And, perhaps, you are.

Everyone will feel they have the right to tell you how to be angry. You are made to feel like you are ungrateful, that you are nothing more than a troublemaker. This is meant to dismiss the amount of time and energy you have spent recovering institutional memory, organizing students and faculty, and advocating for this program. At times, student activism feels like giving yourself endlessly to an institution that insists on misunderstanding you. Making trouble is a kind of care. What the administration willfully interpreted to be a threat, CRAASH understood to be a form of care, not necessarily for the university, but towards the possibilities of the university and the kinds of radical spaces and socialities that can emerge from inhabiting the university subjunctively, to follow the directive of Jigna Desai and Kevin Murphy (2018). To engage in this fight is to reassert the fundamental idea that students can and should shape the content and quality of their education.

CHALLENGING CORPORATIZED DIVERSITY

I offer this brief history of the struggle for ethnic studies at CUNY and reflections on the affective experience of student organizing to evince a particular historical relationship between students of color and CUNY. It is a relationship in which students of color have had to fight to preserve themselves in the university and which has been marked by repeated attempts by the administration to elevate the status of CUNY at the cost of students of color. Betty Lee Sung said in regard to establishing Asian American studies at CUNY, "We were met with resistance everywhere we went" (2017, p. 55). There was resistance at every turn, but, in turn, we also resisted. This fraught relationship between students of color and the university stands at odds against the liberal multicultural public image of CUNY that has become the core of its marketing strategy in recent years.

During my last year at Hunter, when CRAASH faced the greatest hostility from the Hunter administration, I received a collegewide e-mail sent to the graduating class. The e-mail called for students to share personal stories of overcoming challenges to be included in the President's Commencement speech at graduation. The e-mail read, "Stories of success like these symbolize a legacy of triumph and form a memorable centerpiece of the President's Commencement speech," and went on to include examples of what constituted a compelling story. The list included a single mother working two jobs and taking care of her ailing grandmother while pursuing her dream of becoming an astrophysicist, a disabled immigrant from the Dominican Republic who went on to earn a 4.0

GPA, a foster child now going to law school—a list which reduced individuals to their hardships in the face of structural violence to tell a neoliberal tale of aspiration and success.

One story stood out in particular. It read: "A Vietnamese student who survived years in refugee camps, as an undergraduate worked full-time at a hardware store to support his family, graduated with a 4.0, and was awarded a full PhD scholarship to Harvard." It is, with only minor differences, the story of my father, a City College graduate. A story which on paper might read as a success story but is one whose shadow is marked by war and its afterlives, and the maddening violence of the model minority myth. This shadow story is one I have only been able to make sense of and live through in part because Asian American studies gave me the tools with which to understand history.

Other students and I often talked about how we likely would have given up and never made it to graduation if it had not been for the space the AASP created for us. The President has no problem holding up the Vietnamese refugee subject as evidence of the kinds of students that CUNY serves, while actively stripping away the spaces and resources needed for those very students to survive on campus. In other words, CUNY gets to lay claim to students who face adversity and "make it"—in fact, requires these narratives upon which to spin their marketing strategy of CUNY as an engine of social mobility[3]—while doing little to support students materially, and at times actively engineering the very policies that sabotage students' abilities to get through school (Leonhardt, 2017). This is not to deny the profound need for CUNY and public higher education in providing an affordable education for poor and working-class people, but rather to acknowledge how austerity policies and politics have spawned disinvestment at the greatest expense of poor working-class students of color (Fabricant &

Brier, 2016).

As Elizabeth Newton (2016) writes, "The paradox of narratives of ambition is that they require the maintenance of a marginalized position from which subjects can rise." CUNY aggressively markets its diverse student body as a corporate branding strategy, exploiting its status as the "Poor Man's Harvard." In light of the alternate history of CUNY I provide here, I want to consider the revealing differences between the aliases "Poor Man's Harvard" and "The University of Harlem," the name given to CCNY by students during the takeovers of 1969. The former exploits the demographic profile of CUNY students. It defines the value of CUNY and CUNY students through their aspirational achievement and commensurates it to elite universities, the value of which needs no explanation. In contrast, the latter uses the same fact of where CUNY is located as a reminder of its commitments to the children of the people.

This essay is an ode to CUNY students who have resisted and continue to resist the neoliberal logics of the university, particularly given that minoritarian subjects, as June Jordan wrote in 1969, speaking about Black students at CCNY, "can choose to refuse the university only at incredible cost" (1981, p. 51). Students of color who expose the university's contradictions and refuse to fit into its prescriptive and narrowly drawn definitions of success are forced into an antagonistic, and often hostile, relationship with the university— one which it consistently denies.

COUNTERINSURGENCY AND THE NEOLIBERAL IMPERIAL UNIVERSITY: THE THREAT OF ASIAN AMERICAN STUDIES

In September 2016, CRAASH delivered a presentation at the Hunter College Senate reiterating our demands to faculty and administration, including Hunter College President Jennifer Raab. Just two days following this presentation, Jennifer Hayashida, then-director of the AASP, was notified that her contract would not be renewed, essentially firing her from the position and leaving the program without a director. It was a clear retaliatory move; no reasons were cited for the decision. Hayashida's performance was certainly not in question as that very day happened to coincide with the news that Hayashida was awarded a $1.7-million Department of Education grant that would give Hunter College the designation of being an Asian American Native American Pacific Islander-Serving Institution (AANAPISI). In 2018, Kevin Park, a core organizing member of CRAASH who graduated from Hunter and stayed on as staff at the AASP and on the AANAPISI grant, was fired by higher-up administration. It is clear to me that this is an explicit strategy on the part of the university that works according to a logic of counterinsurgency in order to stamp out any trace of resistance or dissent.

In the introduction to their edited collection *The Imperial University*, Piya Chatterjee and Sunaina Maira (2014) conceptualize the U.S. academy as an imperial university given the epistemological and material connections between academic research and the military-prison industrial complex; administrative attempts to censor scholarly and academic dissent; and how the university functions as a site to generate specific knowledges that elide ongoing histories of colonialism, imperialism, slavery, genocide, and state-sanctioned racial and gendered violence. I add an administrative logic and practice of counterinsurgency to the list, by which I mean the active expenditure of time, labor, and resources for surveillance, disciplinary action, and forced expulsion of students, staff, and faculty deemed a threat to "business as usual."

The lens of counterinsurgency is particularly fitting given

CUNY's track record, which includes the CCNY administration's surveillance of the Guillermo Morales/Assata Shakur Community Center, a space on campus where student activists frequently met and out of which they ran a farm share, soup kitchen, and childcare services; the Brooklyn College administration's lack of investigation into, or legal actions against, the NYPD infiltration and spying on Muslim students on campus; the disciplining and slander against Students for Justice in Palestine; and the ties between CUNY security and the police, including their collusion in 2013 in the arrests of students protesting the hiring of David Petraeus, a retired U.S. Army general and former head of the CIA, incidentally the architect of U.S. contemporary counterinsurgency (Kaminer, 2013; Stahl, 2015; Grossman, 2017; Glück et al., 2014).

If there is one thing the university and I agree on, it is that Asian American studies is, at its best, a threat and a disruption to the university's neoliberal imperial project. It is precisely the threat of Asian American studies that marginalizes it within the university and makes it worth fighting for. It is precisely the kinds of solidarities that emerge from crying together in the spaces they've abandoned you to that must be managed and contained. It is imperative for Asian American studies to maintain its critical edge, to keep its "finger on the pulse" of the struggles of marginalized communities on the ground. The finger on the pulse of the community can topple the university.

Notes

1. Shirley Hune urges us to trace the history of Asian American studies (AAS) formations to the first course offered at the university: "I view the initial AAS course as having a distinct history and circumstance, often being taught through an adjunct position by a student, community worker, or faculty member sometimes from elsewhere." Hune notes that getting the university to run a course was often the first struggle and so the first course is a more accurate "origin" point, if one is to be identified, than the date an official program was established. The first Asian American studies course at Hunter College was taught by Professor C. T. Wu from the Geography Department and Fay Chiang, Hunter student and prominent Asian American poet, artist, and activist.
2. See "The Fight for Asian American Studies at Hunter College," *CUNY Digital History Archive*, retrieved

from https://cdha.cuny.edu/collections/show/322.
3. In 2017, it was reported that CUNY propels almost six times as many low-income students into the middle-class and beyond as all Ivy League colleges, plus Duke, M.I.T., Stanford and the University of Chicago, combined. This fact has since become a key feature of CUNY's marketing strategy, appearing in ads across the city's subways.

References

Biondi, M. (2011). "Brooklyn College belongs to us": Black students and the transformation of public higher education in New York City." In C. Taylor (Ed.), *Civil rights in New York City: From World War II to the Giuliani era* (pp. 161-181). Fordham University Press.

Chatterjee, P. and Maira, S. (2014). *The imperial university: Academic repression and scholarly dissent.* The University of Minnesota Press.

Desai J. and Murphy, K.P. (2018). Subjunctively inhabiting the university. *Critical Ethnic Studies,* 4(1), 21–43.

Fabricant M. and Brier, S. (2016). *Austerity blues: Fighting for the soul of public higher education.* Johns Hopkins University Press.

Fujino, D. C. (2005). *Heartbeat of struggle: The revolutionary life of Yuri Kochiyama.* The University of Minnesota Press.

Glück, Z., Maharawal, M. M., Nastasia, I., and Reed, C. T. (2015). Organizing against empire: Struggles over the militarization of CUNY. *Berkeley Journal of Sociology* 58: 51-58.

Grossman, H. (2017, November). Campus reactions to Horowitz posters leave more questions than answers. *The Excelsior.*

Jordan, J. (1981). *Civil Wars.* Beacon Press.

Hong, M. (2017). Dragon ladies. *Open City,* Retrieved June 11, 2021, from http://opencitymag.aaww.org/dragon-ladies/.

Hune, S. (2016). Origins: The first Asian American course at the University of Maryland, College Park. *CUNY Forum* 4(1), 59-63.

Kaminer, A. (2013, October). Protests as City College closes a student center. *The New York Times.*

Kleinman, M. and Arena, S. (1972, April). Demonstrators win, Tong to head Asian Studies." *The Campus.*

Leonhardt, D. (2017, Jan. 18). America's great working-class colleges. *The New York Times.*

Liu, M., Geron, K., and Lai, T. (2008). *The snake dance of Asian American activism: Community, vision, and power.* Lexington Books.

Moten, F. and Harney, S. (2013). *The undercommons: Fugitive planning & Black study.* Autonomedia.

Newton, E. (2016). Representing crisis. *The New Inquiry.* Retrieved June 11, 2021, from https://thenewinquiry.com/representing-crisis/.

Pérez-Peña, R. (2012, May 23). At CUNY, stricter admissions bring ethnic shift. *The New York Times.*

Reed, C. T. (2013). "Treasures that prevail": Adrienne Rich, the SEEK program, and social movements at the City College of New York, 1968-1972." In I. Brown, S. Heim, E. Kaufman, K. Moriah, C. T. Reed, T. Shalev, W. Tronrud, A. Alcalay (Eds.), *Adrienne Rich: Teaching at CUNY: 1968-1974 (Part II)* (pp. 37-71). Lost & Found: The CUNY Poetics Document Initiative.

Stahl, A. (2015, October 29). NYPD undercover "converted" to Islam to spy on Brooklyn College students." *Gothamist*.

Sung, B. L. (2017). Betty Lee Sung: Teaching Asian American studies at CUNY, an interview. In Leong, R. C. (Ed.), *Asian American Matters: A New York Anthology*. Asian American and Asian Research Institute, the City University of New York.

Wei, W. (1993). *The Asian American movement*. Temple University Press.

The Imaginary Place

Palestinian Displacement at the City College of New York

JASMINE HOPE KASHEBOON KHOURY

BRINGING THE IMAGINED PLACE INTO SPACE

My first experience in academia with anti-Palestine remarks was with another student. He and I were waiting to be interviewed for a prestigious fellowship offered at all CUNY campuses. We spoke about the projects we hoped to conduct with the funding. He was over six feet tall, white, wearing a fitted suit, and I was about half his size, Arab with white-passing privilege, wearing dress pants and a casual shirt. He told me his project focused on ISIS, a militant organization that imposed strict Islamic rule—more specifically, how the United States regulated ISIS' movements, who was part of ISIS, and what motivated them to join. I explained to him that my project focused on the availability of health facilities for mentally ill Palestinians in the West Bank. His eyes widened and creases began to form on his forehead. My stomach dropped, my face blushed. I was already nervous about my first academic interview, especially since this fellowship could provide me with the financial stability I needed to graduate from the City College of New York (CCNY).

Despite his reaction, I asked, "What do you think? Do you

think I'll get in?" His reply, "Probably not." After a long pause, he said, "It's too radical and risky for the fellowship," suggesting that the mere acknowledgement of Palestinians in the West Bank would exclude me. Granted, I won the fellowship and he didn't, but that was when I began to realize how most students did not know about Palestine and its history. I believe his reaction to my proposed research stemmed from the lack of conversations about Palestine in CCNY classrooms. This student's proposed project focused on an international issue, yet he had a negative reaction to speaking about Palestine, making it clear that he had not been taught about the complexities of this conflict. However, by speaking about Palestine, I brought into existence a space that is usually unseen.

In the essay "In the Company of Writers," the writer and novelist Kamila Shamsie discusses how she had difficulty wrapping her head around the assassination of Kamal Nasser, a famous Palestinian poet and writer. Nasser was assassinated in 1970 by the Israeli Defense Force (IDF) during a raid where he was shot in the mouth and in his writing hand to represent the end of his writing and speaking on behalf of Palestine. Shamsie used the pages of *Poetry East* to grapple with the injustices of Palestine: "And so I turned the pages of *Poetry East* to find the lines further in which played an even greater role than the story of Nasser's assassination in first taking me to Palestine by making it a place I learnt to imagine…" (2017, p. 100). Shamsie used the words of poet and author, Mahmoud Darwish, to grieve and understand the injustices suffered by Nasser and Palestinians at the hands of the Israeli government. Shamsie's assessment leads me to critique how we use literature as an educational tool at CUNY. Although a class may not directly focus on Palestine, it does not mean that we cannot include it in a syllabus with other authors to allow students to make better sense of a place and group of people that are erased, yet often imagined.

HISTORICAL CONTEXT

On November 2, 1917, the British government signed the Balfour Declaration, which gave Palestinian-occupied land to the Jewish people. Following decades of war between Palestinian and Jewish people, it was only in 1948 that the land became officially known as Israel. *Tihur*, a Hebrew word that translates to cleansing, was used in mid-May of 1948 to describe the ethnic cleansing of Palestinians from Israel (Pappe, 2007, p. 131). Since 1917, Palestinians and the Israeli government have been at war. This conflict stems from Israel's mistreatment of Palestinians in the occupied territories of the West Bank and Gaza Strip. The atrocities include the forced migration of families from their homes, the invasion of Palestinian homes and land by settlers and soldiers, as well as the murder of Palestinians by the Israeli military.

The establishment of the Israeli government in 1948 and Israeli control over a Jordanian refugee camp after the Six-Day War in 1967, now known as the West Bank, created 6.5 million Palestinian refugees worldwide. Of that number, 3.8 million registered for humanitarian assistance with the United Nations, and 263,000 Palestinian descendants were displaced within present-day Israel, also known as Nakba (AUPHR). However, the Arab–Israeli conflict, especially its effects on Palestinians, is barely covered by popular media outlets such as Fox News and CNN. What they focus on instead is the Israeli side of the story, which is state propaganda. "On one level, there's what they call *hasbara*, the Hebrew word for information, which is basically propaganda, for the *goyim*, the foreigners" (Said, 2003, p. 43).

By controlling the media, the Israeli government has created a storyline that appeals to the U.S.' better conscience, which is the idea that Palestinians are dangerous and must be controlled. As a result, "The media are so preponderantly pro-Israeli that ordinary people are not able to voice their support for what in effect is a brave attempt to overthrow a colonial-style military occupation" (Said, 2003, p. 38). What the media decides to present to the public directly affects what a professor and students focus on in the classroom. In my experience, CCNY classrooms lack the narrative of Palestinians, even in courses intended to include Palestine. These classroom narratives influence how Palestine is perceived and spoken about in fellowships and other university spaces.

SUBSIDIARY OF SUBSIDIARY

Jewish studies programs are quite popular at CUNY. Among the twelve four-year colleges, there are more than five campuses that offer Jewish studies, yet only one that has Arab studies. Consequently, most students interested in Palestine or Arab studies take a Jewish studies designated course instead, usually with "Palestine" or "Arab" in the title. As Edward Said argues in an interview with David Barsamian, "[T]he whole subject of Palestine is virtually forbidden in the United States and can only be treated as a subsidiary of a subsidiary of a subsidiary" (2003, p. 57).

Considering my Palestinian background, I insisted on taking a course focused on Palestine during my sophomore year of college. When I told a fellow student that I was thinking of taking "Arab–Israeli Conflict" taught in the Jewish studies program, the student immediately told me not to take the class if a specific professor was teaching it because he would debate me, if he knew I was pro-Palestine and that it would become frustrating for me. I took my peer's statement into account and decided to take a different course, "Literature of the Arab–Israeli Conflict."

However, finding a course that focused solely on Palestine was impossible, and the only way for me to learn more about Palestine was to take a course either taught in Jewish studies or the history program. Unfortunately, the history program only included Palestine in courses that focused on the Middle East, meaning Jewish studies was the closest I could get to the literature, history, and people of Palestine.

The course that first piqued my interest was "Literature of the Arab–Israeli Conflict." We did not speak about Palestinian literature until the last two weeks of class when I finally made a statement about the lack of Palestinian authors. One student said that there were not many Palestinian authors, which is not true. Throughout the course, we had to write reaction papers. To critique and analyze Israeli authors, I discussed Palestinian authors and the history of Palestine. The professor graded my paper and recognized my frustration with the fact that we had not talked about Palestinian authors or the occupied territories, saying, "we were not there, yet," implying it would come later in the semester.

However, the last week was the only time we spoke about the West Bank. This class was supposed to be focused on the literature of the Arab–Israeli conflict, but the professor taught in a way that separated Israel from Palestine, when, in fact, they have been inseparably coexisting since the Balfour Declaration. Considering Israel apart from Palestine disguises the violence, oppression, and lack of human rights enforced on the Palestinian population by the Israeli government. In a classroom setting, this narrative imposes Palestine as an "imaginary place" not connected to the settler-colonial state of Israel.

This constant erasure dehumanizes what Palestinians experience and is further implicated in the showing of films, which provide incomplete narratives that distort perceptions of the Arab–Israeli conflict. Before the semester ended, we were shown *Waltz with Bashir* (2008), an autobiographical animated film about a veteran of the 1982 Israeli war with Lebanon. The main character recounts his memories, and interviews other Israeli soldiers that fought alongside him. The entire film focuses on how Israeli veterans were victims of abuse because they were as young as 19 when murdering people in Lebanon. This film painted Israeli soldiers as the victims instead of considering the loss of Lebanese and Palestinian lives. The film exoticized the Israeli soldier as someone who was only following orders without understanding their effects. While these soldiers may have experienced trauma, it still does not excuse the harm that they inflicted.

Most troublingly, this film was completely animated until the last scene, which showed live footage of Palestinians being killed, along with images of the dead bodies of children, and of a woman, upon finding her lifeless son's body, screaming in Arabic, "Love of my heart" (Folman, 2008, 1:20). The last minutes of the film were extremely graphic and unnecessary to insert. Throughout *Waltz with Bashir*, Palestinian and Lebanese people were barely mentioned, yet live footage of their deaths was inserted at the very end.

This artistic decision removes the stories and histories of Lebanese and Palestinian people and centers upon the experiences of the Israeli soldiers who killed them. Although films should not necessarily have to warn viewers in advance of showing violent images, some of us wished the professor in that class had done so. It is not required for CUNY professors to provide trigger warnings to their students, and I know that many do not, but they do have to preserve the safety of students in the classroom. I felt that a warning to students should have been provided for this film, especially since the class included not only students with Palestinian ancestors, but a Marine veteran.

As the semester came to an end, the professor asked us to critique the course. Multiple students felt the course provided an equal view of both Israeli and Palestinian sides of the conflict in its use of literature and films. I was confused how a course that only spoke about Palestine in the last two weeks could be perceived as equally inclusive of the Palestinian side of the story. This experience led me to conclude that Palestine is so absent from the conversation that two weeks is enough for a student to believe that the course was balanced.

FUNDING FOR UNDERREPRESENTED PROJECTS

In my sophomore year, I received a fellowship that provided funding for students to create their own research projects. Originally, I gained strong support for my project, which focused on the availability of health facilities for mentally ill and dis/abled Palestinians in the West Bank, and how these health issues were caused by environmental racism. However, during my last year and a half in college, I was challenged in a way that made me feel like I was being pushed out of the fellowship, which I relied heavily upon. I was passionate about my project, however, so I stuck through it. The challenging moments included—but were not limited to—being asked to change my project, almost being forced out of presenting at an academic conference and having my funding withheld.

For the last summer of the fellowship, I requested funding to compile a bibliography on Palestine and to conduct interviews with Palestinian-Americans in New York. However, I was the only student denied my funding until the end of the summer, after I had achieved all my summer goals. During this time, I was repeatedly asked if I would be interested in changing my project to focus on something that was more relevant and easier to conduct. I rejected this advice because I was passionate and motivated to speak about Palestine since it was often silenced and overlooked in academia. Therefore, I independently pursued my summer goals, focusing on Palestinian literature and conducting interviews with Palestinian-American women without any institutional support. Though my fellowship was designed to assist students who lacked financial resources to work on projects related to underrepresented communities, the program's administrators forced me to use my own limited personal finances. I completed my readings and interviews and became excited to present my findings at the annual fellowship conference. The readings motivated me to switch to a project that focused on the narratives of Palestinian women in America in the form of "storytime," in which my interviewees told me stories of their life in Palestine, rather than responding to a series of questions by me.

After submitting to a conference specifically designed for fellowship students, the director asked me to redo my abstract because it was similar to my previous abstract, even though the project was basically the same, just with interviewees involved now. When I submitted the new abstract to the director, I was told that it was too late. They said the abstracts of my peers had been submitted earlier that day and that I would not be presenting. I felt the director was failing to make an extra effort to include underrepresented voices, so I reached out to the director at another CUNY campus, and asked if I could present. I was told they were happy to include more students. On the day of the conference, the CCNY director noticed me on the program and confronted the conference's leadership, telling them I had overstepped my boundaries and that I should not be allowed to present my project. In the end, I was allowed to present. However, when I stood up to begin my presentation, the CCNY director left the room. Fellowships such as the one I received are meant to provide resources and support to students who are financially underprivileged; however, during my last two years in this fellowship, I received a lack of support from the director and often felt my project was being negatively targeted.

CONCLUSION

CUNY institutions were created so financially underprivileged students and their parents could afford a college degree. I am grateful for the education I received at CUNY, as well as for the professors who supported me when others tried to exclude me. However, it is important to critique an institution even when it provides a great deal of resources to underrepresented communities. There is no excuse for why Palestine is not spoken about in classrooms and in fellowships. While discussing the absence of Palestine from the conversation, Edward Said said, "It's a challenge that can be met if young people are mobilized and have a critical awareness of what's going on. There's no excuse for not knowing" (Said, 2003, p. 61). Writing this paper is not meant to target anti-Palestinian students and professors but, rather, to raise awareness within CUNY that Palestinians still exist and should no longer be silenced. To ignore this group of people is to ignore an entire history of oppression, settler colonialism, murder, and abuse by the Israeli government.

References

Americans United for Palestinian Human Rights (AUPHR). (2003, May 15). Adapted from "The Palestinian Dispossession."

Barsamian, David. (2003). *Culture and resistance: Conversations with Edward W. Said.* South End Press.

The Editors of Encyclopedia Britannica, Balfour Declaration, Accessed on September 27, 2018. https://www.britannica.com/event/Balfour-Declaration

Folman, Ari. (2008). *Waltz with Bashir.* Bridgit Folman Film Group, Les Films D'ici, Razor Film Produktion, Arte France and Noga Communications-Channel 8.

Pappe, Ilan. (2007, Reprint Ed.). *The ethnic cleansing of Palestine*. Oneworld Publications.

Shamsie, Kamila. (2017). "In the company of writers." In This is not a border: Reportage & reflection from the Palestine festival of literature. Bloomsbury Publishing.

Racial Performance and New History for Korean Americans

LEE PAINTER-KIM

As a queer, non-binary biracial Korean and White American, I am used to my identity being questioned because it doesn't neatly fit into fixed and one-dimensional concepts of sexual orientation, gender, race, and culture. Being asked by more traditional Koreans through the bitter undertow of bias if my omma is really full-blood Korean and if my parents are "still together." Being told by haughty white military wives of older generations that I did not live in South Korea during my childhood while living on U.S. military bases in Taegu and Seoul—well, I'll be sure to inform my relatives who are Korean citizens.

Often, I feel that people who are not aware of nuanced and complex sensitivities with mixed-race identity are not comfortable with who and how mixed people are. Instead, somewhere in-between these fixed concepts of race, culture, and continuing personal efforts to quiet my racial imposter insecurities, I negotiate validation for my mixed and hybrid self because I am tired of feeling shame about my identity. From this perspective, I write to focus on the complicated issues of contemporary marginalization of mixed identity and biracial Korean Americans through concepts of racial performance and the intrapersonal, and on how post-Korean War Republic of Korea (ROK) social policies instruct social norms and mass media representation of biracial Koreans, stunting progress for hybridity in the globalized nations of the ROK and United States.

NEGOTIATING RACIAL PASSING AND PERFORMANCE IN THE MIRROR

In *The Souls of Mixed Folk*, Michele Elam (2011) describes racial passing as a performance continuously enacted over time and also as a tool to negotiate social practices and norms within the focus of "Black-white mixes." From this concept of racial passing and performance as a negotiating tool for social progress, I hope to respectfully extend its meaning to my personal experiences and Korean mixed-race identity. In most U.S. environments, I'm often told that I pass as white, and I'm grateful for the many privileges it allows. For instance, my English language skills are never questioned nor assumed deficient, and I rarely have a conflict with police that ends unjustly. However, there are negative consequences of being a mixed-race Korean, such as being alienated from Korean communities. When I buy baechu from a Korean market, the question, "Are you making kimchi?" is often asked in the context of learning a fun trend. But when I reply, "Yes, my omma taught me," and confirm she's full Korean, the conversation ends abruptly in silence. It's likely this happens because it's a specific 20th-century Korean social norm to not recognize biracial individuals as Korean or a part of the community in the United States. A similar logic of racial performance is present in mixed-race individuals who pass as white or as a person of color, enclosing them within varying benefits and consequences of fixed ideas about race and culture.

Within the context of postcolonialism, Homi Bhabha

(1994/2004) analyzes a similar dynamic in *The Location of Culture*, in which hierarchical and fixed claims of cultural "purity" are inherently flawed. Bhabha produces a concept of the Third Space where ambiguity can be recognized in-between fixed concepts of culture, which can be disrupted and made into something hybrid and new (1994/2004, pp. 54-5). From this, an intrapersonal understanding of how to navigate divisions of race and culture can be found, of understanding what is in-between. With optimism, this understanding can serve as a bridge from a mentality of fixed and imposing assertions of race to a more stable understanding of the many complexities of mixed-race identities. Furthermore, that culture and identity can reach further than the tolerance of multiculturalism, as they can actualize a mixed and hybrid existence that reflects the spectral diversity of people.

It has taken my lifetime to understand that the non-white part of my identity is often negated as a consequence of white privilege. I do not want one-half of my identity to dominate the other in any form; I just want to be my mixed, hybrid self. And yet, there have been far too many instances where I've had to perform as solely white to allow other people to let go of the fact that I am biracial and to let go of my omma's presence in my life, as if she were a souvenir of times past. One example is how a former American roommate, a white male who considers himself far-left politically, would heavily imply that being of mixed-race is an equivalent to the false identity of Rachel Dolezal. "½, ⅓, 1/16—there really isn't a difference, either you're one or the other," he would smirk with condescension, next to his 'ironically' purchased Rachel Dolezal 2018 calendar. Dolezal, a fully white woman who claimed she was of African American descent, was formerly the president of a local NAACP chapter in Spokane, WA, and had changed her name to Nkechi Amare Diallo (Haag). How could it be that such a series of lies to perform a race you're not is equivalent to someone expressing and sharing their mixed-race, culture, family? And yet, I reflexively question myself, asking if I am able to talk about my identity as a person of color because I am half and often pass as white. Moreover, this interaction where my failure to bridge an understanding of mixed-race identity with this person has left me hollow in optimism that most people understand or are even willing to try and understand the nuances of mixed and hybrid life.

NEW HISTORY FOR BUTTERFLY'S KIDS

The need to judge individuals into fixed concepts of race and ethnicity corrodes the beauty of how hybrid identity can bring to light new forms of nuanced, complex life and potential social progress. Similarly, following the Korean War, there is a history of maintaining racial purity in South Korea to further establish national independence from U.S. control; I feel this was dependent on Korea's national pain from the experience of Japanese colonialism from 1910 to 1945.

"The Kinship of Violence," an essay authored by Grace M. Cho and Hosu Kim (2012) offers an invaluable argument that the U.S. military presence during the Korean War resulted in biracial Korean-American children who were subject to discriminatory social policies enforced by the new ROK's Ministry of Health and Social Services. This government justified their actions by interchangeably categorizing these children with the disabled in terms of social status and ability. With the cooperation of a U.S. adoption agency run by Harry Holt, these children were separated from their mothers in Korea, and relocated to the United States. Cho and Kim further argue that, to the new ROK government, these biracial children were representative of the nation's compromised independence from having accepted help from the U.S. military.

This sentiment was driven by Syngman Rhee, the first South Korean president (1946 to 1960), who envisioned a future for South Korea with uncontaminated racial and ethnic purity.

To note, for an individual whose social policies were fixed on maintaining ethnic purity, Rhee received an American, Ivy League education at Princeton and Harvard Universities. Moreover, his second wife, Franziska Conner, born in Austria, was the inaugural First Lady of South Korea.

These Korean social policies from the mid-to-late 20th century constructed a stigma against mixed-race Koreans and enforced social norms that have carried over to the present. For me, it has been a huge relief to learn about this historical context of mixed-race Koreans because it has given breath to my understanding of why more traditional South Koreans act with such slighting discretion around me. It is as if I can see a space in my life where there is a thread to pull its tense structure of guilt loose and into a free play of something new.

As described by Homi Bhabha, the function of ambivalence is a discriminatory power where an opinion or perspective of a subject is left open-ended just enough for the audience or people to rely on oversimplified familiarities, like racial stereotypes, to understand the intended meaning (1994/2004, pp. 93–5). In turn, this reinforces fixed concepts of identity, for instance judging a biracial Korean American as solely American. With this and the historicized biracial Korean identity from Cho and Kim in mind, I offer cultural examples of race performed by biracial Koreans in contemporary South Korea.

A recent popular South Korean TV show *Mr. Sunshine* is an early 1900s historical drama that depicts the geopolitical relations of Joseon with the United States, Russia, and Japan. It was a fraught time and the narrative follows activists fighting for Joseon's national independence. The male lead, Choi Yoo-jin, romanized as Eugene Choi, was a Joseon slave as a child who found a way to run away to the United States. As he grew into adulthood, Choi found a way to join the America Marines despite racial discrimination, and was later stationed in Joseon as an American consul where he learned of plans to colonize Joseon; all the while, he reflected on his related inner conflict. Being a K-drama, the story unfolds with many twists, but, for the sake of brevity, I focus on Choi's supervisor—a white American, Major Kyle Moore, played by actor David Lee McInnis. The major is a supporting character who excites moments of comic relief where he is perplexed and entertained by the foreignness of Korean culture. What is disconcerting is that the actor David Lee McInnis is a biracial Korean and white American who could easily pass as Asian. The actor's father served in the U.S. Army and was stationed in Korea, where he presumably met his mother in Jinju (*Wikipedia*). Without intent to discredit McInnis, the question is why this TV series cast a biracial Korean American in this white American role? The irony is this TV series is clearly focused on depicting national progress as a globalizing country and multicultural acceptance in the ROK, yet it wields a discriminating ambivalence reinforcing stigmas against mixed-race Koreans as a fixed identity to alienate from the Korean community as a means to maintain racial and ethnic "purity." There is a line drawn between the tolerance of multicultural coexistence and the disdain of accepting mixed-race Koreans in society.

This disdain for mixed-race Koreans is certainly not limited to white-Korean mixes. There is an emerging social media project called "The Halfie Project: An Exploration of a New Sub-Culture," where their focus is on half Koreans who reside in South Korea. With only a few halfies interviewed at the moment, there is

Tony Smith—a biracial Korean and African American whose father was in the U.S. Army. He emphasizes that, in Korea, he is usually judged as only Black and is used to people always staring at him. Smith further elaborates on how Koreans often question the validity of his mother's Koreanness to the point where he chose to stop identifying as half-Korean with other Koreans. "Because they would literally tell me, like, 'you're half-Korean? Is your mom Korean? So, are they together, your mom and dad?' Yeah…why would you ever say something like that?" (6:58–7:10) These are very common questions for mixed-race Koreans; I especially relate—this line of inquiry toward those from military families often feels close to the idea of 'Western Princess', *yang-gongju,* however erroneously, inelegant, and offensive.

There are joys that come from being of mixed race and cultural identity, like piecing and connecting the best of cultures, and there are instances of deep pain and sorrow spurned by the need to segregate and maintain false, fixed pretenses of "purity." For me, this is a pain that froths beneath quieted disdain and discretion, and has been corrosive to my sense of self.

So, why not put in the effort to corrode stereotypes and stigmas against mixed-race Koreans? Specific to contemporary South Korean culture and mixed-race Koreans, there is an irony in a parallel of Korean and American social codes—the ROK has been building itself as a globalized country, a leader in international culture that is independent of American control, yet it employs a form of systemic racism reliant on fixed concepts of race evocative of U.S. white patriarchal dominance that is failing its citizens. For me, with my pride and principles of respect, I expect more from South Korean and American cultures. I expect them to be better than petty judgements on race and to advance into fuller forms of hybrid and mixed culture instead of tolerated multiculturalism. I expect them to see the threads that can dissolve structures of oppression and find the logic to render something new from the fat of history.

I leave the last word for Insooni, the biracial Korean and African-American K-pop and R&B singer, translated from her hit "A Goose's Dream":

> One day I will pass over that wall
>
> And be able to fly as high as the sky.

References

Bhabha, Homi. (1994). *The location of culture*. Routledge Classics.

Cho, Grace M. and Hosu Kim. (2012). "The kinship of violence." *Journal of Korean Adoption Studies*, Vol. 1(3), pp. 7–25.

Mr. Sunshine. (2018). Created by Jinnie Choi, written by Kim Eun-sook, directed by Lee Eung-bok. CJ E&M and Netflix.

Donnella, Leah. (2018, January 17). "'Racial imposter syndrome': Here are your stories." *Code Switch: Race and Identity, Remixed*, NPR,.https://www.npr.org/sections/codeswitch/2018/01/17/578386796/racial-impostor-syndrome-here-are-your-stories.

Elam, Michele. (2011) *The souls of mixed folk: Race, politics, and aesthetics in the new millennium*. Stanford University Press.

Haag, Matthew. (2018, May 25). "Rachel Dolezal, who pretended to be black, is charged with welfare fraud." *The New York Times*, https://www.nytimes.com/2018/05/25/us/rachel-dolezal-welfare-fraud.html. Accessed 8 January 2019.

Insooni. "[LYRICS] Insooni - Goose's Dream (Romanized+English translate)." https://eflownworld.wordpress.com/2012/12/10/lyrics-insooni-gooses-dream-romanizedenglish-translate/. Accessed 1 May 2019.

Puccini, Giacomo. (1904). *Madame Butterfly*. Composed by Giacomo Puccini.

Tyson, Lois. (2006). "New historical and cultural criticism." *Critical Theory Today*. Routledge, pp. 281–297.

Wikipedia Contributors. "David Lee McInnis." *Wikipedia*, Wikimedia Foundation, last edited 2 April 2019, https://en.wikipedia.org/wiki/David_Lee_McInnis. Accessed 1 May 2019.

White, Becky. (2019, April 30). "The good, the bad and the ugly of being half-Black, half-Korean in Korea," interview with Tony Smith. *The Halfie Project, YouTube*, https://www.youtube.com/watch?time_continue=891&v=llpVIHRWNuk.

Bridge to Baraka

I Am That Bear

YVETTE HEYLIGER

PREFACE

When I graduated from high school in 1977, I was an emerging artist, activist, and scholar. The way had been paved for me to "have a dream," to vote unimpeded, and to ride the second wave of feminism, which included women of color. Oh, yea... and Black was beautiful.

And then life happened.

Fast forward to 2018. I walked into a psychiatrist's office to determine if I should continue taking medication for depression and, if so, should the dosage be increased or remain the same. I had reluctantly given in to taking medication earlier that year after being diagnosed with "persistent depressive disorder with anxious distress (currently mild) and panic disorder." At my insistence, I was prescribed a low dosage. This is because I am an artist—specifically a playwright. I was concerned about having access to my feelings in order to be able to do my work. I did not want to be floating on a cloud somewhere, disconnected and unable to access my gifts and talents.

The psychiatrist and I were meeting each other for the first time, so before we discussed the reason for my visit, she asked what had brought me there. I summed it up in three sentences. "It is hard to be Black in America. It is hard to be a woman in America. It is hard to be aging in America." I told the psychiatrist that aside from the blessing of family and the measure of "success" I had created by pulling myself up by my own bootstraps, my life had been a series of disappointments in response to obstacles both concrete and invisible. I told her that for a long time, I thought it was me—that I wasn't good enough; didn't jump high enough or run fast enough.

At 60 years old, I now understand that I live in a country where "race" is an invention, a social construct, designed to maintain white supremacy through control of land, labor and wealth. Systematic racism has created a situation where Blacks and people of color "marginalized by those in power experience life differently from those whose lives have not been devalued. They experience overt racism and bigotry far too often, which leads to a mental health burden that is deeper than what others may face" (American Mental Health).

As I consider how the lens of personal experience has illuminated structural barriers to social justice and equity, I realize that marginalization is about a lot of little injustices that happen to a person over a lifetime. When I was younger, I believed these injustices were surmountable. I had the strength and the will to fight or to, as legendary poet, activist, and Hunter College graduate Sonia Sanchez commands, "Resist."[1]

As I've gotten older, I have found it harder and harder "to get back up on that horse." It is only now, through therapy and education about transgenerational racism post-graduation that I am beginning to understand and fully appreciate that maybe *it's not all my fault*. Therapy has helped me through the pain of being Black and female in America. Education about racial bias has given me the language to talk about what I have felt and experienced over my lifetime, including my time at two CUNY colleges, Queens and Hunter.

In 2008, I was heavily recruited for the Queens College English Department's new MFA Creative Writing—Playwriting Program, which I learned about quite by accident. I was doing research for one of my plays which had a character who attended Queens College, "the jewel of the CUNY system" at that time. My interest in the program was piqued because, an actor at New York University, I had never formally studied playwriting. Now, I was a lifelong artist fast approaching 50, who was in need of financial stability. I realized I needed to find a parallel career that not only was salary-based but also provided health insurance. I had BA and MA degrees from New York University but job postings revealed that an MFA or PhD was required if I wanted to teach in higher education. Moreover, with one daughter recently graduated from Vassar College, one still in college at New York University, and my husband a casualty of massive layoffs during the financial crisis in 2009, I was unsure whether returning to school was prudent.

When visiting the Queens College campus, I saw these words embedded in the iron lattice entrance, greeting students as they entered the grounds of the college: *Discimus ut Serviamus*, "We Learn So That We May Serve." Moved, I believed this to be a "sign" that I was in the right place. After all, my work as an artist is all about service! My vision as a playwright has always been to create works of lasting value for the American Theatre, primarily about women, and by uplifting them, uplift humanity. I write plays that enlighten and entertain in the service of social change; plays that are steeped in research and represent issues that I care about as a woman, a citizen, and a human being. So, I accepted the offer to attend the MFA Creative Writing—Playwriting Program at

Queens College.

I had a troubling tenure at Queens College, despite having been heavily recruited for their new program. I felt myself to be the victim of not only racism but sexism and ageism, as well. The experiences I had in the English Department compounded my feelings of isolation and marginalization to the point where I did not know whom to trust when it came time to ask professors to read my thesis project and paper. The thesis project (a new play) and paper had to be submitted in partial fulfillment of the requirements for the MFA degree in the English Department of the Graduate Division of Queens College. My concern was that my thesis be read impartially and judged fairly. Given what I had experienced, I was not sure that would happen. In retrospect (and now that I know what to call it), I believe that institutional racism was at play.

Despite all of the -isms, there were some good things that happened at Queens College. Electives. I really enjoyed taking them because, unlike my required courses, they allowed me to find "my peeps"—like-minded people, whether alive or in a book, that I could be in community with. One elective I took was "Conceptions of Selfhood in African American Literature." Outside of reading Black plays, this was the first time I had studied Black literature. In addition to in-class discussion of the readings and written responses to the work, students had to sign up to present on various topics selected by the professor. I chose the Black Arts Movement, a topic of which I had only cursory knowledge. This opportunity was such a blessing for me, not only as a student but as an artist and a human being. In doing the research to prepare for my in-class presentation, I realized that I wasn't an anomaly in theatre history, standing alone with a message and no microphone. I was standing on the shoulders of the artistic warriors of the Black Arts Movement who, like me, possessed (or cultivated) an entrepreneurial spirit. This knowledge was life-changing. It emboldened me, giving me renewed strength, resolve, and desire to keep going as an MFA candidate. A new world had opened up to me and what I learned later became the foundation for my one-woman show, *Bridge to Baraka* and its spin-off, my performance text, *Bridge to Baraka: I Am That Bear*, which follows.

Fast forward to Hunter College. I was selected for the Lincoln Center Scholar/Hunter College Alternative Certification Program for Creative Arts Education program to become a drama teacher in NYC public schools. In addition to taking required classes in the School of Education, I also took classes in the Hunter College Theatre Department on theatre history and play analysis, among others. In theatre history, students were asked to make a selection from given topics for an in-class presentation. I seized this opportunity to fill a glaring gap in the syllabus, Black theatre. I selected "protest art" as represented in the Black Arts Movement of the mid-1960s to mid-1970s, building on prior knowledge attained in my class at Queens College. In my play analysis class, I decided to narrow the focus of my thesis on the plight of the Black women playwrights who were subject to racism, sexism, and misogyny within the Black Arts Movement. All of this provided excellent fodder for my one-woman show whose mission had only become clearer because of these in-class presentations.

In *Bridge to Baraka: I Am That Bear*, I spotlight the unpublished and minimally published women playwrights from the Black Arts Movement whom I uncovered in writing my thesis, especially and most notably, Sonia Sanchez, a political science major who graduated from Hunter College in 1955. Sanchez also took creative writing courses at Hunter College and often wrote through the lens of personal experience. I had the good fortune to meet and speak briefly to Sanchez after an evening of poetry and performance honoring her at the Schomburg Center for Research in Black Culture.[2] With her blessing, I included a monologue from her play, *Sister Son/ji*, in my performance text. In the monologue, the character by the same name, Sister Son/ji, describes an experience of being marginalized at Hunter. It seems that the professor can never remember Son/ji's name because she and the only two other Black students in the class all look alike. Fed up, Son/ji walks out of the class never to return, explaining, "After all at some point a person's got to stand up for herself just a little…" (Sanchez, 1969 pp. 100-101).

It is likely that the cumulative experiences of interpersonal and structural racism that Sister Son/ji (aka Sanchez) and her fellow classmates had as students in the 1950s were contributing factors, which led to the student protests at Hunter College in the 1960s. Because of the collective experience of marginalization and invisibility, Black and Brown students at colleges and universities around the country protested. My late paternal grandmother, Blanche Barfield Erwin, attended Hunter, as did my late mother-in-law, Cleo Wooldridge Heyliger. If Sonia Sanchez, who graduated in 1955, experienced overt racism and discrimination at Hunter College, I can only imagine what it must have been like for my grandmother and mother-in-law whose tenure at Hunter preceded Sanchez's.

I would be curious to know if Sanchez, or my grandmother and mother-in-law for that matter, knew that CUNY Hunter College was a part of the grand social experiment of CUNY schools to provide a free education to the "children of the people" (that's the "children of the ninety-nine percent" in today's jargon!). It would seem that despite best intentions, this grand experiment called a "public university," which had as its initial goal the leveling of the playing field for ALL in higher education, succumbed to the structural racism that is in the DNA of our country that privileged

White students over Black and Brown students. Had it succeeded, CUNY, our nation's first free public university, would have been a lighthouse on the raging seas of racial injustice—*even a form of reparations.*

Dr. Maulana Karenga, the creator of Kwanzaa, the Nguzo Saba (The Seven Principles), and the author of Kawaida, the philosophy out of which The Seven Principles are created, is an internationally recognized social theorist, ethical philosopher, and activist-scholar. In "Rightfully Linking Reparations and Liberation: Righteously Repairing Ourselves and the World," Karenga (2019) lays out six steps to heal, repair, and transform the world:

> Regardless of the eventual shape of the evolved discourse and policy on reparations, there are six essential aspects which must be addressed and included in any meaningful and moral approach to reparations. They are public dialog, public admission, public apology, public recognition, compensation, and preventive measures against the recurrence of Holocaust and other similar forms of massive destruction of human life, human culture and human possibility.

These steps are instructive to the honest examination of historical racial bias at CUNY colleges. I believe this preface and my performance text to be part of the first step: public dialogue. Plays can be great conversation starters—what happens next is up to the citizenry. Karenga's remaining five steps are the work of the people, our elected officials, and our institutions.

The challenge is clear—to radically reimagine the public university and to discover, as Horace Webster, the first president of the Free Academy said in 1849, "whether an institution of the highest grade, can be controlled by the popular will, not by the privileged few, but the privileged many" (qtd. in Medina, 2014). An incentive to tackle this challenge may be to look at CUNY's mission through the lens of Hunter's motto, *Mihi Cura Futuri*. If, in fact, the "Care of the Future Is Mine," then we as a body of stakeholders (current students, faculty, staff, administrators, and alumni) have an obligation to dismantle and to disrupt racism on CUNY campuses for the benefit and care of future generations.

President Barack Obama once called Hunter "one of the best colleges in the country" (Raab, 2014), but I think he would agree that, like democracy, CUNY schools are a work in progress. For this reason, at my graduation from Hunter in January of 2019, when asked to stand for the singing of the national anthem, I "took a knee"—not physically, but metaphorically. I protested by remaining seated and placing my hand over my heart, while an ocean of purple graduates stood around and behind me in the auditorium. President Jennifer J. Raab, the officiant of the graduation ceremonies, saw me sitting in the front row, hand over heart. I wondered if she wondered why.

Bridge to Baraka: I Am That Bear

<u>AT RISE</u>: *A musical selection reminiscent of the early seventies composed by Larry Farrow called "Black Arts Boogie" plays as lights rise. Music fades as YVETTE X, a guest artist at an institution of higher learning, is dressed in an Afro wig, sunglasses, bell-bottom jeans and a dashiki. SHE plays an African drum.*

YVETTE X

Calling women. Calling ALL WOMEN: mothers, daughters, sisters, wives, aunts, nieces, girlfriends and grandmothers; cisgender, transgender, she/her/hers and they/them/theirs…wherever you are, calling you. Urgent. Come in, you women. Come on in.

Welcome to "Achieving Artistic Parity…by Any Means Necessary". My name is Yvette X, Uptown Artist. I am not a man. I am not White. I am not thin, and I am not young, but I write plays for the American theatre featuring roles for leading women. No doubt you've heard the statistics. It's pretty bleak. In the whole history of the American Theatre, no female playwright has ever been produced to the extent of any male playwright living or dead.

We don't feel it so much here in New York City, the mecca of theater, but if you spread out across the country, you feel it—and you can believe when things are hard for white women, they are doubly hard for women of color. Why, at the rate things are going, women may not see equality in the American Theatre for another hundred years! That's what, like two hundred years for me!

So, you may wonder, what gives Yvette X the determination, the courage, the audacity to write plays for the American Theatre—

to write the plays she wants to write, the way she wants to write them? On whose shoulders does she stand? Tell you what; I'll give you a clue. In order to find the answer to that question, we have to go back—back to Black!

[To the sound booth.]

Hit me!

[Sound cue, James Brown's hit song, "Say It Loud - I'm Black and I'm Proud." YVETTE X dances the "Boogaloo" and/or the "Funky Chicken".]

Did you guess on whose shoulders I'm standing? No? Well, hold on to your seats. This may shock you. I am standing on the shoulders of the Black Arts Movement. Is there anyone here that was around in the sixties? Well, there's a lot more to it than what you might think—more to it than, "Whitey did this to us," and "Whitey did that to us"; more to it than a bunch of angry poems, rioting and finger-pointing. Luckily, I have documented my revelations in my soon-to-be-released, self-published book…

[SHE gets her book, takes in a deep breath, and exhales the title.]

"Yvette X's Evolutionary Pilgrimage to the Black Arts Movement and What Women Playwrights Can Take from It to Inspire Them to Keep Fighting the Good Fight." *(To the light booth.)* Can we bring up the lights a little?

[House lights up.]

Now, feel underneath your seats. Anything there?

[Audience does so.]

Nothing, right? That's because instead of putting a copy beneath your seats like they do on those talk shows, for the price of a theatre ticket, I'm going to lay it on you live, right here in this classroom! Can you dig it?

[Lights restore as SHE returns to the podium.]

Now, in the interest of time, I'm going to give you the CliffsNotes version of my book. Let's see… *[ruffling through her notes to find her place]* dramatic opening, check. Welcome, introductions… Ahh ha! The Lesson.

Picture it. The Divided States of America. Black folks have won the right to vote, to sit at White-Only lunch counters, in the front of the bus, and next to White kids in class. But the day-to-day quality of life for most Black folks was still the same—poverty, unemployment, lack of education, decent housing and health care. You name it—Black folks needed it, couldn't get it, but were expected to pay taxes for it anyway. Institutions of higher learning found themselves subject to Black and Puerto Rican student-led protests which sought to end structuralized racism which disadvantaged them.

Tensions, which had been building up since Lincoln signed the Emancipation Proclamation, were coming to a head in major cities across the country: Atlanta, Boston, Chicago, Cleveland, Detroit, Evanston, Los Angeles, Milwaukee, Newark, New Orleans, New York City, Oakland, and San Francisco!

America had decided we were citizens alright, but was slow to deliver equal opportunity for Blacks. We still had to wait until we got to the gold-paved streets of heaven to get our milk and honey. And to add insult to injury, because only white folks could afford guns, Blacks were defenseless against unchecked violence and murder at the hands of those whose job it was to protect and serve them—

[Assuming the "Hands Up Don't Shoot" position.]

—the police.

[Raising her fist, she chants a slogan.]

"Arm yourself or harm yourself! Arm yourself or harm yourself! Arm yourself or harm yourself!" Because the United States government was either "unwilling or unable" to protect the lives and property of Blacks; because of the violence unleashed on peaceful demonstrators; because we were no longer content to turn the other cheek, *we protested*. The straw that broke the camel's back was the assassination of El-Hajj Malik El-Shabazz, better known as Brother Malcolm X. That was it, baby! That was it! Black folks were ready to take some White folks out.

But dig this, before Malcolm died, he issued a call to action, utilizing the arts to build racial pride and solidarity. He said, "We must recapture our heritage and our identity if we are ever to liberate ourselves from the bonds of White supremacy." "We must launch a cultural revolution to un-brainwash an entire people."

Artists who considered themselves to be "Malcolm's sons and daughters" took his marching orders to heart, avenging his death by choosing the PEN instead of the GUN as a means of armed self-defense against the System. They turned poetry into bullets and called it "Black Art."

[SHE sits at a manual typewriter.]

Black folks were writing *for* themselves, *by* themselves and *about* themselves; not caring what "The Man" thought about it, or if he would ever read it, review it or buy a ticket to see it—

[Manual typewriter out.]

pushing the envelope and breaking every rule governing grammar, style, form, content, and plain old good manners. I'm telling you, Black poets, playwrights, essayists, and novelists were out of control! All up in your face and emboldened by their Blackness, they rejected Western standards, traditions, and values; smashing, burning and looting white ideas, white ways of doing things, white ways of being, white ways of looking at the world; and most importantly, seeing ourselves the way white people see us. Shoot! White folks don't know how close they came—just an ellipsis, an em-dash, or a comma away from meetin' their maker!

The writing that came out of the mid-sixties to the mid-seventies was a militant literary movement, the likes of which America had never seen before. The Black Arts Movement transcended "protest art" to become a "Black aesthetic" proving that African Americans can be the creators of a distinctive culture with its own aesthetic art forms—and writers in particular did this, despite being forced to give up their native languages and culture. They reached back to Africa to gather strength, wisdom, and inspiration from the past. And "Black Power" led to "Black is Beautiful."

Now, you may ask, Yvette X, what about all those beautiful Black sisters writing during the Black Arts Movement? What'd I tell you? *If things are hard for white women, they're doubly hard for women of color.* White women have historically been discriminated against in the literary arts, and in the world of Black literature it was no different. A woman's place was a few paces behind the men who thought themselves to be the definitive voice of the Black experience in America.

But Sonia Sanchez could hold her own with the men and, like the father of the Black Arts Movement, Amiri Baraka, she was adept at crossing literary genres. But because sexism was alive and well in the sixties and seventies, she fought to be taken seriously. She fought to get audiences for her work. She fought against being dismissed or silenced. The Black man's story was only *half* the story, and Sanchez knew that. She not only courageously took on those chauvinistic Black Nationalist brothers who mistreated the sisters in the Movement, but she took on racism too.

In a moment, I am going to share a monologue from *Sister Son/ Ji* by Sonya Sanchez. *Sister Son/Ji* speaks to the racism she encountered during her college days. One reviewer said, "The play typifies Sanchez's bold spirit as it illustrates her early capacity to celebrate the Black Power Movement and critique it at the same time. The patriarchal oppression of women within the Black Power Movement is thus central to the play's impact both in the '60s and today. Sister Son/Ji, in part, explores the vital role in the movement of college students..." (Leskowitz, 2009)

[Street noises are heard.]

SISTER SON/JI

i'm coming nesbitt. i'm coming. Hey. thought I'd never catch you—how are you? *(Looks down for she has that shyness of very young women who are unsure/uncertain of themselves and she stretches out her hands and begins to walk—a lover's walk.)* yeah. i'm glad today is Friday too. that place is a mad/house. hunter college indeed. do u know nesbitt that ole/bitch in my political theory course couldn't remember my name and there are only 12 of us in the class—only 3 negroes—as different as day and night and she called out Miss Jones, Miss Smith, Miss Thomas and each time she looked at the three of us and couldn't remember who was who. Ain't that a drag? But she remembered the ofays' names/faces and they all look alike honey. *(Turns & faces him.)* You know what I did? u know what I did nesbitt? i stood up, picked up my note/book and headed for the door and u know she asked where I was going and i said out of here—away from u because u don't even know my name unless I raise my hand when u spit out three/blk/names—and she became that flustered/red/whiteness that ofays become, and said but u see it's just that—and I finished it for her—I sd it's just that we all look alike. yeah. well, damn this class. (i wanted to say fuck this class honey but she might have had a heart/attack/rt there in class) I said damn this class, i'm a human being to be remembered just like all the other human beings in this class, and with that I walked out. *(Is smiling as she turns her head.)* what did you say? am i going back? no honey. how/why shd i return she showed me no respect. none of the negroes in the class was being respected as the individuals we are—just three/big/blk/masses of blk/womanhood. that is not rt. can't be. *(Stops walking.)* Uh-huh. i'll lose the credit for that course but i'll appeal when i'm a senior and u know what I'll write on that paper. I'll write the reason I lost these three credits is due to discrimination, yes. that's what I'll say and... oh honey. yes. it might have been foolish but it was right. after all at some point a person's got to stand up for herself just a little... (Sanchez, 1969, pp. 97-107).

Yes, at some point, a person's got to stand up for herself. This daughter of Malcolm understood the power of drama and playwriting and its accessibility to the masses. So she continued to write in spite of the racism and sexism she and other women encountered. Perhaps this is why Sanchez fought to get work by Black writers included in college curriculum.

Sonia Sanchez was a part of something bigger than herself. She and the other writers of the Black Arts Movement lived and breathed the issues of their communities and had tremendous faith in the power of theatre to bring about social change. White folks were scratching their heads wondering, "Now, what bear did we poke?" Sweet, sticky honey! I just thought of something. I AM THAT BEAR!

["Baraka Groove" by Larry Farrow is heard.]

I am that bear that writes plays for the American theatre featuring roles for leading women, in a country where no female playwright is produced to the extent of any male playwright, living or dead.

I am that bear standing on the shoulders of artistic warriors whose poetry, plays and essays were like honey from the Tree of Life—recognized, sought after and consumed for the first time in spite of their buzzing, stinging, sticky words.

Carol Freeman, Marti Evans Charles, Alice Childress, Alexis De-Veaux, J.E. Franklin, Aisha Rahman, Beah Richards, Salimu, Sonia Sanchez, and all of the unsung bear-women who got poked, but never got a chance to publish, much less produced or be taken seriously.

These foremothers of multiculturalism and inclusion would not be denied a place in the heretofore lily-white canon of American literature, just as we women will not continue to be denied equal pay and access to America's stages!

For heaven's sake, if Black women facing relentless racism and sexism in the sixties could somehow manage to contribute to, and along with Black men, leave a literary and cultural legacy to the melting pot,

[SHE sits and types; sounds of a manual typewriter are heard.]

then surely we multicultural women in the new millennium can write and publish our own plays *for* ourselves, *by* ourselves, *about* ourselves not caring what "The Man" thinks about it, or if he will ever read it, review it or buy a ticket to see it—pushing the envelope and breaking every rule writing our female leading characters; signing our gender-specific names; writing our plays with or without an agent, a pedigree from a prestigious writing program, or a review from *The New York Times*, and getting those plays to the ticket-buying masses!

Heck, we make up roughly seventy percent of those ticket-buying masses anyway. We bring the men to the theatre! Since we hold the purse strings, why not have more of a say about what we're dragging our boyfriends, husbands, and significant others to see?

Women playwrights are crammed together on the back of a bus filled with plenty of seats for men. We don't have to fight with each other over the few open seats that are left. We don't even have to ride that bus. We can walk—no, *march*—to our destination.

What we women can learn from the Black Arts Movement—writing *for* ourselves, *by* ourselves, *about* ourselves, and getting those plays to the masses BY ANY MEANS NECESSARY—is what inspires me to keep fighting the good fight. *(SHE has a revelation.)* Hey! I'm going to give myself a new name! Black Bear X. And if there is a Black Bear XX *[pronounced "two-x"]* or a Black Bear XXX *["three-x"]* or four-x among you who got poked today, then dig this…

[African drumming is heard.]

Calling you… Calling all you women: cisgender, transgender, non-binary, two-spirit, she/her/hers and they/them/theirs… Urgent. Come in you, "binders full" of "nasty" women. Come on in.

= THE END =

Postscript (Added July 5, 2021)

During his first days in office, President Joe Biden signed an Executive Order on Racial Equity, saying in part, "… advancing equity has to be everyone's job." Five months later, on June 25, 2021, he followed up by signing an Executive Order Advancing Diversity, Equity, Inclusion, and Accessibility in the federal government. President Biden's actions to disrupt institutionalized racism throughout government agencies, ensuring that America's public servants reflect the full diversity of the American people, should inspire our educational institutions both large and small, city or state, public or private, brick and mortar or online, to do the same. These types of transformational changes will take *generations* to achieve. For this reason, it is important that these seeds are planted now. You and I won't see the fruits of this labor, but I draw comfort knowing that my grandchildren's children who are entering college might!

Notes

1. This statement was said by Sonia Sanchez during the live performance of *Shake Loose: A Celebration of Sonia Sanchez*, on April 1, 2019, 6:30 p.m. to 8:30 p.m.; an evening of poetry and performance honoring the legendary poet, activist, and Schomburg Society National Ambassador; Schomburg Center for Research in Black Culture, 515 Malcolm X Boulevard, New York, NY 10037.
2. Sanchez, Sonia, spoken during the meet-and-greet, following *Shake Loose: A Celebration of Sonia Sanchez*, Schomburg Center for Research in Black Culture, April 1, 2019.

References

Karenga, Maulana. (2019, June 6). "Rightfully linking reparations and liberations: Righteously repairing ourselves and the world." *The Los Angeles Sentinel.* Accessed July 2, 2021 from https://lasentinel.net/rightfully-linking-reparations-and-liberation-righteously-repairing-ourselves-and-the-world.html.

Leskowitz, Ali. (2009, July 28). "THE BRONX IS NEXT and SISTER SON/JI Hit Riverside Theatre 8/6 Thru 8/17". *Broadway World.* Retrieved on July 2, 2021 from https://www.broadwayworld.com/off-broadway/article/THE-BRONX-IS-NEXT-And-SISTER-SONJI-Hit-Riverside-Theatre-86-Thru-817-20090728.

Medina, Douglas. (2014). Open admission and the imposition of tuition at the City University of New York, 1969-1976: A political case study for understanding the current crisis in higher education. *New Political Science*, Vol. 36, No. 4, December.

Mental Health America. Accessed on July 2, 2021 from www.mhanational.org/racism-and-mental-health.

Raab, Jennifer. (2017, Jan. 10). Special distribution message to Hunter College community. Retrieved on July 5, 2021 from https://mailcaster.hunter.cuny.edu/archive/communications/special-distribution-messages/2014-0110-132721.354.

Sanchez, Sonia. 1969. Sister Son/ji, *New plays from the Black theatre*. (Ed. Ed Bullins). Bantam Books. Pp. 97-107.

TEACHING AND LEARNING

Dear Sister Outsider

On Audre Lorde and Writing Oneself into Existence[1]

LAVELLE PORTER

Dear Audre,

Two years ago, your name came up in one of the most improbable places. A few weeks before the St. Louis Rams drafted Michael Sam, making him the first openly gay player in NFL history, a White male sportscaster in Texas named Dale Hansen gave a passionate response to Sam's critics: "Civil rights activist Audre Lorde said, 'It is not our differences that divide us, it is our inability to recognize, accept, and celebrate those differences.'" I never thought I'd see the day that a silver-haired, Southern white sportscaster with a Texas accent would publicly quote you, a Black lesbian feminist socialist poet, and would do so in defense of a Black, gay professional football player, but here we are. Hansen's full statement was powerful and drew attention. But the moment also made me wary. I thought about how this story of a gay athlete coming out in a major male sport was indicative of an assimilationist moment in queer politics. I wondered about your being reduced to an innocuous "civil rights activist" and not the militant poet who criticized the U.S. invasion of your ancestral homeland Grenada, who spent time in the Soviet Union, and who might be critical of the macho, brutal sport that the young man plays or the billion-dollar corporation that runs it.

The lines that Hansen quoted are widely attributed to you on the web, but I can't find the original source. Some references cite the 1986 poetry collection *Our Dead Behind Us*, but it's not there. Certainly, the quote sounds like yours, and this idea of "difference" is one you expressed so well in your poetry and essays. Though Nancy Bereano reminded us in her 1983 introduction to the original edition of *Sister Outsider* that you thought of yourself as a poet first and not a theorist, your conception of difference has profoundly influenced feminist thought as a way of articulating the overlapping and intersecting ways in which marginalized people can identify. As you wrote in the essay "Age, Race, Class and Sex: Women Redefining Difference" (1980), in a passage that sounds close to what Hansen quoted:

> Certainly there are very real differences between us of race, age, and sex. But it is not those differences between us that are separating us. It is rather our refusal to recognize those differences, and to examine the distortions which result from our misnaming them and their effects upon human behavior and expectation. (p. 115)

The way you invoked difference was not as mere liberal tolerance and not about a corporate market niche, but as a mode of resistance against white supremacist patriarchal norms. In that essay, you also wrote this:

> Too often, we pour the energy needed for recognizing and exploring difference into pretending those differences are insurmountable barriers, or that they do not exist at all. This results in a voluntary isolation or false and treacherous connections. Either way, we do not develop tools for using human difference as a springboard for creative change within our lives. (pp. 115-116)

Those words feel so necessary right now when any reference to structural oppression or inequalities is met with false equivalences and faulty universalism.

When I heard Hansen's quote, I thought about your 1982 novel *Zami*, an autobiographical book you described as a "biomythography"—a mixture of history, biography, and myth:

> Being women together was not enough. We were different. Being gay-girls together was not enough. We were different. Being Black together was not enough. We were different. Being Black women together was not enough. We were different. Being Black dykes together was not enough. We were different. (p. 226)

My copy of *Zami*, with its distinctive bright orange cover in the Crossing Press edition, is one of my most cherished books. Picking it up again recently, I noticed that in the margin next to that passage I'd scribbled the words *the inevitability of difference*. I must have made the note sometime in 2001, when I was reading your books and work by other Black queer writers, searching for words to help me face my own Black queer self. It was your writing, along with E. Lynn Harris and Samuel Delany and James Baldwin and many others, that introduced to me the possibility of writing myself into existence. From you, I learned that we can work across those boundaries of social difference but never from a belief in color-blindness or a denial of other people's particular experiences in this world.

In her beautiful book, *Warrior Poet*: *A Biography of Audre Lorde* (2006), Alexis De Veaux describes *Zami* as a text that "recovers from existing male-dominated literary genres (history, mythology, autobiography, and fiction) whatever was inextricably female, female-centered" (p. 314). That female-centeredness is at the heart of my favorite volume of yours, *The Black Unicorn*

(1978), a collection of poems that celebrates women's bodies and desires and that creates a "mythworld" in which women's experience and feelings are central.

The poem "Between Ourselves" helped me locate my particular Blackness, helped me articulate my feelings that I was marginal within a community that I still found valuable and important.

> Once when I walked into a room
> my eyes would seek out the one or two black faces
> for contact or reassurance or a sign
> I was not alone
> now walking into rooms full of black faces
> that would destroy me for any difference
> where shall my eyes look?
> Once it was easy to know
> who were my people.
>
> (p. 112)

I came to that poem after having graduated from a Black college, after being schooled in the ways of Black solidarity, and yet learning that so many of us who were queer were shunned and shamed. I believe that now we are in a moment when Black people are questioning what you referred to in that poem as an "easy blackness as salvation," that we are no longer willing to accept that signing on to Black liberation means submitting to heteropatriarchy. I see in the political movements of today efforts to embrace feminism and queerness, even as the respectable mainstays of the Black church and the Black college continue to hold sway over Black political discourse.

When I finally decided to come out to my family, I turned to your words from "A Litany for Survival" for encouragement and support.

… And when the sun rises we are afraid

it might not remain

when the sun sets we are afraid

it might not rise in the morning

when our stomachs are full we are afraid

of indigestion

when our stomachs are empty we are afraid

we may never eat again

when we are loved we are afraid

love will vanish

when we are alone we are afraid

love will never return

and when we speak we are afraid

our words will not be heard

nor welcomed

but when we are silent

we are still afraid

So it is better to speak

remembering

we were never meant to survive.

(*The Black Unicorn*, pp. 31-32)

I've often thought about the multiple meanings of that last line. As Black people in America, we were considered chattel, disposable property, and we were never meant to live free, never meant to grow up, grow old, become educated, write books, become scholars or artists or business owners. It is from that specific condition that we understand the larger universal reality that as human beings in this mortality, we are all blips on the screen of eternity, that none of us were ever meant to survive, and therefore we must speak while we can.

In a 1978 journal entry quoted in *Warrior Poet*, you wrote this while undergoing cancer treatment:

> There's a kind of protection the bleak unfeeling walls of a hospital give that allows me to look into the face of death and still dare to be joyful. I want to move toward death if I must with the certain knowledge that I leave some thing rich and part of the Great Going Forward behind me. (p. 225)

You indeed left a rich legacy behind you. I see your legacy in the work of Alicia Garza, Patrisse Cullors, and Opal Tometi, three Black queer women who gave the Black Lives Matter movement its name and helped galvanize a new era in civil rights activism. I see your legacy in the conversations women are having about white feminism and its complicity with white supremacy, something you also addressed in *Sister Outsider*'s "Age, Race, Class and Sex": "Some problems we share as women, some we do not. You fear your children will grow up to join the patriarchy and testify against you; we fear our children will be dragged from a car and shot down in the street, and you will turn your backs upon the reasons they are dying." (p. 119).

I see your legacy in the voices of overworked, underpaid, unappreciated Black women in academia who insist on self-care as an act of defiance, who keep a close watch over their own fatigue and sickness and despair as a means for survival in a harsh system because, as you put it in the epilogue to *A Burst of Light*, "caring for myself is not self-indulgence, it is self-preservation, and that is an act of political warfare" (p.130).

I see your legacy in the faces of my own City University of New York students, products of immigrant New York much like the ones you taught at John Jay College and Hunter College, students from the Islands, Africa, Eastern Europe, the Middle East,

Asia, and South America, all shades of white, Black, Brown, and Yellow, sitting together in our dingy, well-worn classrooms, living out those same immigrant dreams in the metropolis.

Earlier this year, I attended the first meeting of the African American Intellectual History Society in Chapel Hill, where we watched footage of you in Dagmar Schultz's documentary *Audre Lorde - The Berlin Years, 1984 to 1992*. I was proud to sit among this group of scholars who recognized a Black lesbian poet as an important contributor to Black intellectual history, an acknowledgement that felt unlikely to me when I was an undergraduate history student not that long ago.

Recently, I noticed an image passed around the Internet, emblazoned with your bold words, taken from a journal entry written during the last years of your life, collected in *A Burst of Light*:

> I want to live the rest of my life, however long or short, with as much sweetness as I can decently manage, loving all the people I love, and doing as much as I can of the work I still have to do. I am going to write fire until it comes out of my ears, my eyes, my noseholes—everywhere. Until it's every breath I breathe. I'm going to go out like a fucking meteor! (p. 71)

I think about these lines when I find myself distracted and need to rediscover my purpose in this writing life.

Your legacy lives on in the LGBT movement, even though I often wish we would listen more intently to your voice telling us not to relinquish our difference. These days, the movement seems less about celebrating the unique and particular gifts of queerness and more about integrating into heteronormative institutions. The focus now is on gay athletes, marriage equality, adoption, military service, and the clergy.

Here in your home state, New York, the Empire State Pride

Agenda literally disbanded after the *Obergefell v. Hodges* decision in 2015 set a judicial precedent that recognizes same-sex marriage in all 50 states. In its last statement, the **Pride Agenda** declared that because same-sex marriage had been achieved, its work was done. However, in that same year, more than 20 transgender women in America were murdered, most of them poor women of color. An alarming 41 percent of trans people will attempt suicide at least once, a rate four times that of the general public. Rates of HIV infection continue to climb in poor Black and Brown communities without access to adequate health care and among people who live in states where sex education and LGBT legal protections are being suppressed.

I often wonder what you would think about the current presidential administration, of our beautiful Black president; his smart, gorgeous wife; his two Brown girls who have grown up before our eyes in the past eight years, knowing that this same Black president is also the head of an empire, commander in chief of a military machine that rains down death upon thousands of people caught in the crossfires of conflict.

I think of how your writing is so vital to understanding these contradictions that we live with, that we live in a time when the price of assimilation for people such as Michael Sam is to become one-dimensional heroes and to relinquish the ability to be human and vulnerable. I thought about this as I read De Veaux's *Warrior Poet*. The occasion of a biography is often an awkward airing of dirty laundry, including all the embarrassing details that even the most candid writers want to leave out. I want you to know that De Veaux did you proud, Sister Audre. Her elegant book lets us into your world to reveal the complex, beautiful life you led as a Black feminist poet, making up a life for yourself and carving out possibilities that the rest of us could find and imagine for ourselves. I want the contradictory Audre Lorde, the one who was defiantly promiscuous; who had her moments of jealousy, anger, duplicitousness, and hypocrisy; who had white lovers and did not apologize to her Black friends for it; and who grappled with the meaning of this racial complexity, in the faces of her own children from a Black mother and white father, who raised them despite the divorce and helped them learn to accept her lesbian partners.

I think about your poetry in these trying times, such as the underrated 1974 collection *New York Head Shop and Museum*, a series of poems that express your love and fascination for the city of your birth and yet are imbued with an apocalyptic sensibility.

> There is nothing beautiful left in the streets of this city.
> I have come to believe in death and renewal by fire.
> Past questioning the necessities of blood
> or why it must be mine or my children's time
> that will see the grim city quake to be reborn perhaps
> blackened again but this time with a sense of purpose;
> tired of the past tense forever, of assertion and repetition
> of the ego-trips through an incomplete self
> — from "New York City 1970" (p.1)

I suppose there was never a period when everyone felt at ease with the world, but Audre, these feel like apocalyptic times: daily mass shootings in America so frequent that they barely register anymore; the suicide bombs of jihadists in Nigeria, Somalia, Turkey, Belgium, Iraq, Pakistan; the looming climate changes with unprecedented storms; and the situation in Flint, Michigan, where thousands of children were poisoned with lead while politicians trucked in clean water for themselves.

We need your outrage now in these times when we are encouraged to see our Black president as a symbol of progress even as

Black children are gunned down in the streets. Your 1976 poem "Power" expresses some of the anger we felt decades later at the death of 12-year-old Tamir Rice, shot down on a Cleveland playground by a cop who was never indicted.

> A policeman who shot down a ten year old in Queens
> stood over the boy with his cop shoes in childish blood
> and a voice said "Die you little motherfucker" and
> there are tapes to prove it. At his trial
> this policeman said in his own defense
> "I didn't notice the size nor nothing else
> only the color". And
> there are tapes to prove that, too.
>
> (*The Collected Poems of Audre Lorde*, p. 215)

There are the tapes to prove Tamir's death too, but it has led to nothing. And that's why it is so important that "Power" imagines how our sorrow can turn into an unhealthy despair or a destructive vengeance.

> I have not been able to touch the destruction
> within me.
> But unless I learn to use
> the difference between poetry and rhetoric
> my power too will run corrupt as poisonous mold
> or lie limp and useless as an unconnected wire …
>
> (*The Collected Poems of Audre Lorde*, p. 215)

When I started this letter, I feared that addressing you this way is too familiar. As a teacher, I've often had to correct my students' writing when they casually refer to women writers by their first names: Gwendolyn, Harriet, Zadie. I worried that writing to you this way when I've written about male writers in more formal ways could be interpreted as a lack of respect for your craft. But I also wanted to take this risk. I wanted to speak in the way you taught us in "The Transformation of Silence into Language and Action," when you wrote, "I have come to believe over and over again that what is most important to me must be spoken, made verbal and shared, even at the risk of having it bruised and misunderstood." I wanted to honor your work in "The Uses of the Erotic," when you took the risk of celebrating women's sexuality even though some people felt that by writing about the erotic as a feminine force you were reifying old stereotypes of the emotional woman and rational man.

I am not sure where we are going, dear Audre, Sister Outsider, old courage-teacher. I carry your books around with me on the subways of your city, which is now my city, and I dream about what more I can do to transform my own silences into language and action. I'm trying to learn what it means to be guided by Black feminism in this white man's world. I'm trying to do what you suggested in "Eye to Eye" in *Sister Outsider*: "We can practice being gentle with each other by being gentle with that piece of ourselves that is hardest to hold, by giving more to the brave bruised girlchild within each of us" (p.175). You were speaking to Black women then, but I wonder what kind of world we might create if we all develop the capacity to imagine ourselves as that Black girl moving through the world feeling vulnerable, unprotected, and hated.

We need your hope now, the hope you had when you faced cancer with the same candor and intelligence you brought to every piece of poetry and prose you wrote. When I think about this losing game we all play and how we have to find the courage to play it anyway, I often come back to this passage from *A Burst of Light*.

> This is why the work is so important. Its power doesn't lie in the me that lives in the words as much as in the heart's blood pumping behind the eye that is reading, the muscle behind the desire that is sparked by the word–hope as a living state that propels us, open-eyed and fearful, into all the battles of our lives. And some of those battles we do not win.
>
> But some of them we do. (p. 74)

Notes

1. This essay was first published on poetryfoundation.org in May of 2016.

References

De Veaux, A. (2006). *Warrior poet: A biography of Audre Lorde*. W. W. Norton & Company.

Lorde, A. (1974) *New York head shop and museum*. Broadside Press

Lorde, A. (1978). *The Black unicorn*. W. W. Norton & Company.

Lorde, A. (1978) *The collected poems of Audre Lorde*. W. W. Norton & Company, Inc.

Lorde. A. (1982). *Zami: A new spelling of my name*. The Crossing Press.

Lorde, A. (1984). Age, race, class and sex: Women redefining difference. *Sister outsider: Essays and speeches*. The Crossing Press. (pp. 114 – 123)

Lorde, A. (1988). *A burst of light: And other essays*. Ixia Press (2017).

Thriving on Thin Air

A Black Woman's Journey from Student to Faculty at CUNY

NANCY CARDWELL

INTRODUCTION

I am a third-generation free-born Black woman, the first female PhD in my family, a fourth-generation college graduate and teacher; the great-granddaughter of enslaved Africans. My great-grandparents met while they were students at Hampton Institute (now Hampton University) and later married, becoming teacher educators in Virginia. I grew up in an educated Black, middle-class family, and we lived in a segregated housing development in Central Harlem, down the hill from City College.

My mother attended City College at night, earning her undergraduate and graduate degrees in education during my childhood. My dad took a second job preparing newly arrived immigrants for their citizenship exam so my mom didn't have to work and could take care of me. During the day, my dad managed a branch of a National Savings Bank on 125th Street. It was challenging for her to do her homework for class when I was awake, which was most of the time; so, she would get up before sunrise to study.

At first, she worked at the dining room table but that didn't work so well because, after 15 or 20 minutes, I would show up asking, "Mommy, what are you doing?" One morning, as the story goes, I got up and saw her sitting at the table studying, went to my room to get my biggest book, then returned, and said, "Ok Mommy, I got my book to help you study." Even when my mom tucked herself away in the kitchen to study with a towel on the floor to block the light, I was up within minutes to 'help' her.

As funny as the story is, and despite the fact that we laughed about it for many, many years, the circumstances of her life forced her to make hard choices between caring for me and learning to become a teacher. My parents didn't need to tell me about the importance of education because it was woven into every aspect of my life.

When it was my turn to go to school, my parents chose a predominantly white private school on Central Park West. The Ethical Culture School is a predominantly white private school based on John Dewey's progressive education approach and the Ethical Culture Society's principles. Every day I traveled from my home in Central Harlem to Central Park West, navigating the social divides and paradoxes along the way and struggled to create a cohesive narrative to explain these daily trips to and from school throughout my childhood. Despite this struggle to understand racism, classism, gender, privilege, and belonging, I had enormous protections and privileges in place that allowed me to engage in this struggle. To more fully understand why the City University of New York's radical social experiment was radical, I offer a brief look at the roots of higher education in the United States.

In *Ebony & Ivy: Race, Slavery, and the Troubled History of America's Universities* (2013), historian Craig Steven Wilder provides a groundbreaking study examining how the earliest colonial colleges were rooted in and sustained by the African slave trade and slavery. U.S. colleges stood alongside the church and the state as the third pillar of a society built on slavery. At the same time, colleges challenged the domination of the church with their secular ideas on race science. Colleges were instruments of Christian expansion, and weapons of conquest to subjugate indigenous peoples. To fund these colleges, slave traders and slave owners became college founders and British colonial trustees. The rapid expansion of colleges was fueled by the economic growth of the African slave trade (Wilder, 2013).

Table 1: Establishment of Early U.S. Colleges

Date Founded	Name of College
1636	Harvard College (MA)
1693	William and Mary College (VA)
1701	Yale (CT)
1746	The College of New Jersey – Princeton (NJ)
1749	The College of Philadelphia – University of Pennsylvania (PA)
1754	King's College – Columbia University (NY)
1764	College of Rhode Island – Brown University (RI)
1766	Queen's College – Rutgers University (NJ)

The purpose of the colleges was to advance Christian rule over indigenous peoples. Because of these beginnings, American colleges are enmeshed in the histories of the Europeans and with the peoples of the Americas, making their fates antagonistic and interdependent. The African slave trade funded everything—campus construction, operating expenses, and the building of libraries. Enslaved Africans built the buildings, maintained the grounds, cooked, cleaned, and served the faculty and students (Wilder, 2013).

In the 18th century, colleges earned legitimacy and power by developing the field of race science; the prestige of higher education increased as scholars challenged church authority, demonstrating their willingness to defend slavery to establish the supremacy of whites (Wilder, 2013). By advancing race science, scholars entered the public sphere as they discussed the social dangers and racial threat to whites posed by free Black people. As slaveholding began to decline in northern states following the American Revolution, the idea of sending free African Americans to colonize Africa was offered as an alternative to emancipation in the United States (Foner, 2020; 2014; 2011; DuBois, 1935/1998). Founded in 1817, the American Colonization Society, supported colonization as a means to maintain a homogeneous white population, and were active on three-fifths of the campuses in New England and the mid-Atlantic, and was especially strong at seven Ivy League colleges by the 1930s. They advocated for sending free black peoples back to Africa to promote a homogeneous, white population of Americans (Foner, 2020; Kendi, 2017; Wilder, 2013, p. 265; Painter, 2011).

CUNY: THE RADICAL SOCIAL EXPERIMENT

New York took a phase-out approach to abolish slavery that began in 1799 and was completed in 1827, with formerly enslaved Africans moving from enslavement into indentured servitude. The abolition of slavery created a significant social challenge in the new nation. If the once-enslaved Africans, viewed as not quite human, became free American citizens, they would be viewed as equal to whites under the law (Foner, 2020; 2014; 2011; DuBois, 1935/1998).

While the institution of slavery was repugnant to many, there was little support for relinquishing the legal, economic and social supremacy of whiteness. The abolition of slavery carried the need to institutionally reassure whites that they were superior to Blacks and the government allocated opportunities for advancement to promote European wealth building to demonstrate that superiority. They received this reassurance from scholars in colleges founded and paid for by the African slave trade and slavery (Foner, 2020; Wilder, 2013; Foner, 2011; Painter, 2011; DuBois, 1935/1998; Donald, 1996).

THE FREE ACADEMY'S RADICAL SOCIAL EXPERIMENT

Twenty-two years after the abolition of slavery in New York and ten years before the Civil War, Horace Webster, the first president of the Free Academy said,

> The experiment is to be tried, whether the children of the people, the children of the whole people, can be educated; and whether an institution of the highest grade can be successfully controlled by popular will, not by the privileged few. (As qtd. in Brier, 2017)

The experiment focused on shifting the financial control of colleges from African slave traders and slave owners to taxpayers or the popular will (Wilder, 2013). As a port of entry, New York City struggled to manage the influx of more than three million European immigrants from 1850 to 1900 (New York City Government, 2021). The Free Academy was a long-term, 'radical social experiment' to quell the growing social unrest and support European wealth-building capacity with land and free education, while maintaining the subjugation of blacks in perpetual servitude, cut off from opportunities their labor built over generations (Brier, 2017; Wilder, 2013; Foner, 2011; Van Nort, 2007; Brown, 2001; DuBois, 1935/1998; Donald, 1996).

European immigrants were drawn to the apparently limitless possibilities of a rapidly expanding nation to build wealth through hard work and education because of the rapid expansion of manufacturing and industrialization. The Free Academy provided a chance for whites of every economic class, national origin, and station to improve their social and economic status with a free, publicly funded education while stabilizing the emergent United States (Foner, 2020; Brier, 2017; Foner, 2011; Van Nort, 2007; Brown, 2001).

WHAT MADE THE FREE ACADEMY 'RADICAL'?

When the electorate cast their vote to fund the Free Academy (renamed City College in 1866), the 'common man' and 'the whole people' meant white people. As the numbers of Black and Brown students increased, its reputation as 'the poor man's Harvard' diminished. For 128 years, tuition was free. For 122 years of these 128, generations of European immigrants' children benefited socially and economically from unfettered access to high-quality, tuition-free higher education. For six years, CUNY offered free tuition to large numbers of Black and Brown students (Brier, 2017, Van Nort, 2007).

The social experiment was radical because the New York Federalists borrowed a Republican ideal, characteristic of more rural communities, that is, making education freely available for everyone to encourage widespread public participation (Gerring, 1998). However, in the 1840s' New York City, this radical social experiment may have been necessary to grapple with the complex, rapidly shifting social, cultural and political context (Van Nort, 2007). The U.S. borders had rapidly expanded through a series of treaty agreements and land purchases. These efforts were designed to fulfill the nation's "manifest destiny" to stretch from the Atlantic to the Pacific Oceans.

MY JOURNEY FROM CUNY STUDENT TO FACULTY

In light of the central role of the African slave trade and slavery in establishing and sustaining U.S. higher education, Black people hold a particularly contested space in higher education. After reappointment struggles, I thought seriously about just walking away from a tenure-track position I'd dreamed of, worked for and earned. How I got to this place has to do with who I am and the institutional and societal contexts that surround me as a Black woman in higher education (Esnard & Cobb-Roberts, 2019).

Since the 2016 election, I have been reflecting on the meaning of learning, community, and belonging in the historical context of higher education. The Donald Trump administration's positioning of whiteness as the definition of "American-ness" harkens back to early scholars who advanced race science to promote a white, homogeneous population in the face of a free Black threat (Kendi, 2017; Wilder, 2013; Painter, 2011). Perhaps a safe space doesn't yet exist for a Black woman in higher education, but I hope to contribute to creating that space for those who come after me.

Graduate Student Experience: Reflecting on and re-evaluating my life, I discovered my career in education has been about adapting effective private school practices and approaches in public settings to support every child's learning. I was drawn to CUNY as a graduate student because it was a public institution with a public mission I shared.

As graduate students, we prepared to enter the professoriate to keep the doors of educational opportunity open for people across all identity boundaries. In this space of possibilities and potentials, I was encouraged to imagine the unimaginable; to think the unthinkable; to take critical stances and to interrogate existing dynamics of power and privilege in service of social justice. As a student, I was shielded from the impact of decades of underfunding. At this time, I was only marginally aware of "publish or perish" politics among faculty. From the outside, it seemed that no matter what, everyone kept the needs of the students in the center of their work.

Faculty Experience: As I approached the end of the dissertation defense process, I was awash in emotions—sad that my parents didn't live to see this moment and in shock over finishing. I was thrilled to accept a tenure-track faculty appointment at City College shortly after graduation. Like so many tenure-track faculty of color, I experience my share of challenges and bumps along the reappointment road toward tenure. Some faculty have left, while others remain, but no one is unscathed (Esnard & Cobb-Roberts, 2019). Even though the initial conception of the 'whole people' didn't include me or my people, it does now. There is acceptance of diversity in the student body, but a lingering resistance to diversifying the professoriate, particularly with Black faculty (Clarion Staff, 2019).

Teaching: The primary mission of all educational institutions is to provide meaningful learning experiences for every student who attends. Institutional cultures can afford generosity in times of plenty because everyone has more than enough to do their jobs and fulfill their personal needs; they can be confident that the resources they use will be replaced when they run out without diminishing the quality of their work with students. However, it is difficult to be intellectually expansive and innovative when faculty and students can't count on having a consistent inventory of teaching supplies and adequate salaries in the face of unrelenting austerity.

As a new faculty member, I was told to get office supplies and teaching materials at the department's office. It was a few days before my first class, and I went to get a pad of chart paper, markers, and paper clips. When I asked for the supplies, the secretary told me there were no paper clips, and that I could have only five sheets of chart paper to teach my two classes, with 24 students each, "because faculty waste chart paper." The rationing of chart paper seems less than insignificant until considering the impact on student learning. Five sheets of chart paper meant I had 2.5 sheets for each class. This could be enough if I used teacher-centered teaching methods, positioning myself as the sole source of knowledge in the class. However, I don't teach that way. I model learner-centered teaching approaches encouraged in early childhood classrooms to actively engage learners; these methods include:

- Small group, in-class discussions and projects.
- Hands-on activities to help students construct the knowledge I want them to learn as they experience inquiry-based, hands-on learning.
- Developing relationships with teacher candidates to create a shame-free learning community where taking intellectual risks and making mistakes are the beginning of learning.

The purpose of these approaches is to position the teacher candidates' culturally-based knowledge as resources to build the professional knowledge of teaching. One of the ways students can share their diverse perspectives, without determining the one 'right' answer, is to allow multiple perspectives to be valid simultaneously and to share the discoveries from small group work with charts that outline the varied perspectives.

If I break the classes into small groups, each class will have five or six groups. If each group develops a chart to share the substance of their work with the larger group, then the allocation of chart paper is clearly inadequate. It is important for early childhood teacher candidates to regularly develop charts because they are both an important element of early literacy development and an effective teaching tool for young children because teachers demonstrate the literacy cycle as they record the words young children say as they say them.

There is no formula for creating learner-centered charts because each chart is tailored to the individual groups in the room at that particular moment. There are, however, guiding principles and multiple opportunities to practice, practice, practice. Without chart paper and markers, teacher candidates can't practice and learn from their classmates' approaches. This example is just one of the myriad ways that austerity budgeting negatively impacts practice, as faculty don't have the materials to provide the full range of supports and accommodations necessary to enact high-quality early childhood teaching practices in varied learning contexts.

Faculty Life: I was having lunch with two Latina colleagues in the faculty dining room and I was the darkest person at the table. A white male professor sought signatures to run for faculty senate ombudsman. He approached the table and asked if we were faculty. We smiled, and one said, "We're all professors." He handed her his petition first. After she signed it, she passed it to the person next to her, who also signed. Before the second person could pass it to me, he stood between the two of us and took back his petition. He then walked behind me, from my right side to my left, and asked me directly, "Are you a full-time faculty member?" After I said, "Yes", he placed the petition on the table. I took a moment to read it.

My dad was a lawyer and drilled into my head, "Don't sign anything without reading it!" So, I read. The man interpreted my pause to read his petition as illiteracy. He then leaned over me, pointed out the headings on the petition and read them aloud to me as he moved his finger underneath the words. Then, he pointed to the line for me to sign and then where to print my name, explaining the difference. I couldn't believe what was happening as it happened. I looked at him directly, and said, "I have a PhD and I am literate." He smiled sheepishly, and said, "Oh, I didn't know." I declined to sign his petition.

The language of his behavior offers some insights on the narratives and perceptions that shaped this experience. One narrative he enacted was that Blackness and being a member of the professoriate are mutually exclusive. If a Black person is in the professoriate with a PhD, they must have weak or non-existent academic skills. Even though I said I was a professor, for him, my color disqualified me from my role, education and degrees (Esnard & Cobb-Roberts, 2019).

It was disappointing that my Latina lunch partners didn't stand with me and take back their signatures. At the same time, I can understand it. Their road is no easier than mine. Sustained scarcity prevents a cohesive community because it requires a culture of everyone for themselves in order to survive. In that moment, they were probably relieved that it wasn't them. This is another impact of scarcity on collegiality and a cohesive culture.

When I returned to campus after summer break, the first day of the fall semester was an August day that was anything but a fall day. By 11 a.m., a heat advisory had been issued, and the hot, humid wind whipped through the covered, open-air plaza, offering little relief, as I walked toward the entrance of my campus office building. To my left, I noticed frenzied activity as scores of smiling people, wearing uniforms and food service gloves, were popping popcorn, arranging balloons, moving cold drinks out of the sun, and clearing space for platters of food yet to arrive, as dance music played in the background to welcome the incoming students for a new academic year. Welcoming new students is a moment of renewal, filled with possibilities and hope that energizes the whole campus.

I smiled, took a deep breath, turned, and opened the door to my office building. I was greeted with a frigid gust that was an immediate relief. I showed my ID to the public safety officer and headed upstairs to my windowless office to prepare for the year's first division meeting. I entered the meeting room, seeing clusters of faculty and staff chatting over sandwiches, smiling, and waving their greetings as each person entered the room. I found an empty seat, placed my things on a chair, and was greeted with surprise by a colleague who said, "Oh, I'm surprised to see you because I heard you weren't coming back." It felt like a punch in the face. Then, I smiled, realizing there were no more illusions of welcome and, if I wanted to stay, I would have to fight hard. This was a generational battle, and I am only one among many engaged in the struggle. Despite the past, I am still standing, drawing strength from the knowledge that I come from a strong and determined people.

Establishing an inclusive learning environment for Black and Brown students and an institutional culture for Black and Brown faculty creates two interacting phenomena that construct a particularly difficult working context for tenure-track faculty of color. Tenure-track faculty occupy positions of public trust with their curriculum and policy-making responsibilities. However, people of color, and Black women in particular, don't enjoy the privilege of an assumption of public trust in U.S. society. The devaluation and dismissal of Black women's value surfaces in higher education in the forms of low pay, assumed incapacity, few supports, difficult reappointment, tenure and promotion experiences. Depersonalization perpetuates myths of objectivity, reinforcing discriminatory practices that maintain white dominance of the professoriate (Esnard & Cobb-Roberts, 2019). However, I believe there is hope…

A RADICAL SOCIAL EXPERIMENT FOR THE 21ST CENTURY

Public funding of CUNY was never restored to pre-1975 levels following the fiscal crisis. Even now, CUNY functions on a small fraction of the budget it needs to fully support faculty and staff to meet the range of learning needs among the increasingly diverse student body. The true cruelty and oppression of sustained austerity budgets is not the lack of supplies or even the gratuitous acts of disregard and meanness, but rather the constrained resources and crumbling infrastructure that teach us not to imagine, dream, or seek. In not asking or seeking, our dreams, imaginations, and innovations shrivel. Educating the children of the whole people means recognizing and valuing the intersectionality of class, culture, language, and immigration status. In this way, the former Free Academy, now City College, was and remains a site of struggle to expand the definition of 'the children of the whole people' to include everyone's child regardless of race, culture, or language. In doing so, CUNY can establish an inclusive enactment of the radical social experiment for everyone's child (Van Nort, 2007).

DIVERSITY AND INCLUSION AT CITY COLLEGE

The lifeblood of U.S. strength and prosperity has always been its diversity, even though historically, that diversity hasn't been valued or supported. We now know that attending to and promoting diversity and inclusion in organizations throughout the United States is key to sustained economic and social success in the 21st Century. Currently, the new president of City College has made diversity and inclusion a priority of his administration—for students and faculty. This year, he initiated a College-Wide Diversity and Inclusion Working Group with three subgroups to create a framework for policies and practices to guide interactions and to positively impact institutional culture. An interdisciplinary group of staff, students, and faculty is collaborating to promote diversity in the recruitment and retention of students, faculty, and staff to promote an inclusive culture with ongoing professional development, and to pay attention to intervention and compliance.

A diversity of ideas, culture, experience, and expertise is especially important for the professoriate when there are students from around the world with first-hand experiences of the major global dilemmas that we examine and discuss in class. In this context, the traditions of absolute professorial authority as "the one knower" are ineffective. We must now approach this work with clarity on our expertise, and self-awareness and openness to the lessons our students have to share and learn. At its best, teaching and learning in culturally, linguistically, and economically diverse learning environments is a reciprocal exchange, acknowledging the multi-vocal and multicultural funds of knowledge that students provide. To me, the radical social experiment of today is to value, recruit, retain, and promote a professoriate that reflects the diversity in the student body and society.

DISCUSSION

The primary mission of educational institutions is for faculty to provide meaningful learning experiences for the students. Education has been a site of social experimentation, including the Free Academy, designed to knit together the new American nation-state by providing the opportunity of a free, fully funded public education for the 'common man' and their children to improve their lives and station. This freely available opportunity to transcend one's station through education was only open to European immigrants and withheld from the formerly enslaved Africans whose labor and trade built this nation (Foner, 2020; Kendi, 2017; Wilder, 2013; Van Nort, 2007; Brown, 2001).

It is easier to be generous and magnanimous in times of fiscal strength. Taking a risk on a radical social experiment that might fail in 1847 was worth the financial risk because the loss was affordable and the European immigrants were worthy of the investment. In times of fiscal austerity, it is difficult to be generous and the suffering of those who are of questionable value and worth is tolerable, permissible, and acceptable.

CUNY was supported as a worthy radical social experiment for 122 years when the beneficiaries were European immigrants and their children. This benefit was available for Black and Brown students for six years until free tuition was eliminated due to fiscal hardship in 1975, then never restored (Brier, 2017; Van Nort, 2007). This sustained fiscal austerity undermines CUNY's radical social experiment for students and faculty. The fraught, contested position that CUNY currently occupies is emblematic of the broader context of public education across the United States as students became increasingly Black and Brown; state legislatures became disinclined to invest public money in their education and the faculty who teach them (Larabee, 2012).

My students will become the next generation of early childhood teachers and leaders, and the young children they teach will do great things in the future. In this way, my research and teaching will touch a future I will not live to see. It is also an opportunity to sustain and expand radical social experimentation to include everyone's child. In my students, I see shadows of my mother and father in their perseverance, dedication, and intelligence.

It is challenging to navigate the vestiges of this nation's early reliance on the African slave trade and slavery for its development since this erasure has been solidified by scholars who constructed a race science providing evidence of Black inferiority, a perspective that is deeply interwoven into the foundation of U.S. higher education (Esner & Cobb-Roberts, 2019; Wilder, 2013). This adversity forced me to look within myself to identify my purpose, commitment, and inner strength. In the process, I discovered my great-grandfather's voice and had a glimpse of his life that allowed me to clarify my own voice (Blassingame, 1977).

I bring my expertise, knowledge, questions, and experiences to my teaching, and invite my students to do the same. Together we can teach each other who we are and use that understanding to examine the course content in new and useful ways. In this practice, I create spaces for my students to step in and take my place, so they can open space for their students to follow them in greater numbers. My hope is that they will establish CUNY and City College as a model of high-quality inclusive higher education for everyone's child.

CONCLUSION

The early radical social experiment was to determine if the opportunity of a quality, publicly funded higher education could be beneficial to European immigrants and society across the economic spectrum—and the results showed it was. Now, we are in a time when Rep. Alexandria Ocasio-Cortez (D-NY), a well-educated former bartender, has reminded us of all of the dreams and possibilities for the nation with her policies and hope for a brighter future as a new member of Congress. In the 21st century, the radical social experiment has expanded to offer publicly funded higher education opportunities to everyone so they can contribute to a shared, more prosperous future. Building on the expansion that includes Black and Brown students, the 21st century's radical experiment would mean significantly increasing the number of Black and Brown members of the professoriate. This would make the promise of the United States as the land of opportunity a reality for everyone, at long last. CUNY's contribution could be to lead the way in building a strong, diverse professoriate, reflecting the range of diversity in the student body and society in service to a stronger, more just society. The diversification of the professoriate is the next chapter of the radical social experiment yet to be written, and I believe CUNY is up to the task.

References

Blassingame, J.W. (Ed.) (1977). *Slave testimony: Two centuries of letters, speeches, interviews and autobiographies.* Louisiana State University Press.

Brier, S. (2017). Why the history of CUNY matters: Using the CUNY digital history archive to teach CUNY's past, *Radical Teacher,* Vol. 108:28-35.

Brown, D. (2001). *Hear that lonesome whistle blow: The epic story of the transcontinental railroads.* Henry Holt.

Clarion Staff, (2019). Lacking black faculty, *Clarion,* December 2019, p. 10. Retrieved from https://www.psc-cuny.org/clarion/december-2019/lacking-black-faculty.

Donald, D.H. (1996). *Lincoln.* Touchstone.

DuBois, W.E.B. (1935/1998). *Black reconstruction in America, 1860-1880.* The Free Press.

Esnard, T. & Cobb-Roberts, D. (2019). *Black women, academe, and the tenure process in the United States and the Caribbean.* Palgrave Macmillan.

Foner, E. (2020). *The second founding: How the Civil War and Reconstruction remade the Constitution.* W.W. Norton & Company.

Foner, E. (2014). *Reconstruction updated edition: America's unfinished revolution 1863-1877.* Harper Perennial Classic.

Foner, E. (2011). *The fiery trial: Abraham Lincoln and American slavery.* W.W. Norton & Company.

Gerring, J. (1998). *Party ideologies in America, 1828-1996.* Cambridge University Press.

Kendi, I.X. (2017). *Stamped from the beginning: The definitive history of racist ideas in America.* Bold Type Books.

Larabee, D.F. (2012). *Someone has to fail: The zero-sum game of public schooling.* Harvard University Press.

New York City Government (2021). *1790-2000 NYC total and foreign-born population.* Retrieved, 6/24/21,

Retrieved from https://www1.nyc.gov/assets/planning/download/pdf/data-maps/nyc-population/historical-population/1790-2000_nyc_total_foreign_birth.pdf.

Painter, N.I. (2011). *The history of white people*. W.W. Norton & Co.

Van Nort, S.C. (2007). *The City College of New York*. Arcadia Publishing.

Wilder, C.S. (2013). *Ebony and ivy: Race, slavery and the troubled history of American universities*. Bloomsbury Press.

All Roads Lead to CUNY

EMILY SOHMER TAI

Long before there was "take our daughters to work day," my father took us to where he worked: the City College of New York. Over a fifty-year career at City College, my father served, variously, as professor of Mathematics; a Dean and Vice-Provost of Students; and, finally, as a faculty governance leader for City College and eventually the whole of CUNY. Growing up in the 1960s and 70s, City College seemed to me and my younger sister to be a fairy-tale complex of fabulous towers and labyrinthine passages, a magical mystery world. My sister and I grew up sampling the lavish greasy spoon fare of the City College cafeteria, listening to the cheerful, jostling arguments my father would enjoy with colleagues over a clatter of breakfast dishes and endless cups of coffee; playing tag and hide-and-seek in the cavernous wonderland of his neo-Gothic office upstairs in Shepard Hall. I remember how disappointed I was when City College's president, Robert Marshak, moved my dad's office to a more modern building that lacked all those beguiling nooks and crannies.

My sister and I were raised in a modest Queens apartment that somehow accommodated a grand piano and an overflowing library of books. It used to fascinate me to run my fingers over their spines along the bookshelves that lined our living room, sounding out the names of authors I would come to appreciate: Balzac, Hugo, Dickens, Rumor Godden (a favorite of my mother, Hunter, Class of '52); Howard Fast—together with endless titles on the history and literature of Judaism that my sister and I would ultimately donate to the Kupferberg Holocaust Center at Queensborough Community College, where, decades later, I would teach history.

My sister and I grew up in a home where the arts, ideas, and the searing political issues of the day were freely and contentiously discussed. Nothing was ever sugar-coated or hidden from us as children. We knew that when our dad pulled an all-nighter at work, the same tensions we saw on television were playing themselves out at City College. However, what consistently distinguished my father's perspective was the humor and sympathy he brought to the endless student confrontations he was hired to diffuse. The year I turned 13, my mother was laid low by Guillain–Barré syndrome. While care for this disease has since advanced, my mother landed on the wrong side of medical history. For three months, she hovered between life and death at a Queens hospital, suffering from a comprehensive paralysis that compromised even her ability to breathe. She then spent another eight months re-learning ambulatory skills at the Rusk Institute of Rehabilitative Medicine. My father went to see her every evening after work, bringing my sister and me to visit on alternate weekends. My father would cheer us both up with uproarious tales of students with fierce dispositions and soaring agendas on the way home. But there was always affection in his voice as he described the students whose frustrations and grievances he respected. Like them, my father had also been a first-generation college student, the son of a Russian Jewish printer and a Romanian Jewish seamstress; like them, my father had worked a variety of odd jobs to put himself through NYU's old

University Heights campus at a time when Jews were no more welcome at America's elite institutions than the Hispanic and African-American students whose demonstrations he so colorfully detailed. Years later, my father would write of the principled "idealism" that drove student calls for an expansion of their input into the CUNY curriculum; of their just opposition to "the horrors of a foolish war...."

Under his guiding hand, programs like Open Admissions and Search for Elevation, Education and Knowledge (SEEK) came to City College. While some might have chafed that such measures lowered academic standards, they widened the doors of opportunity for students and affirmed the true, transformative promise of higher education: the promise that a college education would not merely certify what a student already knew, but teach them something they hadn't known before—the promise my father sought to affirm every time he wielded a piece of chalk to teach algebra to a student who swore they'd always hated math.

My mother's illness hurtled me, as a 1970s' adolescent, into a strangely bifurcated world. On the one hand, reports of violence at the local junior high school to which my sister and I had been assigned had fueled my mother's decision, shortly before her hospitalization, to remove us from the New York City public school system to the private preparatory institution where we would complete our secondary schooling. On the other, my mother's illness meant that neither my sister nor I would ever truly identify with the privilege that surrounded us. Many of our fellow students, residents of wealthier sections of Queens, or Long Island, shopped with their own credit cards, drove automobiles they received as gifts in our senior year, and, occasionally, dabbled in recreational drug use without penalty. Most of them could count on housekeepers to do the work my sister and I took up as my mother returned home, gamely hobbling on a cane, and dogged by a new incapacity that necessitated our takeover of the cooking and cleaning. By the time I was 16, I was preparing dinner for the family, and juggling academic work with domestic tasks—a skill that would come in handy years later when I defied professional norms to start my family while still a graduate student. But the immediate importance of my labor to our family also meant that the sort of residential college to which most of my high school friends were bound after graduation was not an option for me. CUNY it would be!

My decision to attend Queens College reflected my own struggle with a dilemma I had not quite yet resolved: whether to pursue a career in history, a field I had come to love, or in the performing arts. Throughout my high school years, I had been studying voice and composition at Mannes School of Music. To the extent that a singing and acting career continued to beckon, I had not ruled out continuing these studies at Queens College's conservatory-quality Music Department—now the Aaron Copland School of Music. And yet, high school had also been the place where I fell gradually in love with academic research. First, it was hours spent in the closed carrels that graced our private school library, working my way through thick tomes on the history of Elizabethan England; then, it was clandestine forays to the New York Public Library on 42nd Street. Since the library was, in those days, off-limits to younger students, I used to fill in the name of my mother's alma mater, Hunter College, where request slips asked for the name of each reader's affiliation. Finally, it was a project I'd pursued in music history: a study of troubadour music that launched me on a campaign to teach myself Old Provençal and read everything about medieval southern France I could get my hands on.

For years, I had watched my father revel in mathematics, often pulling a pad and pencil out to play with formulas as our family listened to chamber music at the Washington Irving People's Symphony Concerts. It may have been my father's delight with the precision of numbers that enabled him to recognize the point at which my love of history was pulling me toward the same decision he had made so many years before, to immerse himself in the life-long study of a single subject. I vividly remember the afternoon I first began to seriously consider this step as a high-school junior. My mother and sister were both away; my father and I had decided to attend a concert of the Queens Symphony Orchestra in Flushing. As I peppered him with questions about the mechanics of earning a doctorate, my father sugar-coated neither its rigors nor the slender likelihood of employment thereafter. But the man who had prodded thousands of students toward the careers that best suited them did not discourage me, either. "I put it to you," he said to me, "that virtue is its own reward."

When I was ready for college, the pressure to commit to one professional track seemed inexorable. At Mannes, the Julliard-trained director of our Madrigal Group would stride up and down our studio as we rehearsed, hectoring us with the mantra he'd heard during his own conservatory days. "Are you singers?" he'd bellow, "or are you *musicians*?" By my junior year in college, I finally had an answer to that question: I was a singer who preferred to be a scholar. In the days before the Internet, I would trudge upstairs to the Microfilm Reading Room in Klapper Hall (Queens College's library before the construction of Rosenthal Library in 1988). I was now a history major, ploughing through Calendars of the State Papers Foreign Series to complete a research paper for a course taught by Stuart Prall. On the days I didn't need to come to campus, I worked at the microfiche machines at New York Public Library, where one of the librarians I'd befriended during my high school forays fended other patrons away from the machine I was using. John O'Brien, a professor of medieval history at Queens College, laughed when I told him about how she'd hover, protectively, to keep my workspace available. "Someone like that," he commented, with a conspiratorial smile, "can be more helpful than a department chair."

My arrival at Queens College in September 1977 nevertheless coincided with some of CUNY's hardest times. A brutal shortfall in New York City's finances, immortalized in the October 1975 *New York Daily News* headline, "Ford to City: Drop Dead", created a necessity for the first-ever imposition of tuition at the traditionally free university; massive layoffs of untenured faculty; workload increases and the threat of pay furloughs for the tenured faculty who remained. Morale among students and faculty was terrible. I'd hear about promising scholars who had been forced from CUNY, their stories recited in hushed, funereal tones. Some faculty shouldered on, repelling the new conditions of austerity with a reserve of kindness and undeterred enthusiasm. They, together with my father, became my role models.

One such professor was Paul Avrich, an international expert on the history of anarchism, whose oral history research ingeniously applied a sociologist's methodology to enhance a historian's tale. Every Monday and Wednesday, Dr. Avrich left his office door defiantly and reliably open, with chairs invitingly arranged to entertain any students who might wish to drop by. Robert Haan, a professor of early modern history, who helped to administer Queens College's still-flourishing Humanities Program, similarly made himself available to students, whether they were enrolled in the Humanities Program or not (I wasn't). In the five years I studied French literature with Jack Reilly, I never saw him ever tell a student their answer was wrong, no matter how outlandish or off-base it might have been—always, Reilly would only smile, flexing his hand up and down, as he offered a gentle correction: *pas exacte-ment* (not exactly). At a time when the methodology of undergraduate research was barely a gleam in anyone's eye, Robert Clark found ways for his students to take on original projects in medieval art history. And finally, in my senior year, Frederick Goldin welcomed me, a mere undergraduate, to his Graduate Center seminar in Provençal poetry—offering me the chance to study the poets I'd been reading since high school in a classroom setting at last.

My father, who networked furiously to get me into Goldin's seminar, was weathering his own challenges during these years. In 1976, my father ended his tenure in City College Administration, only to be swept up into the hurly-burly of faculty governance as chair of the City College Faculty Senate (1977–1979; 1985–1991; 2002–2004); and member of the Executive Committee of the University Faculty Senate (1980–1998)—an organization my father had helped to found in the 1960s, and ultimately chaired, from 1998–2002. These commitments once more propelled my father into a storm-center of controversy, as he was obliged to defend the free-speech rights of two eccentric members of the City College Faculty: Michael Levin, a professor of philosophy who argued for the superiority of white intelligence; and Dr. Leonard Jeffries, chair of City College's African-American studies department, whose tirades against "Ice people" and Jews (my father, in particular), elicited the unhappy outcome of a lawsuit that upheld a university's right to remove an elected chair.

In the years that followed, my father would weather a number of additional attacks on CUNY's traditions of what the Professional Staff Congress's first president, Belle Zeller, termed "Access and Excellence"; a new round of faculty terminations and program elimination, under the CUNY Chancellor Ann Reynolds; and a

1999 report produced by former Mayor Rudy Giuliani's Advisory Task Force on the City University of New York that pronounced CUNY "An Institution Adrift." My father's final years as a governance leader were consumed by a struggle to defend CUNY that included a fraught debate, sponsored by the Manhattan Institute, with the current Board of Trustees Chair, Herman Badillo, on a sticky summer evening at the Roosevelt Hotel, a year after the report appeared.

The circumstances of my own life as these events unfolded had placed me in the center of a tug-of-war between my father's battle to affirm CUNY's ideals of public service, and the opulent, privileged world of private education, which I, myself, had re-entered. My senior year in college had been an eventful one, as I had at once met my future husband, and been admitted, with a generous fellowship, to the doctoral program at Harvard University. Paul and I met as classmates in a year-long sequence in Ancient Greek. Ours was a typical Queens romance, which is to say an unexpected alliance between two people of different classes and ethnicities: Where I was Jewish, American-born, and preparing for a career as a second-generation academic, my husband had been raised in Vineyard Town, a working-class neighborhood in Kingston, Jamaica, as a child of mixed Asian and African descent. In 1978, Paul's family had fled political violence in Jamaica to settle in Miami, Florida. Enrolling at Miami-Dade Community College, my husband had stunned his family by abandoning the practical computer science degree his Chinese-Jamaican father had hoped he'd pursue to study with Thelma Altshulter, founder of Miami-Dade's Humanities program. Gifted at languages, my husband mastered French, Italian, and Spanish, then followed his heart to CUNY to complete a BA in Ancient Greek and Latin. Like most CUNY students, my husband had worked the while, advancing from clerk to classical buyer at downtown Manhattan's earliest 80s' icon, Tower Records, by the time he finished college.

Nearly twenty years after *Loving v. Virginia*, in the ostensibly liberal bastions of New York and Boston, our marriage raised eyebrows—and the occasional menace—of strangers and police. At the same time that my father was navigating the storm of the Jeffries affair, my parents were obliged to parry the disapproving questions of friends and relatives, while I sadly saw a few friendships with Black women end abruptly. Not only had I chosen a partner outside my race, religion, and class that would cost me some of the support system I'd relied upon in high school and college, I was entering a social and professional environment where women were discouraged from having any partners at all.

Harvard University, in the 1980s, was radically different from CUNY—not only in the sense that there were few female role models (although female graduate students were admitted in rough parity to males the year I arrived, my advisor, the late Angeliki Laiou, had been the first woman to be tenured in the Harvard Department of History in 1981), and few doctoral candidates of color—but in the way faculty approached teaching, and advising. Most professors adhered to old traditions in keeping guidance to a minimum; the purpose of the program, I quickly discovered, was not so much to enhance our existing knowledge as to determine what we already knew. In such an environment, students who had been undergraduates at Harvard often thrived, while those less accustomed to the Harvard approach were challenged to find their footing on uncertain ground. The alienation I remember feeling around fellow graduate students who'd attended private, elite undergraduate institutions was only compounded by a tense situation at home, where my mother barely hid her anger at what she considered to be my abandonment of household duty, while my poor father tried to mediate between us.

As in college, Harvard's libraries provided a social refuge—I met one of my dearest friends, to this day, pouring over multiple dictionaries to translate a Byzantine saint's life at the library of Harvard's Divinity School. Another colleague in Comparative Literature, who shared my carrel in Widener Library, attended my wedding. However, these varied pressures propelled me in an untried direction that ultimately built a bridge between my father's experience and my own: I became involved in governance, specifically in the group that offered advocacy to graduate students in the 1980s, Harvard's Graduate Student Council, for which I served as secretary between 1982–1984. There, I met colleagues from other disciplines, several of whom became lifelong friends, men and women who, like me, had come to Harvard's Graduate School of Arts and Sciences from less elite institutions. Undergraduates at Harvard socialized through a system of "houses." In meeting after meeting with Harvard administrators, the Graduate Student Council worked to establish what eventually became Dudley House—a place where young scholars could unwind and make friendships beyond departmental boundaries—as well as a peer counseling network for GSAS students struggling to negotiate the often yawning chasm between the professional demands of their doctoral programs and the day-to-day challenges of their personal lives.

When my advisor moved to Washington, D.C. to head Harvard's Byzantine research center at Dumbarton Oaks, I moved back to New York, married my husband, and started a family. For the next several years, we lived alternately in Queens, close to my husband's work at Tower Records; then in a small town in Italy, close to the archives I commuted to as a Fulbright scholar. While my husband served as principal parent while we lived in

Italy, upon our return to New York, I became a full-time mother and full-time graduate student, staying awake every other night to write my dissertation from 10 p.m. until 4 a.m. Occasionally my youngest, a night owl herself, would rise from her bed to join me as I worked in the kitchen; we'd sit companionably across from one another as she drew crayon pictures and I transcribed four-teenth-century notarial petitions. Constant sleep deprivation took its toll in a series of hospitalizations and health problems I have been obliged to manage ever since.

By the time I earned my doctorate in 1996, these experiences had seeded my commitment to return to CUNY to assist students living the life I had lived in college and graduate school: caring for family members by day while being a student by night; try-ing, as my husband had, to make their way in a foreign country as a first-generation college student; choosing partners and career paths that skirted the boundaries of parental disapproval. Over the years, Queensborough students have shared stories of incarcerated spouses, mentally ill parents, finding themselves homeless when parents disapproved of their sexual orientation, their decision to continue a pregnancy, or when a parent prioritized a relationship with a new partner. Some students staggered to my class exhaust-ed after working a night shift; others hadn't had anything to eat. I began to keep cookies and tea in my office to feed the hungry ones, but wondered how else I could help.

My father's experience and my own convinced me that the answer might well lie within the structures of shared university governance. Governance could create a space for faculty to com-plement the intellectual support they provided for students in the classroom, facilitating strategic approaches to overcoming ob-stacles to student success. In contrast to the hierarchical dynam-ic established when an instructor evaluated student work, shared governance opened opportunities for egalitarian exchanges with students that solved problems and built trust. Shared governance fostered similar camaraderie between colleagues and even administrators, creating opportunities for collaboration rather than competitive or adversarial exchanges.

It was hard to watch CUNY's best traditions of shared governance tested by the controversy over the CUNY Board Resolution on Creating an Effective Transfer System, better known as the Pathways Curriculum, during the final year of my father's life (2010), and my first years on the UFS Executive Committee (2010-2018). Argued then litigated until 2013, Pathways not only threatened the intellectual rigor of a CUNY education, but engendered bitter disputes that sundered collegial associations and friendships of decades. But governance also offered a way through this troubled period, as it created opportunities for divided faculty and administrators to reconnect over the moral grandeur of CUNY's mission.

It was with this goal in mind I became involved in two projects as a faculty governance leader. As an incoming member of the UFS Executive Committee, I was assigned the role of secretary to a committee founded by UFS Chair Manfred Philipp (2008–2010) on Higher Education in the Prisons. In 2011, the UFS organized a conference on this topic, where we welcomed specialists in prison education and formerly incarcerated students from the tristate area, and especially from CUNY's famed Prisoner Reentry Institute (now the Institute for Justice and Opportunity) at John Jay College of Criminal Justice (its founder, former John Jay President Jeremy Travis, was our keynote speaker). The momentum of the conference, which brought an unpresented registration of 175 faculty and administrators, including a local legislator, led to the persistence of the committee as an ad-hoc consortium sponsored by the University Faculty Senate. As of this writing, the UFS Committee on Higher Education in the Prison continues to function as a locus of information and exchange for faculty involved in teaching in various state and federal correctional faculties in New York, as well as those who mentor students with a history of criminal justice involvement. Faculty on the committee have established educational programs in local correctional facilities like the College Justice Program at Edgecombe Correctional Facility, established by my colleagues at Queensborough; or La Guardia's program at Queensboro Correctional Facility; taught in John Jay's Prison-to-College Pipeline at Otisville Correctional Facility, and College Way at Riker's Island; authored books and articles on pedagogy and curriculum for incarcerated students; and sponsored at least six conferences over the last decade on aspects of prison education at John Jay, Borough of Manhattan Community College (BMCC), and LaGuardia Community College.

A second committee with which I became involved at Queensborough grew from faculty concerns over student hunger. By 2015, with tuition and the cost of living spiraling ever higher in New York City, research was showing that approximately 40% of CUNY students suffered from food insecurity. Once again, faculty, students, and staff banded together to solve this problem through governance. The faculty, working through Queensborough's policy-making body, the Academic Senate, formed a nine-member Committee on Food Insecurity, which brought together student government, staff, and the College's Single Stop office, to collect food and personal hygiene items to fill a walk-in closet, a space donated by Queensborough's former President Diane Call, while faculty members each volunteered an hour of their time weekly to staff it. As of this writing, Queensborough's Committee on Food Insecurity is fully integrated into the fabric of the college.

Its mission and charge are listed among Queensborough's Academic Senate bylaws, while the pantry itself, sustained by faculty donations and generous grants from the New York City Council and the Petrie Foundation, has been moved to a more capacious location. Efforts to keep track of the number of students the pantry serves will, meanwhile, support the research of colleagues who study poverty and its impact upon health and nutrition.

When BMCC opened their food pantry in 2018, former Interim President Karen Wilks spoke of creating "a culture of care." Over the years that I've studied and taught at CUNY, and elsewhere, I've become convinced that the campaign to create such a culture should be central to the practice of any institution of higher education. While, as a historian, I curate and analyze the artifacts of the long past, I draw as an educator, not only upon my vocabulary of experience, but upon what I've learned from my students to look for ways to engage them in the study of history. What makes CUNY unique is the way our faculty marry university traditions of intellectual rigor to our equally cherished institutional traditions of social justice. Through CUNY's shared governance traditions, we can uphold these twin pillars of access and excellence to realize the aspirations of the nineteenth-century Free Academy to educate "the children of the whole people."

Disappearing in Plain Sight

Developmental Education, Distance Learning, and the Covid-19 Pandemic

JASON VANORA AND EMILY SCHNEE

INTRODUCTION

The City University of New York (CUNY) is both the birthplace of basic writing and the university whose open admissions battles of the 1970s inspired Adrienne Rich's classic chapter, "Teaching Language in Open Admissions." We write this essay to reflect upon the dismantling of remediation at CUNY, the nation's largest public urban university, and to affirm her legacy. Rich was among the first to write about the challenges and possibilities of teaching what were then called "basic writers." We are struck, even after so many years, by how our experiences as community college professors, whose pedagogy and research focus explicitly on the needs and challenges of developmental readers and writers, parallel those of Rich, who sought to guide the most educationally disenfranchised students to develop the reading, writing, and critical thinking abilities necessary to reimagine their worlds and provoke positive social change (Rich, p. 55). By engaging with Rich's foundational writing from the 1970s, we consider what has been lost with the elimination of developmental education at CUNY and reflect on the structural changes needed to reshape higher education to more authentically support student learning.

Rich's essay has become all the more relevant as we consider what the precipitous move to online education as a result of the Covid-19 pandemic means for underprepared students at CUNY and beyond. Though much ink has been shed about the ways in which the move to remote instruction has exacerbated existing educational inequities, we have yet to read a consideration of what it means for the most academically marginalized college students, those previously classified as developmental learners. Not only do these students face all the same technological, financial, and motivational challenges as many college students in the United States, they are much more likely to come from those communities hardest hit by the Covid-19 pandemic. Black, Latino, English Language Learners (ELL), and low-income students have consistently been among those most likely to be designated "academically underprepared" for college-level work and in need of remediation (Flores and Drake; Jimenez et al.; Sparks and Malkus). Now, they are also the most likely to be doing essential work as cashiers, Uber drivers, janitors, home health aides, fast food and delivery workers, rendering them disproportionately susceptible to contracting Covid-19 (Feldman and Blumgart). Thus, it is not surprising that these students—those with the deepest academic challenges who are also working on the front lines—appear to be having the greatest difficulties adjusting to the new distance-learning format of higher education.

As community college faculty working on a different kind of front line, we can attest that those students who in a previous era would have begun college in developmental education are the ones who are disappearing from, or struggling most mightily, in our online classes. They are the students with the flickering Wi-Fi connections, who are trying to type essays on their phones as they supervise their younger siblings' online education because their parents don't speak English. They are the ones who seem stymied by our text-rich Blackboard sites despite the instructional videos and PowerPoints we post in a last-ditch effort to explain what would have taken five minutes to model in a face-to-face class. These are the students who went "missing in action" all semester, submitting no work, only to resurface with two weeks left to go, asking what they can do to make up the lost time and learning. As we struggle to respond to this new reality, our university has not said one word about these students or their future in a dramatically changed higher education landscape. But, in order to look forward, we must look back from where we came.

BACKGROUND

In Spring 2009, we began teaching in a first-semester learning community program designed specifically for students placed into the lowest level of developmental reading and writing at Kingsborough Community College, Brooklyn's only community college. Like CUNY in the 1960s, we had committed ourselves to open admissions, which both Rich and Mina Shaughnessy recognized as "openly admitting" that our city had failed to provide high school students with the academic fortitude needed to succeed in higher education and become civically engaged members of their communities (Rich, p. 61). Perhaps naïvely, we were convinced it was the university's responsibility to provide compensatory education so our students could develop what Rich described as a "special conception of what it means to be released into language...learning that language can be used as a means of changing reality" (Rich, p. 67). While certainly not a quantifiable outcome, or one valued in the paradigm that governs community college education today, we saw this potential within our students, and it kept us going as educators. What we did not know back then, over ten years ago now, is that this would be one of the last full-fledged developmental cohorts at our college, and one of our final opportunities to enact a curriculum designed to empower, awaken, and inspire those students who had been most marginalized and underserved in their prior educations.

In this essay, we reflect upon what feels like a lost opportunity—and one we mourn—to enact our commitments to student-centered, collaborative, and liberatory approaches to education with the most academically disadvantaged students at CUNY. Like Rich's Search for Education, Elevation and Knowledge (SEEK) students of the early 1970s, we know that none of the students in our developmental education learning community, "would have come near higher education under the regular admissions programs of the [four-year colleges of the] City University" with their abysmal test scores and multiple life challenges (Rich, p. 55). Some barely satisfied the requirements of a NYC high school diploma, while others stopped out of high school altogether because of limited resources, family challenges, and an overall lack of trust and engagement in the educational process. Like Rich's students, ours have "...held dirty jobs, borne children, negotiated for Spanish-speaking [*and Urdu- and Uzbek-speaking*] parents with an English-speaking world of clinics, agencies, lawyers, and landlords, had their sixth senses nurtured in the streets..." (Rich, p. 58).

Furthermore, our experiences with these students provoked us to engage many of the same questions Rich faced: "What are the arguments for and against...[t]he English of academic papers and theses? Is standard English simply a weapon of colonization?" and "How does one teach order, coherence, the structure of ideas while respecting the student's experience of his or her thinking and perceiving?" (Rich, p. 56). Yet, in our English and psychology classes, in fits and starts, we found ourselves, together with our students, enacting the messy, incomplete "reflection, criticism, re-naming [and] creation," that higher education necessarily involves (Rich, p. 68).

In our face-to-face learning community, we were able to deflect attention from test scores and outcomes to focus instead on empa-thy for Charlie in *Flowers for Algernon* in whom we saw Howard Gardner's theory of multiple intelligences come to life (Gardner). We moved beyond student resentment at being assigned to an eight-hour (yes, eight hours!), non-credit developmental course to debate the ethics of Jane Elliott's "blue eyes, brown eyes" experi-ment, and shared our dismay at the Clarks' famous doll test and its 21st-century reenactment captured on *YouTube* (Clark and Clark). Our learning community was *far* from perfect. But, we were there, two full-time professors, in the weeds with our students, physical-ly and psychically, as they grappled and grew, enlarged by what was perhaps their first encounter with an educational enterprise that respected their capacity to read, write, think, and question. We were there intentionally, willingly, often joyfully, locating our students' intellectual development at the epicenter of the social justice mission of our open access, public community college.

As we write this, we pause to wonder how it is possible that we are already nostalgic for *classrooms*? And for our learning com-munity experience of just a decade ago? How quickly, and how far has CUNY moved from its commitment to developmental educa-tion as part and parcel of its dedication to open admissions, social justice, and racial equity? With these questions in mind, we exam-ine more closely how developmental education has been phased out, specifically within CUNY.

PHASING OUT DEVELOPMENTAL COURSEWORK

Over the past decade, a growing chorus of critics of remediation has bombarded us, along with our students, with the message that developmental education is *not* "a necessary component of higher education (and) one with deep historical roots" (Attewell et al., p. 887). Rather, in the pervasive parlance of student success, remediation is considered both a "curse" and a "stumbling block," keeping students from achieving their goals of social mobility (Kirp; Smith). Critics often point to a few large-scale, quantitative studies that show negligible gains, or even negative results, for students in remediation (Calcagno and Long; College Complete America; Martorell and McFarlin). They also cite the low graduation rates among developmental readers and writers, lamenting the waste of money and resources spent on developmental coursework (Barry and Dannenberg; Calcagno and Long; Complete College America; Douglas-Gabriel; Mangan; Martorell and McFarlin). Arguing that "students get bogged down taking multiple remedial courses, leading many to give up and drop out," they conceive of developmental education as "a hoax perpetrated upon academically weak students who will be unlikely to graduate" (Attewell et al., p. 887). These critics of remediation almost universally fail to acknowledge critical research revealing that once academic performance and preparation are accounted for, college remediation no longer predicts graduation rates (Adelman, p. 75; Attewell et al., p. 889).

At CUNY, the remediation wars began to stir in earnest in 1999 when the Board of Trustees mandated that only community colleges would offer developmental classes (McCormack et al.). Though faculty fiercely and vociferously pushed back, arguing that developmental education was critically important to both CUNY's two- and four-year colleges, policymakers called these claims "a defense of failure," and placed the blame on students rather than the primary and secondary institutions that *truly failed* to provide students with the reading, writing, and higher-order, think-

ing abilities they would need to succeed in credit-bearing higher education courses (Giuliani; McCormack et al.). By 2011, in
line with national trends, CUNY had already begun to implement
policies intended to compel underprepared students to complete
remediation within their first academic year, while threatening to
implement "registration stops" on students who failed to make expeditious progress (Crook et al.; McCormack et al.). From the top-
down, our chancellors, administrators, and outside experts were
telling us that, in the best interest of our students, remediation can
(and must) be circumvented, replaced by "refresher" workshops
and limited academic supports, all aimed at helping students complete 15 credits per semester so they could graduate within two
years (Utakis). The final blow came in a 2018 memorandum from
the City University's Associate Provost for Academic Affairs and
CUNY's Director of Policy Research that announced the end of
full-fledged developmental education:

> ...CUNY's strategic goal is to phase out stand-alone non-credit remedial
> courses over the next several years and replace them with corequisite
> courses, in which students receive additional developmental supports
> while enrolled in credit-bearing math and English courses, or with target-
> ed developmental workshops taken before they enroll in credit courses
> (Crook and Truelsch)

These policy changes reside in stark contrast to recent research
revealing that CUNY community college faculty, across academic disciplines, are "advocat(ing) for more developmental coursework, more reading and writing instruction in credited courses, as
well as the need for higher academic standards" (Schrynemakers et
al., p. 24). These faculty members—the very ones who work with
community college students in their (now virtual) classrooms on a
daily basis—"stressed the need to keep or expand developmental

education" (Schrynemakers et al., p. 24). And yet, faculty were barely consulted when policymakers chose to phase out remediation at community colleges within CUNY, and across the country, rendering Rich's and our commitments a relic of the past. In short, even before the pandemic, our life's work had been hijacked by educational imperatives that privileged efficiency and productivity over student learning (Levin, p. 12). By all reports, this move away from a focus on student learning and towards quantifiable completion outcomes will only worsen with the higher education budget crisis nipping at our heels as a result of the economic collapse triggered by the pandemic (Pereira; Sandoval; Smalley). Simply put, we fear that we might be fighting just to move our teaching back into real classrooms.

When we need it most, few appear to remember that George Zook, the former President of the American Council on Education, declared in the 1940s that "the modern community college was theorized quite deliberately as a way to systematically address 'social problems' and help promote 'a fuller realization of democracy'" (quoted in Sullivan, p. 153). Again, we pause to wonder, how did we get from there to here? In the next section of this essay, we find a partial answer by considering how higher education—and in particular community colleges—have been reorganized to reflect a new paradigm, one that borrows heavily from business, and leaves little space for the kind of thinking and learning that was originally part of the community college's mission (Levin, p. 23).

NEW COMMUNITY COLLEGE PARADIGM

John Levin, in attempting to address how community college has lost sight of its original vision and embraced a business model of education, reminds us that the relatively recent focus on productivity and completion outcomes over students' learning and development is one facet of larger structural changes in our globalized economy (Levin, p. 11). As the neoliberal shift from collegiality and professional consensus toward "hard managerialism" and "autocratic control" impacts all areas of the economy, we should not be surprised that it has seeped into the pores of higher education, especially community colleges (Levin, p. 12). This pervasive culture of academic capitalism—replete with new accountability measures based on corporate completion agendas—prizes efficiency and competition over student learning. The space we created in our classrooms for reflection, agency, community, and social change are sacrificed to a new mission: to maintain the tuition dollars and state and federal funding attached to student enrollment and retention as students are prepared to enter—at the bottom rungs of the ladder—a globalized labor force (Levin, p. 13).

As education continues to move online, and the fight for students' tuition dollars intensifies, we anticipate that these trends will become increasingly intractable. Already we are being told that "continuity of instruction" must be maintained at all costs during the pandemic, and that we are responsible for holding on to and retaining students, whose learning appears to be placed last in the long list of institutional priorities. Students have been re-conceptualized as "consumers" and "commodities," rather than agentic persons with the power to read, write, think, reimagine their worlds, and provoke social change (Levin, p. 17). Thus, in this time of Covid-19, budget cuts, and continued disinvestment in public higher education, the emphasis on retention and enrollment take on ever-increasing importance and precedence over our students' academic needs. Consequently, our students have become the widgets in a dramatically underfunded public higher educational institution that is defined, almost exclusively, by its numerical "outcomes." Moreover, as the likelihood grows that across

CUNY course sections will be cut, class sizes increased, and portions of its campuses sold to stave off budget shortfalls, we find that opportunities for "automated teaching" have begun to flourish (Campanile; Knox et al.; Sandoval; Smith and Sandoval).

On a regular basis, we are offered rescue by educational technology companies chomping at the bit to design and grade our classes, and even to provide students with "Robotic Tutors," who might be better able not only to teach but also to "empathize" with students' challenges (Serholt, p. 77). If we have truly reached the point at which students are simply consumers and education a commodity to be taught by artificial intelligence, then perhaps we should stop worrying. Maybe the kind of relational, empowering, and human pedagogy that Rich called for in the 1970s has already been lost, and Covid-19 has simply forced us to a quicker reckoning with it.

But before giving up entirely, we share what we learned from our developmental students' experiences about the value of a more relational and less outcomes-oriented approach to higher education. We offer the following student narratives with the hope that if we cannot reclaim what has been lost, we might use this history to collectively reimagine some new paths forward.

LISTENING TO DEVELOPMENTAL STUDENTS

The students whose stories we share in this essay were one of the last cohorts of students at our college who had the benefit of a full complement of developmental courses and began their college experience in a learning community that offered a rigorous, interdisciplinary approach to developing their reading, writing, and critical thinking abilities. Fortuitously, they were also participants in a qualitative study we conducted from 2009 to 2012, and their stories of remediation were preserved through three years of longitudinal interviews (Schnee, 2014, p. 242; Schnee & Shakoor, p. 85; VanOra, 2019, p. 59). Little did we know at the time that their experience of developmental education would so soon be relegated to the history books. We bring in student voices here precisely because they are often excised from the contentious educational debates swirling around them—especially now, as these classes, and the students who were once in them, disappear in plain sight. While faculty perspectives on remediation have been largely ignored, we have yet to find evidence that the experiences of a *single developmental student* were considered when deciding that they would be better off without developmental coursework. We attempt to share those experiences now.

The data we collected in our study confirm that our students entered community college having already accepted the "common sense" notion of education as an exchange of commodities in which tuition dollars should earn them college credits. Non-credit developmental education classes explicitly challenged this conception and, not surprisingly, elicited student resistance at first. Fueling this fire were the pervasive negative stereotypes about remediation and the students assigned to what we called, perhaps euphemistically, always aspirationally, developmental education.

Latisha,[1] an African American woman with ambitions to become an attorney, told us that she "just kept kicking myself because (of) the way I kept hearing people talking about (developmental English)…that it was for dumb students who couldn't spell and people who were illiterate." Similarly, Eduardo, a young Latino who connected his motivations for attending college with the desire to make his parents proud, said he "felt real bad…felt kind of dumb" when he learned of his placement in developmental English. Jessica, a young Latina who describes stopping out of a dangerous high school in which she was "not going to be able to learn anything," went so far as to proclaim that she was "devastated" by her placement in developmental courses, while Yuri, a Russian student who describes coming to college in order to overcome what felt like stagnation and laziness, stated, "Obviously I got upset when I learned that I had to take these classes that give me absolutely no credits...I am a college student, but then I got these (remedial) classes...and it's time wasted and it's not giving me any credits, you know."

However, as the semester progressed, and as students moved further in their academic careers, they developed a different conception of what it meant to begin their college careers in "zero credit" developmental English classes. Almost unanimously, students declared that developing their critical reading and writing abilities superseded their initial desires to graduate as expeditiously as possible. Jessica no longer felt "devastated." In fact, she declared, "I don't care about it anymore, to be honest. I don't think about, oh my God, I have to finish in two years, or a year and a half, anymore. It doesn't bother me anymore." Similarly, Victoria, a young Latina, who described having no contact with a family of origin, unconcerned with her well-being, asserted, "I can start from absolutely nothing, and then work my way up. Like, I don't care how much time I spend in the remedial course, because I know that I (am) going to benefit." Latisha went so far as to proclaim that "maybe every student should have to take (developmental) English...they should know how to write papers before they go to other classes." It is important to note that these retrospective convictions about the need for remediation, and the value of spending this extra time, were identified across students' narratives. Jeremy, a white man, who discussed college as a vehicle for overcoming drug addiction and changing the direction of his life story, demonstrated a dramatic shift in his initial belief that remediation would be a "complete waste of time," when he told us, "I think (the first-level developmental English class) is probably one of the, *the* most important classes there is."

Why were these students able to embrace this slower, less ex- pediency-oriented journey toward a college degree, despite living and learning in a culture that conceives of them as "consumers" and "commodities" with little "time to waste" on non-credit-bear- ing classes (Levin, 2005)? It probably begins with the trust that we established as a community and our "fundamental belief" in our students, which Rich conceived of as "more important than any- thing else" (Rich, p. 66). Though we tried very hard to emanate radical kindness towards our students in this moment of pandem- ic, it remains deeply challenging to create trust via video confer- ence, and our efforts to do so often end in miscommunication and frustration on both sides. In our face-to-face classrooms, we, like Rich, tried to assess the strengths and challenges with which each student entered the classroom, while "never losing sight of where he or she *can* be" (Rich, p. 66). On a daily basis, we attempt- ed to enact a pedagogy of "critical care" that combined respect, compassion, and academic rigor (Allman and Slavin, p. 237). We remained empathetic to our students' daily struggles, while refus- ing to lower academic expectations or perpetuate the message that they were second-class academic citizens whose writing would be simply passed along for a modicum of effort.

Consequently, students' positive experience with education, possibly the first of their lives, outweighed the more transactional and instrumental motivations that initially brought them to com- munity college. In fact, students embraced the opportunity afford- ed by developmental coursework to learn to read, write, and think in ways that would enhance their lives. When reflecting on their emerging abilities to write more effectively, Ari, a relatively new language learner from Israel who struggled to pay tuition without the benefit of financial aid, told us that he "feel(s) much more freedom when I want to express myself in the writings," while Jessica has transitioned from a state of "panic" when it comes to writing to feeling confident enough to "start trying to write a book" about "me as I…get older, or how I wish my life will turn out." Students attributed much of their growth as writers to the time, attention, and meaningful feedback that they received in their developmental English class. Reflecting upon the opportunities to revise, collaborate, and think deeply in a developmental context, Victoria said:

> I think that everything seems a little bit more clear. Like, what is it that someone else would find to be good writing…I learned how to be a better writer…Honestly, I didn't know you could actually draft like, five times, and then be like, oh yeah, here is my final revision, like no one ever gave me the opportunity to do that. So, like, how could I be a better writer or know my mistakes if you don't give me that opportunity to allow myself to do better?

In addition to their newfound confidence as writers, some students also discovered joy in reading, both academically and for pleasure, through their experiences in developmental coursework. We were particularly struck by this part of students' narratives, given the evidence that developing college-level reading abilities might be the strongest predictor of retention and success among community college students (Fike and Fike, p. 75; Schnee, 2017). Interestingly, many students described an initial dislike of reading, while others reported that reading was simply, "not something I had done before," even in their high school English classes. For example, Hakeem, a young man, who seeks to earn a nursing credential so that he might help those struggling to obtain adequate medical care in his hometown in Guyana, said:

> (I came) from never reading a book, I never read a book, like I (was not)
> a big reading fan...In (developmental English) I had to read books and
> write about them. It was, it was transforming...I would say the experi-
> ence was good.

Similarly, Annamaria, a young Latina, who described struggling
to obtain enough money to pay for "bills, Metrocards, and books"
found that, as a result of the books she read in developmental English, she no longer "loses track of details that are important," and
instead, "pays pretty close attention to everything." Ari journeyed
from having conceived of books as "the enemy" to taking pleasure in reading, even when the books have not been assigned for a
class. When asked about the most significant experience from his
semester of developmental English, Ari said:

> The books. I read two, two books. Books, they (were) my enemy. I hat-
> ed books. I hated them. I never read books...I couldn't sit in one place
> and read (but in developmental English) it was very interesting...it was
> interesting. Yeah, I liked it. And now, I know when I have free time in
> August...I (will) go to the library and take a few books and I will read
> them. For pleasure (because) I enjoyed the experience with the books.

Of potentially the greatest significance is that some students reported planning to pass on their positive experiences with reading to their own children so they too might discover the benefits
and joys of reading. For example, Latisha was overjoyed with the
Barnes and Noble gift card we offered as compensation for participation in our research and used it to buy her daughter a book
for Christmas: "I bought my daughter (a book) so she could start
reading already, so I can get her ready for what I'm gonna teach
her, so I can teach it to her early, so she'll always have a love of
reading and writing and learning."

Also notable is that many students reported beginning the term with the sense that they did not need developmental coursework, and, thus, were surprised and disappointed by the placement. However, by taking developmental English, students became better able to assess their academic strengths and weaknesses, and to view their placement as an appropriate one. For example, Latisha said, "I saw that I did have weaknesses, I wasn't as good as I thought I was. I had myself at a high level, in my opinion; but I was at a lower level than I thought." Had this cohort been interviewed about remediation before (or without) having taken a developmental English course, they probably, without exception, would have declared that they did not need remediation, that their skills were already college-level, and that this would simply slow down their time to degree.

It was only through the experience of remediation that students recognized its value, and the reality that, without it, they would not have been prepared for higher-level academic coursework or, we might add, the literacy demands of a democracy. This insight reinforces our steadfast belief that we must reconsider the notion of students as consumers to whose immediate desires we must cater. Rather than simply "giving the people what they want," educators and policymakers need to "mediate student demands and endeavor to shape responsible curricula that maximize educational attainment" (Levin, p. 13).

LOOKING BACK TO LOOK AHEAD

How do we reconnect with the "hidden veins of possibility" that Rich alludes to in her essay, especially in the face of Covid-19's reshaping of public higher education (Rich, p. 67)? It is overwhelming, she admitted almost half a century ago, to teach under conditions at a large, underfunded, urban institution; today, even more so. How do we not let the cynicism of our current situation define our relationships with our students, or our aspirations for them? How do we center social justice in all of our teaching, even when to do so has been positioned in opposition to our institution's, and even our students' stated, or implicit, desires for individual "success"? How does one reimagine possibility when confronting an entire economic system that threatens both our vulnerable public educational institutions and our students? And what might it look like for us to take on these challenges remotely without sacrificing our commitments to relational pedagogies and genuine collaboration?

Training our gaze on the social justice opportunities of our current teaching lives, we both resist and accommodate the opportunities and constraints presented to us. In meetings, now virtual, we bring a critical perspective to the notion that any intervention that hastens students' graduation is a successful one, and urge our colleagues to think more critically (and creatively) about what it means to educate community college students in a pandemic. We continue to conduct research that shows that students' work and family obligations may make it impossible for them to complete fifteen credits per semester, despite the "fifteen to finish" campaign that pre-pandemic we found plastered all over our campus (often in the form of glossy posters with the vaguely menacing message, "The Longer You Stay, The More You Pay"). We try to maintain academic integrity and standards in our online classes, despite recognizing that our students did not sign up for this and are not learning what they would have in a face-to-face class, especially without the additional (and critical) supports developmental courses provided.

We also acknowledge that many of our students do not have the privilege to "shelter at home" and that they are among the most likely to be caring for (and losing) family members with

Covid-19. Thus, we adjust expectations, extend deadlines, and sometimes just let things go, while reminding ourselves that we make these accommodations in response to our students' needs and *not* because of administrative pressures to retain students and increase enrollment at a time when first-time enrollment at community colleges is down 21% (Lanahan).

We also attempt to understand the dismantling of remediation and the push towards expeditious graduation rates through a (critically) historical lens. We remember that Rich wrote at a time when CUNY was tuition-free, and that this was a significant factor enabling students to move at their own pace, without fear of losing financial aid if they did not complete their studies within a predetermined time frame. Without the burden of tuition, we might stop worrying about students wasting financial aid dollars on remedial coursework and, rather, enable our students to move slowly and steadily towards developing college-level reading and writing skills, while continuing to work and fulfill their familial obligations.

Structural changes aimed at reinforcing a mission that both admits and supports all students would necessarily include smaller class sizes, reduced teaching loads, and additional class time for students in foundational courses. As long as CUNY community college faculty continue teaching a minimum of 12 credits per semester, with over 45 students in a class, it will remain exceedingly difficult to engage students in the critical reading, writing, and thinking opportunities that remain an integral part of higher education in better-resourced institutions. We also need to fight against what some consider the inevitability that many colleges and universities will continue the "restructuring of higher education around online instruction and learning" after the current pandemic has been contained (Brightbill; Wright). Before CUNY even considers moving in this direction, serious research would need to be conducted on the impact this transformation might have on those students who are already the most marginalized and least academically prepared. As mentioned earlier, it is precisely those students who have been unable to successfully (or even moderately) transition over to remote learning in our classes.

Of course, the changes that we propose demand significantly more financial support from the city and state, at a moment when discourses of austerity and scarcity continue to dominate. We refuse to accept the notion that draconian budget cuts to public higher education are the only possible response to the economic devastation wrought by the virus. We note that CUNY opened three new colleges during the Great Depression, all while maintaining free tuition. A wealth tax, such as that proposed by former Democratic presidential candidate Elizabeth Warren, could allow for massive new investment in public higher education and a vision of CUNY as central to the economic revival of our city.

Such macro-level changes might also enable us to (re)conceptualize the social, political, and intellectual culture at our community college and across CUNY. What if we imagine a system in which the value of learning supersedes quantifiable outcomes, and faculty and students across disciplines collaborate in working through the dilemmas, challenges, and contradictions that we face at this crucial juncture? We might draw upon our disciplines' and students' wisdoms to generate ideas for resistance and change. We might dare to speak openly and substantively about the long-term impacts of racism, injustice, and inequality and their influence on how we relate to this fraught institution. Ideally, these conversations would begin in real classrooms and travel upwards, ultimately reaching policymakers, who continue to make high-stakes decisions about our students' lives, without input from them or us, even though we have the greatest degree of insider knowledge and first-hand experience.

Of course, these imaginings continue to feel "radical" and far afield from where we are today. Like Rich, we worry that the future of public higher education, especially in a post-Covid world, might be "already too determined…(with) too great a stake in keeping things as they are" (Rich, p. 68). And yet, we continue to believe that fighting for change is our only option—even as each new expediency-oriented initiative and automated teaching option makes us feel like we are attempting to halt a tsunami with our bare hands. But following Rich's lead, we will do what we can to provide students with access to the linguistic and intellectual tools needed to reflect, critique, (re)name, and (re)create. With the complicated gift of language, we trust that our students might join us in this fight or perhaps take the lead in fomenting changes that we, as CUNY faculty, have not yet brought to fruition. We continue this work with much worry and some hope for our students, our university, and the future.

Notes

1. All students were assigned pseudonyms, which we use throughout this chapter.

References

Adelman, Clifford. (1999). "Answers in the toolbox: Academic intensity, attendance patterns, and bachelor's degree attainment." *Washington, DC: Office of Educational Research and Improvement, U.S. Department of Education.*

Allman, Kate R. and Robert E. Slavin. (2018). Immigration in 2018: What is a teacher educator to D\do? *The Teacher Educator,* Vol. 53 (3), 2018, pp. 236–243.

Attewell, Paul., et al. (2006). "New evidence on college remediation." *The Journal of Higher Education,* Vol. 77 (5), 2006, pp. 886–924.

Barry, Mary Nguyen and Michael Dannenberg. (2016). "Out of pocket: The high cost of inadequate high schools and high school student achievement on college affordability." *Education Reform Now.* (https://edreformnow.org/policy-briefs/out-of-pocket-the-high-cost-of-inadequate-high-schools-and-high-school-student-achievement-on-college-affordability/). Retrieved February 1, 2021.

Brightbill, Gregory. (2020, March 24). "A post-COVID-19 higher education." *The Elm.* Retrieved Feb. 1, 2021. (https://elm.umaryland.edu/voices-and-opinions/Voices--Opinions-Content/A-Post-COVID-19-Higher-Education.php)

Calcagno, Juan Carlos and Bridget Terry Long. (2013). "The impact of postsecondary remediation using a regression discontinuity approach: Addressing endogenous sorting and noncompliance." *Community College Research Center.* (https://ccrc.tc.columbia.edu/publications/impact-remediation-regression-discontinuity.html) Retrieved February 1, 2021.

Clark, Kenneth and Mamie P. Clark. (1950). "Emotional factors in racial identification and preference in Negro children." *The Journal of Negro Education,* Vol. 19 (3), pp. 341–350.

Complete College America (2012). "Remediation: Higher education's bridge to nowhere." (https://completecollege.org/wp-content/uploads/2017/11/CCA-Remediation-final.pdf). Retrieved February 1, 2021.

Crook, David and Sarah Truelsch. (2018, Dec. 13) "Changes in CUNY's remedial assignment practices for spring 2020 admissions." *Memo to CUNY's Chief Academic Officers.* Retrieved from Kingsborough Community College's faculty listserv on January 9, 2019.

Crook, David. et al. (2011, August). "Proposals to improve success rates for students in developmental education at CUNY: Report of the working group on remediation." *CUNY Office of Academic Affairs.* (https://www.cuny.edu/wp-content/uploads/sites/4/media-assets/Report-of-the-Remediation-Working-Group.pdf). Retrieved February 1, 2021.

Campanile, Carl. (2020, March 15). "CUNY considering selling off properties." *New York Post.* https://nytimespost.com/cuny-considering-selling-off-properties/). Retrieved February 1, 2021.

Douglas-Gabriel, Danielle. (2016, April 6). "Remedial classes have become a hidden cost of college." *The Washington Post,* April 6, 2016. (https://www.washingtonpost.com/news/grade-point/wp/2016/04/06/remedial-classes-have-become-a-hidden-cost-of-college/?utm_term=.27a5e91b192d). Retrieved February 1, 2021.

Feldman, Nina and Jake Blumgart. (2020, April 2). "'Essential and unsafe:' Frontline workers of color face compounded risks." *WHYY, National Public Radio (NPR.* (https://whyy.org/articles/essential-and-unsafe-frontline-workers-of-color-face-compounded-risks/). Retrieved February 1, 2021.

Fike, David and Renea Fike. (2008). "Predictors of first-year student retention in the community college." *Community College Review,* Vol. 36 (2), pp. 68–88.

Flores, Stella and Timothy A. Drake. (2014). "Does English language learner (ELL) identification predict college remediation designation." *The Review of Higher Education,* Vol. 38 (1), pp. 1–36.

Gardner, Howard. (1983). *Frames of mind: The theory of multiple intelligences.* Basic Books.

Giuliani, R. W. (1999). "An agenda to prepare for the next century." *1999 State of the City Address. Archives of the 107th Mayor.* (http://home2.nyc.gov/html/records/rwg/html/99a/stcitytext.html). Retrieved March 15, 2021.

Jimenez, Laura, et al. (2016, September 28). "Remedial education: The cost of keeping up." *Center for American Progress.* (https://www.americanprogress.org/issues/education-k-12/reports/2016/09/28/144000/remedial-education/). Retrieved February 1, 2021.

Kirp, David. (2017, June 10). "Ending the curse of remedial math." *The New York Times.* (https://www.nytimes.com/2017/06/10/opinion/sunday/cuny-ending-the-curse-of-remedial-math.html). Retrieved Feb. 1, 2021.

Knox, Jeremy et al. (2019). *Artificial intelligence and inclusive education: Speculative Futures and emerging practices.* Springer Publishers.

Lanahan, Lawrence. (2021, January 15). 'It's just too much': Why students are abandoning community colleges in droves. *The Hechinger Report.* (https://hechingerreport.org/its-just-too-much-why-students-are-abandoning-community-colleges-in-droves/). Retrieved Feb. 11, 2021.

Levin, John. (2005). "The business culture of the community college: Students as consumers; students as commodities." *New Directions for Higher Education,* Vol. 129, pp. 1–26.

Mangan, Katherine. (2012, December 13). "National groups call for big changes in remedial education." *The Chronicle of Higher Education.* (*https://www.chronicle.com/article/National-Groups-Call-for-Big/136285).* Retrieved Feb. 1, 2021.

Martorell, Paco and Isaac McFarlin, I. (2007, September). "Help or hindrance: The effects of college remediation on academic and labor market outcomes." (https://ncde.appstate.edu/sites/ncde.appstate.edu/files/Martorell%26McFarlin.pdf). Retrieved Feb. 1, 2021.

McCormack, Tim, Emily Schnee, and Jason VanOra. (2014). "Researching up: Triangulating qualitative research to influence the public debate on literacy, standards, and access." *Teachers College Record,* Vol. 116 (4). (http://www.tcrecord.org). Retrieved Feb. 1, 2021.

Pereira, Sydney. (2020, May 7). "CUNY braces for anticipated budget cuts due to coronavirus pandemic." *The Gothamist.* (https://gothamist.com/news/cuny-braces-anticipated-budget-cuts-due-coronavirus-pandemic). Accessed on Feb. 1, 2021.

Rich, Adrienne. (1972). "Teaching language in open admissions." *On secrets, lies, and silence: Selected prose 1966–1978.* W.W. Norton & Co.

Sandoval, Gabriel. (2020, May 4). "Looming CUNY budget cuts have faculty and students fearing for the future." *The City.* (https://thecity.nyc/2020/05/cuny-budget-cuts-have-faculty-and-students-fearing-future.html). Retrieved Feb. 1, 2021.

Schnee, Emily. (2017). "Reading across the curriculum at an urban community college: Student and faculty perspectives on reading." *Community College Journal of Research and* Practice. Vol. 42 (12), pp. 825-847.

Schnee, Emily. (2014). "A foundation for something bigger: Community college students' experience of remediation in the context of a learning community." *Community College Review.* Vol. 42 (3), pp. 242–261.

Schnee, Emily and Jamil Shakoor, J. (2016). "Self/Portrait of a basic writer: Broadening the scope of research on college remediation." *Journal of Basic Writing.* Vol. 35 (1) pp. 85–113.

Schrynemakers, Ilse et al. (2019). "College readiness in post-remedial academia: Faculty observations from three urban community colleges." *Community College Enterprise.* Vol 25 (1), pp. 10–31.

Serholt, Sofia. (2019). "Interactions with an empathic robot tutor in education: Students' perceptions three years later." *Artificial Intelligence and Inclusive Education: Speculative Futures and Emerging Practices,* edited by Jeremy Knox et al., Springer Publishers, pp. 77–99.

Slaughter, Sheila and Larry L. Leslie, L.L. (2001). "Expanding and elaborating the concept of academic capitalism." *Organization Overviews,* Vol. 8, (2), 154–161.

Smalley, Andrew. (2020, December 28). "Higher education responses to Coronavirus (COVID-19)." *Na-*

tional Conference of State Legislatures. (https://www.ncsl.org/research/education/higher-education-re-sponses-to-coronavirus-COVID-19.aspx). Retrieved Feb. 1, 2021.

Smith, Ashley. (2018, August 10). "CUNY's intensive remedial ed semester showing success." *Inside Higher Ed.* (https://www.insidehighered.com/news/2018/08/10/cuny-initiative-sees-early-success-remedial-education). Retrieved Feb. 1, 2021.

Smith, Rachel Holliday and Gabriel Sandoval. (2019, October 11). "CUNY vies to cash in on its prime west side real estate." *The City.* (https://thecity.nyc/2019/10/cuny-vies-to-cash-in-on-its-prime-west-side-real-estate.html). Retrieved Feb. 1, 2021.

Sparks, Dinah and Nat Malkus. (2013, January), "First-Year undergraduate remedial coursetaking: 1999–2000, 2003–04, 2007–08. *National Center for Educational Statistics, 2013–013.* (https://nces.ed.gov/pubs2013/2013013.pdf). Retrieved Feb. 1, 2021

Sullivan, Patrick. *Economic inequality, neoliberalism, and the American community college.* (2017). Palgrave Macmillan.

Utakis, Sharon. (2018, May). "Opposing a 'one size fits all' education." *Clarion.* (https://www.psc-cuny.org/clarion/may-2018/opposing-'one-size-fits-all'-education). Retrieved February 1, 2021.

VanOra, Jason. (2019). "It's like one step for me to go forward: A longitudinal study of community college students' perceptions on the value of developmental education." *Community College Enterprise,* Vol. 25 (1), pp. 59–76.

Wright, James. (2020, April 6). "Social justice, online learning, and post-COVID-19 higher education." *The Elm.* (https://elm.umaryland.edu/voices-and-opinions/Voices--Opinions-Content/Social-Justice-Online-Learning-and-Post-COVID-19-Higher-Education-.php). Retrieved Feb. 1, 2021.

7.9.6

BRYANNA FLORES, WITH A PREFACE BY CHAMUTAL NOIMANN

"Teach them how to fish," is what they tell us. That is a good metaphor. "Fishing" will allow them to feed themselves, you see. The assumption is that students come to us with hungry, empty stomachs. But we can't simply feed them; that would be a temporary fix. We are to teach them how to be fishermen. For English departments, "fishing," often and exclusively means "teach them how to write college essays" so they know how to do it in their other classes. Sometimes, we are asked to teach them how to write emails or resumes, technical writing, because then they will be able to catch a better job. But we English folks (most of us, I believe) still see that as just feeding them fish. Students come to BMCC having been hungry for years. Most begin their journey in developmental courses, a year's walk to the nearest river, where fish might be abundant. Developmental writing classes are supposed to be what pre-fishing training looks like. We spend much of our time finding ways to convince students that they have the strength to walk to the riverbank.

English 088 at BMCC was our first-level English writing course. Students were supposed to learn basic sentence- and paragraph-level writing skills that lead to personal narratives and descriptions. For the final exam, we prompted them with "people change as they grow older. Tell of a time in your life that shows this change" or "describe a family member whom you consider successful." Personal. Where does one begin to teach them to fish for that? They try to respond to these prompts with what skills they bring, what they think we want to hear.

We can see our job as simply pointing to the subject-verb disagreement or punctuation issues. We ask them to review their peers because that is supposed to train them to spot these issues on their own. But we are often disappointed. Their responses are often "I was shy and now I'm not," and "my mom is the best mom in the world," and "Jason did a good job." We are disappointed in ourselves because subject-verb agreement instruction doesn't teach creativity, empathy, perception, self-analysis, reflection, criticism. For us English folks these are the beginnings of true fishing.

I first encountered Inuit songs in the *Norton Anthology of World Literature* (Second Edition, Vol F). The Inuit are Indigenous cultures, who live in the northernmost parts of the Earth: Northern Canada, Alaska, Greenland and Siberia. They are the First Nations of the Arctic. The songs included in the Norton anthology are called ID songs. These songs are performed in the communal feasting house, accompanied by drums and dancing. The audience joins in with the refrains. The songs are composed to commemorate important personal or familial events, solitary moments of great emotions, important life transitions and other subjects that are often very personal and difficult (2001, pp. 2036-37). Performing these songs publicly allows the individual to connect with the community. It allows the community to listen and offer support. The song becomes its creator's identifying song.

In spring 2014, I gave my ENG 088 students a handout containing three Inuit ID songs: "The Longspur's Incantation," "The

Lemming's Song," and "I Remember the White Bear." We talked about the songs, their purpose and power, and then I ask them to write their own ID poems. No rules. Poetry resists standardized spelling, punctuation, capitalization, or grammar. It has no regulated format, nor organizational expectations. It demands no supporting details or examples. I asked my students to define themselves and share that definition with their classmates. ID songs celebrate everything a fisherwoman requires: freedom to explore, patiently, internally, intently. My students understood right away.

The poem included here, "7.9.6" by Bryanna Rosemarie Flores, is one of fifteen, including mine. We shared and commented on each other's songs. We looked into ourselves and into each other honestly. We created a community of non-judgmental awareness in the classroom. I then felt confident to ask them to walk to the river with me, together. That is where I left them. Learning to fish. And here is what I also know: when you ask those who fish what makes a good fisherman, the answer consistently has nothing to do with casting technique, or bait selection, or gear, or subject-verb agreement. The answer is always "patience." Other answers include "willingness to learn," "respect," "adaptability," "creativity," "self-confidence," "respect." We teach our students about fishing, but we should not, cannot, try to control their casting, or which bait they use, or the variety of fish they catch, or how they cook them. We help them see their inner Angler because that they already are.

References

Lawall, Sarah N., & Maynard Mack (Eds). (2001). "Introduction to Inuit songs." *The Norton anthology of world literature*. Second edition, Volume D. W.W. Norton & Company.

7.9.6

Bryanna Rosemarie Flores, A name that means everything to me.

To friends, it's comfort.

To family, it's love.

To you, A possible friend, and to the world...something.

My superiors see clay, something they can mold, employers see a cog...

more money they can hold.

To all I am something, and to all I am nothing...and to the system, A number...

that is all that they see.

A Handicapped mother...A Distant father.

Beautiful son...Crude father.

I am that cog, support for my child.

I am that clay, better future to be had.

Not a number...I have a name...I have a self...I'm not the same.

Everywhere i go...it's always the same.

"I need help", "please mam, enter your social".

Buying a metro, please type in your code.

Buying some clothes, "let me validate your card".

"Have a rewards card"? ..."left it at home",

"No problem mam...just tell me your phone".

My son had a number...before he was a name,

he's still a number...though Manuel's his name.

Bought diapers the other day, "please mam, sign your name",

wait what did you say...that's right...I am a name.

"Thank you mam, card please, i must validate"...

Shoulder's fall, for fuck's sake.

Bryanna Rosemarie Flores, A name that meant everything.

Angry…tired…faith for humanity all but well.

Maybe that's why forensics, my future to tell.

Condemning man…criminals to others,

am i any better ?…turning them into numbers.

No longer matters, son is all that i need,

"i'll protect you from a system…that just wants you from me".

"I'll be your number, and i'll be the same…but you can't have him…he's a name".

You want him to be like every other guy, "run faster, jump higher, believe a man can fly",

Jordans, Fitted, True Religion…hundreds of dollars for "made in China" shit.

You want him to fight for you…and be proud to die…"your son was a true hero mam",

…all in the name of lies.

"I won't let you do that…you aren't the same…let me suffer…just so you can play"

Bryanna Rosemarie Flores, I'll always remember that name.

Between me and the lord…i am not the same, and in the end…i shall hear my name.

Today i am a number, XXX-XX-XXXX is what they say…

"thank you mam, and have a nice day"…

Writing "Our Stories"

Turning Individual Stories of the First-Year Transition at City Tech into a Web of Belonging

SANDRA CHENG, KAREN GOODLAD, JENNIFER SEARS, MERY DIAZ, MARIAH RAJAH, PHILIP KRENISKE, AND ASHWIN SATYANARAYANA

> There is no greater agony than bearing an untold story inside you.
> — Maya Angelou

The 21st century has seen the rise of digital instructional technologies that deliver wholesale, austerity-inspired academic instruction, often originating from top-down directives. Many faculty and higher education advocates view this massification of education as further deepening the marginalization and educational inequality experienced by poor, working-class, and minority students, especially those who rely on public universities. In response, they have argued for more faculty-led innovative instructional technologies and projects that emphasize developing the students' writing and critical thinking skills and building open, collaborative relationships among students and with faculty. All these characteristics are reflective of good scholarship, as well as just and effective pedagogy.

In Fall 2017, students in First Year Learning Communities (FYLC) at New York City College of Technology (City Tech) had the opportunity to participate in such a project designed by faculty who strongly believed in the potential for writing to transform a student's experiences. A program designed to help new students adjust to college, FYLC assigns two cohorts of students to share two or more classes linked by an interdisciplinary theme, thereby creating a community where students are encouraged to learn and bond with one another through the common coursework. For example, an introductory psychology course was paired with an introductory English composition course and titled *Emotions 101: Learning to Navigate the Challenges of College and Life*. In the psychology class, students learned about the emotional and physical effects of stress on the mind and body, while in their composition class, they reflected on the stress of their own transition to college. Each fall, City Tech offers fifteen learning communities co-developed by teams of FYLC faculty.

As an urban commuter college, City Tech lacks the physical space to bring students together. However, by utilizing the OpenLab digital platform, we hoped to virtually bring together students via a shared website. In creating the digital platform titled "Our Stories," we wanted students to share their experiences of transitioning from high school to college. This multi-year collective writing project offered students a means to reflect on their college experiences, and also for faculty to better understand their students' needs. We designed the platform, believing that the writing and sharing of stories would positively influence the students' transition to college. We thought it would help students seek out college resources; to make sense of the social, emotional, and bureaucratic challenges in their transition to college; and, ultimately support their academic achievement.

It is critical to learn more about this early, pivotal phase of college experience, especially at a public university serving working-class and minority students, often the first in their families to attend college. Minority students rely heavily upon public institutions for higher education, and research shows the transition to college is a precarious time. One student wrote:

> Well to begin with like most of you know college is nothing compared to high school. Everything is so different you become more responsible for your own things, the professors expect you to walk in to class knowing how to use black board what is Cuny first etc., but it's not like that.

In this essay, we as the faculty and staff who initiated and implemented the program, share how our digital writing platform offered a means to help develop a sense of belonging among our students; we also share what we learned from their writings. The collected stories document the challenges faced by new students in significant detail, capturing our students' voices as they express their concerns and aspirations. Their experiences must be understood within the context of continued disinvestment in public higher education over the last 40 years; and, simultaneously, the growing demographic diversity among CUNY students due to post-1965 changes in immigration laws. These ongoing trends highlight the need to increase advocacy for academic, economic, and social supports for our students.

SHARING STORIES IN THE CONTEXT OF SOCIAL JUSTICE EDUCATION

"Our Stories" was developed bearing in mind the tenets of social justice pedagogy, which emphasize community-building, participatory education, emancipatory initiatives, the humanizing of student experiences, and a democratizing school culture. The project sought to give voice to students and to bear witness to what they had to say. M. Diaz and B. Shepard (2019) note that this type of narrative approach is one way to give voice to compelling, yet often unheard and marginalized voices. By centering the students' stories, we sought to engage and learn from students, especially those from communities whose voices often are unheard. We also wanted to build upon interpersonal interactions taking place on the digital platform, and, further, to explore how to best meet the students' needs.

Over three semesters, students shared their stories via blog posts on the online platform. Faculty and students in learning communities were able to read and respond to the posts. The stories revealed multiple aspects of the first-year experiences of students enrolled at an urban campus that has few physical markers to distinguish the university grounds from the hustle and bustle of downtown Brooklyn. Many expressed surprise over how different college was from high school. Some of the recurring themes included (1) the challenges of navigating the bureaucratic processes of financial aid and registration; (2) the difficulty of balancing family pressures, a situation often unique to first-generation college students; (3) concerns about fitting in socially and succeeding academically; and (4) the struggle to engage with the varied teaching styles and diverse student body.

Their stories reveal an institution with a large immigrant population, evoking questions of vulnerability, cultural adjustment and unspoken uncertainties about legal status as documented or undocumented persons. The narratives also reveal the potential of digital writing to help students take a step towards self-advocacy through the expression of their thoughts.

GOING DIGITAL TO FOSTER COMMUNITY

We designed "Our Stories" to support student engagement and to learn directly from students about their college experiences. From the start, we were committed to FYLC as a high-impact practice that makes significant, positive impacts on student learning, especially for those from underserved communities. We also recognized the powerful potential of reflective writing as a first step towards self-advocacy for students in the initial stages of college. We believed asking students to reflect on their transition to college, thereby sharing their triumphs and apprehensions with a larger audience, would expand the network of support and foster a stronger college community.

Unlike Blackboard and other academic learning management systems, OpenLab is an open-source, digital platform for teaching and learning. All FYLC faculty and students use the platform in their courses. This decision was inspired by the work of Philip Kreniske (a former member of the OpenLab support team), particularly his findings on the efficacy for CUNY SEEK students to reflect on their college transition; FYLC faculty leaders adapted Kreniske's model in developing "Our Stories."

GROWING LEARNING COMMUNITIES BEYOND THE CLASSROOM

By extending the learning community beyond the physical and temporal limits of class meeting times, "Our Stories" complemented the community-building efforts taking place within the learning communities. In the early weeks of the semester, first-year students were directed to tap into the college-wide digital support network to find students facing similar challenges. Over the course of the semester, students were prompted to tell a story about their transition to college; they received the same assignment three times—at the beginning of the semester, roughly in the middle, and in the last weeks.

Some students responded to all three prompts, and others submitted only one post, or none. Peer mentors (FYLC upperclassmen) were trained to monitor and comment on the posts. The students' posts were visible only to faculty, staff, and students who joined the website. An important aspect is that no one outside City Tech has access to this reflective writing; only students in a learning community can read and comment on posts by fellow students.

Due to privacy concerns, the writers of the excerpted student comments are not identified here, although any member of the City Tech community could create an OpenLab account to access the posts. With hopes of acquiring more insight into the students' needs, we received Institutional Review Board (IRB) approval to analyze the students' responses. The IRB certification was a mixed blessing; though it allowed us to utilize student writing for research, the legal language of the consent process proved to be a deterrent for many students, and some who posted about their transition experience did not wish us to publish their words. Therefore, this essay only includes excerpts from students who gave their consent.

Readers of our students' posts will recognize some of their anxieties as universal to all new college students. However, the details offer broad insight into the challenges that City Tech students face in balancing their academic and personal lives. Their writings are a refreshing reminder to faculty that college life is more than covering the curriculum; it must include the social fabric of our students' lives. Our team appreciated the honesty of the student participants. Their reflections on college life strengthened our commitment to the value of providing a digital space for students to voice and work through pressing personal and political issues, while simultaneously cultivating personal writing as a means of agency and self-empowerment.

HOW STUDENTS EXPERIENCE DIFFERENCES BETWEEN COLLEGE AND HIGH SCHOOL

The majority of student posts highlighted the differences between college and high school. Students expressed how their adjustment to the college's physical space was connected to their emotional adjustment to college life. For many students, the sheer size of the campus—ten buildings scattered across several city blocks—was intimidating. One student wrote about his first day on campus, describing nervous emotions, and contrasting the college's physical appearance to his former high school:

> While I was walking down the hall to get to my first class, I was nervous. I did not know what to expect on my first day. I walked in nervous and excited. I noticed that everything was different. No posters on the wall, no bell to indicate when the class starts, and, most differently, no friends. High school was a place where I had teachers look after me, and making sure I was in school every day. My first week at college made me notice that all of that was over, and that if I wanted help I'll have to seek for help myself.

The poor state of the elevators was a common complaint in the posts, and brings to the forefront how a campus environment, in particular, CUNY's distressed physical facilities, negatively impacts the student experience. Students were overwhelmed by the queues for elevators. One student wrote:

> Also, the amount of students in this school is tremendous so the elevators are always packed. This puts me at a disadvantage because I try and come in on time, but I can't even do that since the elevators are always full except for when you don't need them.

Another wrote, "I never knew how bad an elevator line can be until I saw city techs line,"; many blamed the elevators for making them late to class and recognized the lines as symptomatic of overcrowding.

Students found the flexibility of college schedules—in contrast to the regimentation of high school—both frustrating and liberating. One student lamented: "There is new responsibility to get to class on time every day and the fact that the start time for class is different depending on which day it is can be disruptive." The dawning awareness of the need for self-actualization to achieve success in college is evident in this and other similar statements. For some, the change from a high school schedule meant the upending of everyday routines, like lunch. One student wrote about skipping meals because there were no preset lunch periods, and because her classes started at different times, depending on the day. Some students, however, liked the flexibility of designing one's own class schedule and thought it was an empowering benefit of college life, writing, "I feel like I'm in control of my life and my schedule."

The longer length of classes, compared to the standard 45-minute high school class, was another common issue. Several wrote about how it was a big challenge to transition to classes that could be three hours long, or more. One student descriptively compared the adjustment to this change, using video gaming terminology:

> I still haven't gotten used to sitting in the same classroom with the same teacher along with the same students for more than forty-five minutes. To transition from less than an hour to three of them with an extra thirty minutes is taking a big step. That's like changing a video game's difficulty setting from easy to extra hard while skipping every setting that is in between.

The switch from shorter intervals to traditional college schedules demanded extensive re-adjustment from the learning strategies acquired and reinforced in their K–12 experience.

The diversity of the student population was another major difference that students discussed. Students wrote about being one of the few new students in their courses, and about how many classes had students, ranging from first-year students to seniors. Incoming students were uncomfortable with the diverse age range of the student body, especially the much older students. One student wrote:

> This was the day where I saw a old person in my math class. I seriously thought that old man was a teacher, but he was a student like the rest of us. It's weird being in a class with people of all age ranges.

This student, like many others, revealed an assumption that everyone in college would be of similar age. Being one of the youngest in a classroom added to student distress. A student wrote about not liking a class specifically because of the older students:

> I didn't like my Friday class bcus (sic) their were some old people such as moms, it made me feel nervous because I wasn't familiar with that type of surrounding in a class. I wasn't use to it. I was also the youngest in the class (18) everyone else was older than me.

These posts reflect the inherent diversity of a typical CUNY classroom, filled with students at different academic stages, and of various ages.

STUDENTS WRITE ABOUT "FITTING IN"

It is common for new students to worry about being socially compatible with their peers when they start college. Since City Tech students belonged to immigrant communities, they expressed concerns not only about fitting in socially, but also about adjusting academically to the American university system. Feeling foreign in an already unfamiliar educational setting can exacerbate the sense of alienation. One first-year student wrote:

> Coming from a different country, I didn't know what to expect. As I walked into the building on my first day, the halls were flooded with new students, I was one of them. I thought to myself, am I dressed accordingly? Do I look worried?

Questions of belonging arose, repeatedly. The posts that expressed concerns over "fitting in" often got responses from other students who had experienced similar worries. Notably, many responses communicated support and shared solidarity over being immigrants, and attempted to reassure the fellow student that the uncertainty over navigating new cultural experiences was a shared concern.

Posts later in the semester showed that students became more comfortable once they learned of other students from their home countries, and realized they were not alone. As students got to know each other, they also learned many of their peers were immigrants, or the children of immigrants. This recognition, though, was dependent on students being exposed to and communicating with a large number of students. This level of exchange shows the importance of having a platform where a student can write to their peers. One student illustrates the importance of having such a resource, writing, "I know more people now that I noticed some of them are from the same country I am from."

The posts revealed that students faced unique demands as immigrants and the children of immigrants, including dealing with international travel, learning in English, and negotiating legal processes. Students sometimes came from families with multiple cultural backgrounds, and were required to travel to important family events, more than peers from non-immigrant families. One student shared her story of falling behind because she had to travel home for an important family event:

> My first few weeks at City Tech have been stressful. I have social anx-
> iety, so in all my classes I mostly remained silent. Everyone else was
> quiet too, which made me feel better and relieved. After the first week at
> school, I had to go to Honduras for my sister's quinceneara during labor
> day. I caught an infection on my trip and had to miss a whole week of
> school (and work).

Not surprisingly, the posts revealed how reading and writing in English is stressful for students who have only recently mastered the English language. A student wrote:

> I've been living in the United States for only 5 years, and I never attended
> school here in the U.S, so I had no idea how the education system worked,
> and to make it even harder on myself English is my second language.

While it was challenging for new students to navigate the unfamiliar American college system, CUNY's complicated administrative processes added another obstacle, as discussed next.

ADMINISTRATIVE CHALLENGES FOR STUDENTS

Glitches in the registration process can be intimidating and frustrating for all students. However, this project revealed that such problems are particularly troubling for immigrant students who must answer questions about their legal status; additionally, they worry about how their answers will impact their financial aid. One student recounted the anxiety of receiving a letter demanding that he prove his legal status by bringing in his green card and passport. In addition, he was threatened with losing his financial aid if he did not take a set number of credits. He wrote that he took several days off work to submit the required paperwork and to meet with college administrators, which ended up straining the relationship with his employer. Questioning a student's legal residency appeared to be a systemic problem that was confirmed by other students who had received similar letters. Students were greatly stressed by the danger of not receiving or losing financial aid.

Many students expressed frustrations with paperwork (an eternal student lament). They also complained about long wait times for IDs or meetings with college administrators. One wrote, "I would wait hours just to get service for something that would take no more than fifteen minutes." Students were forced to make time to visit campus to fill out requisite forms, but each visit often negatively impacted home and work schedules. The frustration with the administrative process and wait time was palpable. A student complained, "I had to come back multiple days to fill out paperwork for registration, admission, and financial aid. This sucked because I didn't know anybody and so I'd feel like a whole day was wasted every time I came in."

Frequently, students began college life at a disadvantage because they were not aware of the administrative and academic requirements and available options. The lack of a central location for advising, registration, and financial aid compounded the confusion for new students.

FINDING A SCHOOL-WORK BALANCE

Many students constantly worried about having enough money to attend college, and many students, even first-year students, held jobs. Most worked part-time, and others had full-time positions to help finance college. In the posts, students discussed the expenses of college beyond tuition, lamenting expenditures for transportation, housing, and books. Coping with academic- and work-related demands, students described personal sacrifices that highlighted the many challenges of the first-year experience.

One student said that taking care of herself was secondary to her school and work commitments. She wrote about how school and work consumed her time, leaving her fewer hours for sleep and forcing her to skip meals. Although being able to choose courses offered flexibility in scheduling, many students struggled with finding a sustainable balance between college and employment. One student wrote:

> There were two things I was extremely unexpected. Firstly, I was in trouble with the school and works' schedule. I thought three days in school would help me have a flexible time at work, so I agreed to work after school until midnight; as a result, I was so tired after work and unable coming to class on the next morning.

As the semester progressed, the challenges of balancing work and college were exacerbated by the increase in academic demands.

A SENSE OF BELONGING IN LEARNING COMMUNITIES

A number of posts highlighted the benefits of being in a learning community. Many students said seeing the same cohort in more than one class was the main advantage of FYLC courses; and that the sense of community lessened the stress and helped ease their transition. It was comforting for them to see familiar faces of fellow first-year students in several classes, in contrast to other courses where students were of various ages, and at different stages of their education.

In one post, a student writes positively about belonging to a community of people, all starting college:

> Another thing about college is that many will be nervous on meeting new people. In fact that didn't matter to me but once I found out about my learning community classes, I was amazed on how it works too. For

a whole semester I will have the same students in those LC classes. It is very nice because many of us are coming out of small high schools where we saw a lot of our friends for multiple classes.

Another student thought her first semester at City Tech felt like high school, and said that she easily transitioned into college life. She wrote:

My first months at city tech didn't feel much different from high school. The reason as to why it didn't feel different from high school is because am in a learning community. This learning community helped me adapt to college at a fast pace because I saw familiar faces every day, so I got comfortable quickly.

Another student thought college was very different from high school, but felt encouraged and a level of comfort seeing the same faces in different classes. He wrote:

The first Learning community is something that is so beneficial to people who are introverts. Seeing the same faces in 2-3 classes made communicating more easier…. I hope more kids take the opportunity of joining the FYLC because it really does make a difference. You get to connect with other people and not feel as timid as you would only seeing them once a week.

Finding a sense of belonging is important for all incoming students and the numerous positive references to learning communities, as well as other academic support programs such as ASAP and SEEK, reflect the desire for more one-to-one connections at the university. The built-in routine of seeing the same faces across multiple classes helps to construct a support network for first-year students.

REFLECTIONS ON THE IMPLEMENTATION OF "OUR STORIES"

Implementing this project involved challenges that directly relate to the themes and vulnerabilities opened by issues of student diversity. Each semester we made adjustments to fine-tune the project. As mentioned previously, City Tech students represent diverse cultural and educational backgrounds. Some students feel self-conscious about their language skills, and, therefore, are reluctant to express their views to other students; they are intimidated to reveal their writing level. Other students may have concerns with the public format, especially if they have a legal concern, such as over immigration status. In fact, nearly all students who posted about immigration-related issues refused to consent to having their writing published.

Some FYLC faculty members also expressed reluctance to participate in the platform. One reason was that this project, as it involves one to two class sessions, might consume too much valuable classroom time during semesters that already feel rushed in terms of meeting the demands of course curricula. Like our students, some faculty members have less familiarity and willingness to learn how to navigate the OpenLab website.

As faculty and staff members who have helped to initiate and implement this project, we have made changes that have smoothed out this process. Currently, we have students answer the prompt twice during a semester, rather than three times; this change was made in response to time constraints of students and faculty. Regarding concerns about the quality of student writing, many classes now have students begin the writing assignment in class, which gives students some time to reflect on how they might compose their post. Though we encourage faculty to allow students to write spontaneously, some faculty allow students to seek editing or tutoring help to write posts in a manner that they feel comfortable sharing. We have also had faculty and staff assist with navigating the platform.

One crucial aspect of this project is the requirement that students comment on the posts of their peers. When this happens, many more responses stream in, and the enthusiasm for writing increases. Peer mentors who actively comment on student posts make a big difference in building this momentum, too. We hope to develop a better way to encourage and manage the responses among students to make this project more successful. Consistent commenting by peer mentors is critical to building a sense of belonging among students.

THE IMPORTANCE OF DOCUMENTING STUDENT STORIES

"Our Stories" is a developing project that is continually modified in hopes of making it more effective for our students, and also easier for faculty to implement. This writing project has immense potential to help students make connections and to feel less isolated, as they navigate the challenges of entering an unfamiliar environment. The project has helped us to learn more about how students virtually reach out and help each other, at all hours of the day and night. We have seen how the administrative complexities that are a routine part of attending CUNY colleges negatively impact cultural stressors already being shouldered by our students. We have also seen ways in which students reflect on their own progress, and are sometimes surprised by what they have written in their own posts earlier in the semester.

"Our Stories" has proved a meaningful tool to give voice to first-year students. In reading their stories and hearing their voices, we believe we are better prepared to support our students as they transition into college. Our students have shown us the need for continued support, advocacy, and funding for innovative programs that attend to their academic, economic, and social needs. In sharing their stories, we hope to nurture a more welcoming environment for students at City Tech.

References

Aisch, G., Buchanan, L., Cox, A., & Quealy, K. (2017, January 18). Some colleges have more students from the top 1 percent than the bottom 60. *The New York Times.* Retrieved from https://www.nytimes.com/interactive/2017/01/18/upshot/some-colleges-have-more-students-from-the-top-1-percent-than-the-bottom-60.html.

Columbia University (2014, June). *The effects of co-location on New York City schools ability to provide all students a sound basic education.* The Campaign for Educational Equity, Teacher's College.

Diaz, M., & Shepard, B. (2019). *Narrating practice with children and adolescents.* Columbia University Press.

Gonen, Y. (2013, March 7). Nearly 80% of city public high school grads at CUNY community colleges require remediation for English or math. *New York Post.* https://nypost.com/2013/03/07/nearly-80-of-city-public-high-school-grads-at-cuny-community-colleges-require-remediation-for-english-or-math/.

Graduate NYC. (2016). The state of college readiness and degree completion in New York City: Readiness and enrollment. Retrieved from http://www.graduatenyc.org/wp-content/uploads/2016/05/GNYC-Report-Brief-2.pdf.

Fabricant, M., & Brier, S. (2016). *Austerity blues: Fighting for the soul of public education.* John Hopkins University Press.

Hanzapolous, M. (2016). *Restoring dignity in public schools: Human rights education in action.* Teachers College Press.

Kreniske, P. (2017a). "How first-year students expressed their transition to college experiences differently in two writing contexts." *Computers and Composition,* Vol. 45, pp. 1–20.

Kreniske, P. (2017b). Developing a culture of commenting in a first-year seminar. *Computers in Human Behavior,* Vol. 72, pp. 724–732.

Kuh, G. D. (2008). *High-impact educational practices: What they are, who has access to them, and why they matter.* Association of American Colleges and Universities. National Center for Education Statistics.

New York City College of Technology. (2018). *Fact Sheet (2018–2019).* Retrieved from http://www.citytech.cuny.edu/about-us/docs/facts.pdf.

Shapiro, Dundar, Huie, Wakhungu, Yuan, Nathan, & Hwang. (2017). *Completing college: A national view of student attainment rates–fall 2010 cohort* (Signature Report No. 12). National Student Clearinghouse Research Center.

Rosen, J. R., & Smale, M. A. (2015). Open digital pedagogy critical digital pedagogy. *Hybrid Pedagogy.* Retrieved from http://hybridpedagogy.org/open-digital-pedagogy-critical-pedagogy/.

Black and Latino Studies

An Empowering Vocabulary

REGINA A. BERNARD-CARRENO

"Black Studies is under threat!" my Ethnic Studies professor declared furiously, angry at no one in particular and everyone in general. After his outcry, he slammed his book on the desk. There we were, heading into our twenties, most of us already working full-time jobs and carrying a full load of classes. Full-time enrollment was possible because we could work eight hours during the day and take four classes spread across four to five nights a week. This was—and still is—a workaholic's dream come true. But there was an exchange for choosing that pathway. The perk of attending the City University of New York, then, inspired working-class people in their 20s to get a college degree for advancement.

When my Ethnic Studies professor made that declaration, I thought about how I could best get involved in a topic that I had loved studying, even before I got to college. The professor told me in his Caribbean-inflected accent to "try and organize some students." He was treating Ethnic Studies as a subject that students would mobilize around, solely behind the idea of a looming threat. He didn't understand that students worked full-time, and were also enrolled in school full-time, that some had children, and that all of life's difficulties were at every corner, waiting to deter us from finishing our education.

My first idea was to major in the field, hoping to broaden the army. However, the school didn't offer a major, and even if it had, there were no clear examples of what to do with such a degree. I had fantasies about attending law school or working for the New York Police Department after graduation. So, I majored in criminal justice for practicality and general interest, and spent my nights in a torrid love affair with the works of Zora Neale Hurston, James Baldwin and all the Black literature I could fit into my bag.

Thinking I had figured out my master plan, I rushed to the college's English department, with hopes of majoring in African American literature. I had a desperate need to satisfy my real desire, which was to read books for a living. I was already working 40 hours a week for a tyrannical lawyer, and imagined his life would be my future if I kept the same path, without at least exploring my other interests while in school. Unfortunately, there was no such major, so I continued to study criminal justice, and minored in English literature, developing my own reading list as time went on. A handful of English professors inspired me with special topic courses in African American literature; they were also researching and writing about the very subject. Two professors in particular became my literary cues, as they offered new courses every term and kept the readings relevant to urban experiences. Fully aware of who they were teaching, they taught Shakespeare in a way that opened up dialogue, rather than turned off students, even the cop who was taking a class between rotating shifts.

After graduation, I continued to work for lawyers. I departed from the idea of attending law school and decided to pursue a graduate degree in African American Studies. Quickly exhausting my search, none of the CUNY campuses offered African American Studies as a graduate endeavor; so, I earned my first Master's in African American Studies at an Ivy League school. I was the first graduate of their program, which heightened my self-awareness of my position.

I returned to CUNY for a doctorate in urban education. The program I applied to had just started its second year, and gave me the opportunity to study the philosophical and sociopolitical areas of urban education, or what I like to think of as city schooling. In the program and within my research, I was able to return to the Black studies and Latino studies area of work, which inspired my book *Nuyorganics: Organic Intellectualism, the Search for Racial Identity, and Nuyorganic Thought* (2010). Much of what I discovered as I researched my dissertation topic, and then later for my book on Nuyorican poets, was that my life and social experiences were heavily involved in my scholarship towards my degree. The scenes in the book that describe community, senses of place, and how one's body acts when in familiar spaces, were not just collections of scholarly research, they were examples of my own life growing up in New York City.

Unsure of how it all really happened, except for getting my first break, teaching a course on the diversity of American schools as an adjunct, I became an academic, a career lasting nearly twenty years now. Holding my doctorate in education, I felt as though I had again gathered my practical tools; but the pulse of the community was calling me. There were other things related to Black studies in the world that seemed to be under a looming threat. I ventured off the path of teaching about schools, like so many of my colleagues, and fell into the world of teaching about Black and Latino/a communities. Although the politics of pedagogy and local schooling were always on my mind, the issues of race, racism, and community were at the forefront of my work. The inequalities in schooling was just one tentacle of the broader issue that people of color were facing.

I treated my syllabus like a tour guide or map, exploring the beautiful works of Black and Latino/a literature, history, art and politics. Yet, the inequalities of it all began to keep me awake at night. There were obvious inequalities everywhere. Predominantly Black and Latino/a spaces, such as public schools, low-income neighborhoods, and work industries, were riddled with injustices, yet somehow it seemed like a sleeping giant. The issues were being glossed over, and things were as they always were without any serious attention to them. Sending out my curriculum vitae to various Black or Puerto Rican studies programs throughout New York City, I got a call from one school that urgently needed an adjunct. I immediately took the job, making it the fifth class that I was teaching, while enrolled in my full-time PhD program. Having just completed my academic experience learning from Black scholars that others were only able to read, I developed a dynamic syllabus, like a mix-tape with community-based final projects.

The undergraduates first moaned at the workload I had designed for them. It took careful reminding that our focus and our work together was more than just college class-work. We were to alter the experience of Black studies or Latino studies for the community and through this agreed understanding, we began to get stronger. In a sense, the students and I had a duty like no one else on campus, and the weight of this work and the pressure of representation began to mount on all of us.

My once literary desires had now turned into a desperate desire to address community issues. The students who researched and found hidden problems in their neighborhood had erupted inquiry that was unmatched in any other class they were taking. They were designing the first parts of an imaginary textbook that was riddled with case studies of urban communities. After adjuncting for a few years, I landed a job in the same department, but as a substitute lecturer. The highlight was teaching five classes that attracted about one hundred students per semester. While celebrating the small army of students in the discipline, I quickly recognized it as an extremely heavy load while also completing the doctoral degree requirements. Eventually, and after quite a haul of work-life imbalance, I went from adjunct to substitute lecturer to assistant professor to associate professor with tenure; I also served as chair of the same department for a short stint. The students remained faithful to the classes I offered, and, in turn, I remained loyal to offering as many as possible, so they could have the necessary classes to complete their minor in ethnic studies.

Early in my teaching, the students, mostly Black and Latino/a, were excited to have a space within their classroom to talk about the social issues plaguing their communities and sometimes their own lives. Their gratefulness far outweighed any differences between us, though as a woman of color, we shared invisible bonds. We began every semester with the guidance of Paulo Freire's *Pedagogy of the Oppressed*. I promised the students that although the translated text might be challenging, that once they studied it, they would feel a critical, informed sense of understanding about the world. Reading the book was often transformative, helping to define the oppression around them or within them. By the term's end, the students usually agreed that the book did resonate with them, though oftentimes, the students did not see themselves as able to address social ills head on.

I tell students in my classes that complaints about our society are not allowed unless they can think of interesting ways to resolve, remedy, or at least address the problem. It was a new approach where we replaced exams with projects and shared the burden of cost for class materials. They worked harder each week on the areas of our inquiries they could find results for. Our classroom became a haven for the public sharing of racial, socioeconomic and gender panic, paranoia and discomfort. There was always a heavy sadness within the walls of the Black studies classroom.

Together, the students and I were beginning to uncover acts of racism. For many, it was a revelation. For others, it was shocking. For the rest of us, we were still looking for more vocabulary to define our community's problems. For others, they were finding words to identify their own personal problems. Using Dr. Beverly Daniel Tatum's book *Why Do All the Black Kids Sit Together in the Cafeteria*, we delved into the psychological approaches to racism, and began to confirm her ideas even on our own campus. I, too, began to see racism in a different light.

At the start of the semester, I had told the students that whether we made any impactful change or not, we had to redesign the class's goals so that our class was different from the others they were taking. We had the personal and the academic on the table. By that point, the students had already developed the new vocabulary I had been harping on all semester. They were both identifying their experiences inside and outside of the classroom, and addressing societal issues that deeply affected them. The result was the re-naming of the world, according to their position in it. Students, many of whom majored in business, would trudge into class after a bad day at work in their corporate jobs, and say they were going through a "particular stage of self-identification," as we had talked about in Tatum's book. A hearty roar of laughter would fill the class; essentially, we had built a disciplinary code to discuss our daily lives. We were learning how to live in a world that was—and, still is—unjust and unsettled, but that allowed us to carve out a space for our intellectual growth.

Given the history of the City University of New York and its historical relationship to people of color, students who chose to pursue studies that make them critical of their communities often find themselves at a crossroads of guilt and freedom. While examining an entire failing district of New York City public schools that housed mostly Black and Latino children, a handful of students advocated for the school's closure. They supported their position, arguing that the students who were achieving would be re-integrated into schools that were doing better. "What about the rest of the children?" I protested. Jonas, a student, responded, "If we don't do this, then how we gonna eat, Professor Bernard?" Their real lives had never been addressed and most of the successes they had seen were examples in a textbook they couldn't necessarily afford. They had been given a plan on how to gain competitive, perhaps even successful employment and to secure the best pay on that plan, but they were looking for a space where they could be themselves, too.

Meanwhile, in my class, and later privately on a seat on the city bus or among the CUNY library stacks, they write personal narratives about their favorite books, about growing up in the Bronx, with family who are incarcerated, about dealing with homelessness while trying to attend school, of being hungry, or of being Black and upper-middle class and suffering at the hands of peer teasing for the stigma of "trying to be white." They needed filters, coded language, dual citizenships on campus and in their neighborhoods and a tangible example of freedom. They needed to learn how to be comfortable in rooms where they were the only of their kind, their type, their "breed," as one student referred to himself.

Black and Latino studies is not just an academic discipline. It also serves as a hub for students of color who are the mission of the City University of New York. Many of these students struggle to see themselves reflected in living color on campus, so they create clubs, and form alliances with other students who share a similar cultural perspective, if not the same one, and gravitate towards classrooms like mine where they can take off their other persona. This is not to take away from the service-based programs in place across the schools to address the needs of students of color. Rather, it should reinforce the understanding that Black and Latino students still need multiple spaces to delve into these topics.

To do this work and to curate these spaces, however, is to carefully consider what students bring to the classroom when designing the course itself. Though many would argue that conversations and teachings about Black or Latino studies are just as easily covered in other classes, we know that there are limitations. Students in the discipline rarely find themselves embraced by the syllabus, unless it is a special topic as in my earlier college experience. For many of my students over the years, it is the first time that the students are encountering seminal texts written by scholars of color who should be more widely known across all areas of study. We cannot be taught or learn about ourselves in a single survey course.

The unfolding of our class discussions and the work that is later produced by the students are true forms of liberation pedagogy. Black and Latino studies have made that possible for untold numbers of students over the years. I have witnessed students discovering a new sense of freedom in our classroom spaces. The commitment of students to their communities throughout the city, particularly places that need their voices and perspectives, has encouraged me and kept me loyal to the discipline.

Every semester, I continue to develop new syllabi for every class I teach, even if it's a class I have been offering for sixteen years. Students from previous semesters always inspire new ideas for age-old classes. The freshening of ideas and revamping of pedagogical tools has allowed the classroom and the discipline to amplify its possibilities. Less and less students feel disconnected from the neighborhoods where they spend so little time these days. In a sense, Black and Latino studies has become a theory-to-practice approach to the collegiate experience for many of us, both faculty and students alike.

College Adjunct

CONSTANCE H. GEMSON

I appear as daily faculty, an ordinary feature,

Then disappear, no Houdini, just reality:

rationed work in a rationed world.

I may or may not appear next semester.

I sign up for assignments, take crumbs of time:

least desired hours in a country of rich feasts and famines.

My students speak English as a second or third choice.

The minds move fast and fluid or careful and measured to master the new place

new space of this new world.

What is red tape? What are the secrets all Americans know?

What are the idioms easy to know for those born here?

I ask my students before they sleep,

What language do they dream?

Adjunct Blues and Class Notes

CONSTANCE H. GEMSON

In 2014, my adjunct teaching career came to an end. For seventeen years, I had taught for-credit classes on how to choose a career, but LaGuardia Community College's Cooperative Education Department was closing, and my students' internships were being reassigned to other programs. Contingent faculty for this program were no longer needed.

To get to my campus, I traveled from my Upper West Side apartment home in Manhattan to Long Island City, Queens, taking the #7 train known as the " *International Express.* " This name was due to the varied immigrant groups who used this route to go to school and work and to return home. The languages, clothing, and ethnicities of my fellow passengers were always changing.

I taught back-to-back late afternoon or evening classes, or on weekends. I always wanted to make sure to get an early start on the endless trek. A bagel could be lunch or dinner. On Saturday mornings, I greeted the security guard and glimpsed a colleague in a classroom while passing by. I missed the vibrancy of academic life when I worked the off-hours.

I recalled the song "9 to 5", the spirited anthem about the daily grind—with its computerized world of work, job stability, and specific hours. A set place and time for action are foreign to to-day's adjunct world. For part-timers, classes can be canceled due to low enrollment, with the instructor, usually the last to know.

After my 45 minutes—or more—trip, I would arrive at Rawson Street, the subway station. I'd see the Swingline factory: massive, dusty, red. Once 450 people had worked there producing staples and staplers. The business opened in 1925 and closed in 1999. The brand Swingline remains well-known. Decades ago, these assem-bly-line jobs promised security. A factory job meant steady work, a set paycheck, and maybe more money with paid overtime, and a chance for one's children to do better. Following the passage of the 1994 *North American Free Trade Agreement* (NAFTA), these factory jobs migrated to Mexico and other countries, leaving many workers stranded without employment. I empathized with the changes these workers had undergone. In a playful mood, I imagined the shuttered factory as a great disco! Bring back flam-boyant nights with Donna Summers' sexy singing! This site could become affordable housing or serve as a visible symbol for educa-tion. The theme was clear: worker security is an illusion in a dis-posable-employee economy. The future was a script that needed to be rewritten constantly; security was written in invisible ink.

I got my job at CUNY the old-fashioned way: through the switchboard. In 1997 I was looking for an in-service education-al program for the large organization where I worked. I called LaGuardia and the switchboard operator transferred my call to the Cooperative Education Department. It was the wrong department, but the right time. I spoke to Paula, a social worker, which was my profession, too. She said the historical mission of internships was unusual for a two-year college. She sounded so enthusiastic I asked if I could meet her for a drink or a cup of coffee after work.

We met at an Italian restaurant a week later. Paula shared many recollections of the college's mostly new immigrants. "Their internships helped define their careers," she said. Paula told me about the six-session seminars, unlike the typical classes, which were fifteen weeks long. These abbreviated classes emphasized how to choose a career, assess personality style, and obtain additional education. Students would seek to resolve a personal career dilemma; their dreams, desires, and future plans varied.

Three weeks later, I met with the dean and, yes, I was hired! A department professor had written the textbook. I received course outlines used by my colleagues and then created my own syllabus. My first class was *Fundamentals of Career Advancement*. The book explained the *Myers-Briggs Type Indicator*, highlighting emotional qualities. The *Holland Profile* defined personality styles, such as realistic, investigative, artistic, social, enterprising, and conventional. I used TV shows to illustrate these qualities. These classes served as an introduction to American life for my mostly immigrant students. For example, one Chinese student wanted to know the meaning of the phrase "red tape." I learned to slow down my rapid city speech and to use the chalkboard as well.

Later I taught other career-based classes that studied John Dewey to help initiate students into the world of work. I defined the differences between goals and values. Goals were specific, tangible and numerical; values were a source of meaning. I described the difference in values between a cloistered nun and a corporate leader. The class immediately understood this difference. When the college began in 1971, students spoke about being born and raised in Queens. Now their origins were different: Poland, Argentina, India, Greece, the Dominican Republic, China and Nigeria.

During my early years, many students worked at LaGuardia Airport. I recall one African-American flight attendant who wanted to become a psychologist. "I want to handle bigger problems," was her thoughtful remark. For a class assignment, she interviewed a Black Panther. Would today's students think a Black Panther was a car or a movie?

Early on, my students perceived college as a short stint during which to mull over post-high school vocational choices. Later my students became more aware of precarity in an ever-turbulent economy. A few began in four-year colleges and dramatically changed directions. Some motivated students were over 40, like a woman who had worked at Aqueduct Racetrack and been everything but the jockey. As police and legal TV shows proliferated, forensic psychology became a growing field of interest.

For new arrivals, their educational orbit was often narrow. For many, the United States still felt foreign and strange. They had survived the major transition to the challenges and contradictions of this country and now wanted stability and affordable choices. For many, their dream school was Baruch College. It was rare for students to discover academic opportunities at elite private colleges like Barnard or Vassar. One student showed me his acceptance letter from Morehouse College, where Martin Luther King had studied. He was very proud when I acknowledged the hard work necessary to win his admittance.

A tech support internship was highly desired and well-regarded by students. Often my young college students were more knowledgeable about computers than older workers. Internship responsibilities differed: administrative assistant, teacher assistant, and legal assistant. The placement sites included Lenox Hill Hospital, Queens Community House, Black Entertainment TV (BET), MetLife, and local public schools. Students valued healthcare settings, but direct experiences with patients' healthcare treatments were not included. The internship did not include hands-on clinical work, and was intended as an opportunity to see if a career fit and if they wanted to wear it. They had the opportunity to observe and become more aware of careers in a medical setting.

Daily college life at LaGuardia lacked the romance of a rural college. There were no dorms to meet fellow students for casual conversations or a beer in the student union. The place operated on quick entrances and exits. Posters of student clubs and performances decorated the hall, but the internal mantra was simple: no time, no time, no time. The small green grass courtyard was barely visible. Work, school, and family composed the complicated triad.

My college offered classes that trained students to become veterinary technicians. These classes involved more than how to pat a bunny. This competitive program required many heavy-duty science classes. One student who had a PhD in literature enrolled in this program. Another lived in northern Westchester county; her field-work experience sounded like an experience at a serene horse farm.

Students lived with constantly competing demands in their lives. When babysitting plans crashed, the overworked parent brought the offspring to class. Almost always, the youngster was given paper and crayons and told to behave well. Children usually remained quiet.

When I enrolled in college, my sole responsibility was to be a student. My heroes—whom I met briefly—were Michael Harrington, who wrote about U.S. poverty in *The Other America* (1962), and Cesar Chavez, who became a labor activist organizing farmworkers. I earned my Master's degree in Social Work at Stony Brook University, an affordable choice for my school-teacher parents. I lived at the rural campus in a small dormitory room for one.

My goal was to be a social change agent. We can change the world, I believed! My younger brother was being groomed for a medical school future. My students' lives were more complex and demanding than I'd imagine possible in college. Back when CUNY was tuition-free, many of my friends, first-generation college students, found enrolling in classes an alluring offer. They were grateful to continue their education while staying at home and expanding their boundaries in their own urban community.

My ambitious grandfather Irving, my father's father, arrived from Russia in 1889, when he was two years old. He graduated from City College at 19 in 1906. Even with free tuition, higher education was a financial stretch for him. He tutored immigrants in English for 25 cents an hour, back then, a high rate of pay. My grandfather's education eventually bumped the whole family into the middle class. City College was a vital lifeline for immigrants, then and now. My grandfather taught at Boys High School of Brooklyn in 1910, and retired in 1953. Both my father and uncle attended the school, and were proud alumni. My grandfather's graduation from a public college provided the opportunity for my own future. I was a romantic realist about the different and demanding futures current college students faced.

My grandmother Evelyn, my mother's mother, completed two years of college at Adelphi College in Brooklyn, now Adelphi University on Long Island. She taught kindergarten for over 40 years. Below her college yearbook picture is the wonderful phrase, "Independence now, independence forever, Evelyn knows what she wants." What a great legacy to come from three generations of teachers. My family regarded teaching as a noble calling and valued their students. For my grandparents, teaching provided security during the Great Depression.

My personal history would be different from theirs. At the beginning of my college teaching experience, the dreaded word was "outsourcing," as jobs went overseas. Later, it was "precarity," the tenuous nature of work itself. Then, the "gig economy," as ordinary jobs became more piecemeal, reminding me of garment workers in an earlier century facing uncertainty about their futures. Today, the working world is a world of mini-jobs or jobettes: part-time assignments with little—if any—security or benefits. Precarity is a familiar concern at my school for students, and part-time faculty as well. This theme is universal. Adjuncts—migrant PhDs roving the college dust bowl—became the new poor, searching for new options in teaching or other fields. In my classes, I discovered that the students' written work varied greatly. Newcomers struggled with the demands of English. Noun and verb tenses did not agree. Word usage could be imaginative or awkward. The college offered students additional help with their writing.

I assigned a classic writing prompt to interview someone you admire. I valued their choices. One student interviewed a physical therapist and an occupational therapist because she was interested in both careers. A young woman who worked on John McCain's first campaign for president actually interviewed McCain. I wish I had saved her essay. Another student interviewed a Legal Aid lawyer because he admired his idealism. One woman featured an assistant teacher of children with special needs, describing the stresses of a typical day. One man chose a police officer whose name he would not reveal; the officer's partner had been killed when he was present and the officer still felt devastated. His brooding essay read like a Raymond Carver story of the urban working class. Another paper's subject had worked as a production assistant on the film *Malcolm X.*

One assertive student examined the organizational chart at MetLife where he was an intern and saw his dream job: CFO, the chief financial officer. He called up the man for an interview and was delighted when this high-level executive said yes. The student wore a jacket and tie for the big occasion and noted the administrator had not. "Yes, but you did the right thing," I said. He was very pleased with this important meeting. His paper was excellent.

A student from India admired a doctor. He was moved when the physician shared his favorite quote from Hillel, a Jewish sage, "If I am not for me, who will be? If I am for myself alone, what am I? If not now, when?"

The classroom experience changed after 9/11. Before, many students wanted to use their language skills to be travel agents or work at hotels. I remember one woman, so disappointed about her hotel experience." I'm 21! I wasted so much time!" she said. I encouraged her to think differently: "Now, you are clear about what you don't want to do." She hated the idea of working holidays or being on a changeable schedule. Many clients were demanding and not interested in finding a solution. She began researching other professions.

After 9/11, students viewed police and accounting jobs as being more steady and secure. The friendly skies of strange places seemed more frightening and dangerous. The college provided students with free counseling, a vital service. Most students did not seem interested. Therapy was often not a comfortable experience with their backgrounds.

I asked my students to interview each other. To decline to answer a question was always fine. I was concerned about certain Muslims who would be identifiable based on their clothing. I did not need to use the brake. Classmates were kind. Careless comments did not come up at all.

When the school produced the play, *The Vagina Monologues,* I wondered if this was the right choice for my students when Muslims valued the idea of modesty. One friend said, "Well, they are in America now." I felt the need to be aware of the world of newcomers and to ease their adjustment. Most students came to class in jeans and casual shirts.

Students discussed problems at work. Joe, an American-born student, was the only Latino working in a men's clothing store. As he began sharing his experience, I wondered if his recollection was going to include a Jewish stereotype. "I am the only one who can speak Spanish to the customers," he said. "Everyone else is Muslim." The diverse group suggested he read about Muslim traditions and ask polite questions of his colleagues.

Sometimes, a student sought me out for a private meeting. I remember Rosa, a woman in her 20s, asking me after class. "Professor Connie, I know you worked with cancer patients. Maybe you can help me. My mother died of cancer when I was eight. My dad never told me she was sick. He just told me to go out and play. Why did he do that? I just wanted to spend more time with her. I didn't know she was dying."

I listened, and tried to be helpful. "Rosa, your dad didn't want to worry you. Now, parents are encouraged to share more openly when a family member is sick. Things were different back then. Your dad was trying to do the best he could."

Rosa looked unconvinced. She seemed shy about describing her immense loss. "I'd like to give something back. Maybe I could volunteer for one of those marches against cancer."

"Rosa, that would be a great idea." I gave her information about cancer advocacy organizations.

Later, I thought about that encounter, and how so many of my students reach out to get the help they need yet fail to receive it. Only in retrospect did I realize that joining the march would mean a major financial commitment and require free time.

In class I loved dividing students into small groups, enabling them to become more active. This method also was an easy way to manage over 30 participants and to encourage more autonomous learning. Dividing the class into three groups, I would ask them to consider what factors were important in choosing a senior college. I created roles: a leader to keep the conversation on track; a recorder to write down the findings; a speaker to summarize the results; and a scribe to record the results on the blackboard. Each group chose their own name establishing a sense of friendly competition and ownership. The groups often cited convenience, classes in their major, and cost as significant factors. CUNY, with its relatively low tuition, was still pricey for blue-collar participants born in the United States, as well as more recent arrivals.

Supervising the groups, I answered the students' questions, and added missing information. I reminded them that online classes could be useful in organizing their multiple scheduling demands. Very often, sleep was the first casualty. Their lives were just too busy.

One student said to her group, "My friend said he wouldn't want to go to Brooklyn College. He said there were too many Jews there." This remark was seemingly accepted unquestioningly by her seven colleagues.

Well, I overheard it. If a similar comment were made about any ethnic group, I would tactfully deal with this situation. Now I was the unknown target. I had an ethnically neutered name. I did not discuss my religion in class. I needed to make the student aware and yet not make her uncomfortable or embarrassed.

"That's an interesting perception," I said, softly. "What percentage are Jews in the United States?" One class member stated confidently, "Oh, at least 20 to 30 percent." The others nodded in agreement.

"No, Jews represent less than three percent in this country," I replied. "I am Jewish and feel uncomfortable with that remark."

The group paused and listened. Then the discussion continued as before.

After fifteen minutes, the group work ended. Throughout the entire class, I emphasized the diversity of our college and our city. I wrote one of my favorite quotes by James Baldwin on the board. "The role of the artist is the same as the role of lover. If I love you I have to make you conscious of things you don't see." The statement underscored a valuable lesson. The class ended and the students left the classroom.

I was busy packing up my load of books and belongings in my backpack when the student who had made this initial remark entered the room. "Professor, I am so sorry I hurt your feelings," she said. "My friend said that about Brooklyn College. I didn't." I looked her in the eye. "You showed a lot of gumption to come back here. I accept your apology." I held out my hand. We shook hands firmly. I admired her courage. She felt she was respected, as well.

I walked out into a beautiful spring morning. I noticed lively students moving their hands, creating their own geometry. All the students were deaf; my college has a well-known program for individuals with hearing loss. I admired their exuberant communication.

As my final class ended, I felt a sense of completion. I wondered how my students' lives would turn out. I assessed how much I had learned, shared, and experienced in this box-like setting once a candy factory. I recall the Swingline Factory, a formerly empty space. It took over nine years before that empty space became a warehouse and furniture store. I think of the former candy factory, today LaGuardia Community College, a place where students and faculty are changing lives.

Twenty Years at CUNY

A Political Coming-of-Age

ROSE M. KIM

On November 4, 2008, in my darkened studio apartment, I sat hunched at my desk, glued to the bluish screen of my small laptop showing a brightly colored TV studio set emblazoned with stars, stripes and the U.S. presidential seal. Minutes before polls were to close in five western states, Wolf Blitzer, the white, white-haired, white-bearded CNN news anchor, told the audience that when the clock hit eight on the west coast, the next president would most likely be instantly known. As the on-screen digital clock ran down, Blitzer said, portentously, "This is a moment that could potentially be rather historic." As predicted, within seconds after the clock hit 8 p.m., my home state California weighed in with 54% for Barack Obama and 38% for John McCain; yielding 55 electoral votes, it was enough to establish a clear victory for Obama, the very first Black president of the United States.

The screen switched next to Grant Park in downtown Chicago, where an ocean of people packed the lawn. In a frenzy, the undulating crowd was screaming, chanting, waving flags and banners, pumping fists in the air, clapping their hands. Parents carried young children awake past their bedtime, on their shoulders; couples and strangers alike hugged one other; and, senior citizens sat in wheelchairs or leaned on canes, all having waited for hours for a chance to glimpse Obama and to be in the presence of his magic. In New York City, more than 800 miles away, I too felt viscerally swept up in the excitement, a Durkheimian moment of cultural efflorescence.

Today, more than twelve years later, re-watching that moment on the Internet, it's hard not to feel moved, yet again, seeing that sea of people screaming, "Yes, we can." I remembered the hope and purpose I had felt, making oatmeal raisin cookies and lemon bars to sell outside a Brooklyn coffeehouse in a nationwide bake sale to raise campaign funds. I remember colliding into one of my students on the street on Election Day when she grabbed me by the arm, a wide smile stretched across her beaming face. "I voted—for the first time!" she said breathlessly.

Eloquent, smart, and graceful, Obama exuded style and intelligence. And, what a desire there always is for such a hero, some handsome knight in shining armor, or some indefatigable superhero, to rescue us. It's a yearning fueled by a mass pop culture industry that makes billions, selling us easy entertainment and facile, unrealistic resolutions. Rather than critically examining the real-life, monumental social problems of war, inequality, racism, and climate change that require a radical change in human consciousness and our ways of being, it's easier to just hope for a telegenic savior to save the day.

Today, in the wake of Donald Trump's presidency, it's hard not to feel nostalgia for the elegant Obama, his brilliant wife, his two lovely daughters, and the seductive lie that theirs was a better time. While Obama did deliver beautiful speeches, ones that I relished rereading and studying for the cadence of their words, the truth is a critical assessment of his administration shows an uninterrupted commitment to militarism and the corporate accumulation of wealth that has led to 750 U.S. military bases spread across the planet on virtually every continent. Furthermore, the Obama administration executed the 2008 bank bailout, using the taxpayers' money to rescue major banks, while failing to prosecute financiers who criminally exploited the financial, banking, and mortgage-lending system, then abandoned the individual homeowners, who had been their victims. It also oversaw the suppression of the Occupy movement in 2011, a violent, nationwide assault carried out in the early morning hours, coordinated by law enforcement, the local and federal government, and business interests. It also deported more than five million people from the United States, making Trump's subsequent assault on immigrants and refugees nothing new (Wolf, 2019). Of course, it was moving and meaningful to hear an American president say, "Trayvon could have been my son…", and I'm glad Obama was the first president to ever visit a prison. Yet, his governance yielded no appreciable change to policing or police violence and failed to act as if Black lives truly mattered.

Despite the dominant corporate media's constant fixation on the next, always upcoming presidential election, the office is essentially the figurehead of a vast, complex government that cultural critic bell hooks rightly identifies as an "imperialist white supremacist capitalist patriarchy" (Yancy & hooks, 2015). It is a state bent on dominating the market, without sincere, thoughtful concern or consideration for issues of justice, equality, democracy, or even the value of life—the longstanding ideals used to justify past U.S. interventions and wars. Currently, in a period that anthropologist David Graeber has called "savage capitalism," the pursuit of wealth and power doesn't even seem to require any camouflage or pretense (2014). The 2018 Senate appointment of Supreme Court Justice Brett Kavanaugh, despite credible allegations that he sexually assaulted three women, attests to the contradictory lip service given to true justice at the highest level.

My emphasis on the larger, structural forces shaping U.S. society is a perspective that has been cultivated over my nine years as a doctoral candidate at The Graduate Center, CUNY, and then honed by my subsequent thirteen years as a sociology professor at the Borough of Manhattan Community College (BMCC).

In writing this essay, I realized what a transformative experience studying and teaching at CUNY over the last twenty years has been for me. My education here has radically altered my views of society and social justice and taught me the importance of public engagement. It has especially made me value the important role of public higher education in developing a critical perspective. As befits such a complex, pluralistic society as ours, it is essential to cultivate critical perspectives so we can have a well-rounded, balanced assessment of our collective social situation; such an orientation also helps us to better plan our future goals and actions. I'm grateful to have studied with brilliant, self-reflective faculty members who nurtured critical perspectives of society not typically covered in the popular or corporate media; and, also, for my fellow classmates who represented a broad swath of human experience and taught me even more.

I entered graduate school relatively late in life. At 36, I was significantly older than many in my cohort. I had dropped in and out of The University of Chicago, striving to be a novelist, and also struggling to earn money to pay for my tuition. For my last several years, after my parents had gone bankrupt, I had worked full-time as a secretary at the college to get a 50% discount on my tuition. After I finally earned my BA at 28, I worked as a journalist, most substantially for six years at *New York Newsday*, a daily newspaper in New York City. Amidst a massive corporate downsizing of the newspaper that was killing a job I had once loved, I decided to quit my job, get married, and apply to graduate school.

Like so many other significant moments in my life, my enrollment at The Graduate Center was a fortunate turn that yielded prospects and outcomes I had never anticipated. Until then, I had generally thought positively about American society. I was aware of inequalities and injustice, having personally experienced them as the youngest child in my family, as a girl, and as an Asian American, but I had directed most of my anger and resistance toward my parents and the Korean culture they represented, rather than wondering about the social forces that had divided their homeland into warring states and brought them to this country. I embraced the United States' myth of national progress, seeing this country as an escape from my parents' traditional constraints, and as a place where my dreams might flourish and unfold. My success in school and in journalism reinforced my generally positive assessment of U.S. society.

I'm not sure why—perhaps it was the influence of my older brother, or maybe it was the times, but I was politically engaged from an early age. At 11, I volunteered in the first of three political campaigns for Jerry Brown; a few years later, I worked on *Proposition 14*, the 1976 ballot measure to promote labor rights and unions for farmworkers, and participated in marches to better fund public education and to desegregate schools. In college, I developed the idea of pursuing a journalism career after working as a reporter on the campus newspaper. I was committed to the idea that journalism was the "Fourth Estate" and that documenting social problems and challenging abuses of power would lead to peaceful, democratic, social change. Lacking a fully developed sociological imagination, I thought history was shaped primarily by individuals—autonomous, rational agents—rather than larger social structures and history itself.

In graduate school, my view of the dominant mainstream corporate media, of which I'd been a proud, badge-carrying member, altered radically. By studying a rich array of critical social theorists, from Karl Marx to Frantz Fanon to bell hooks, I deeply considered how violence, oppression and exploitation structured our social reality. I grew increasingly aware of how denigrating narratives of "the other"—whether "poor", "Black", "woman", "Asian", "Korean", "immigrant", or disabled—were deeply interwoven into the social fabric and culture of the United States. I learned about the Korean War and the role of the United States in dividing the country, propping up military dictatorships, and occupying it to this day. My parents had rarely spoken about their lives in Korea or during the war, so I was well into my 30s when I first asked about their experiences and learned that American bombers had killed my paternal grandmother and uncle.

For my doctoral dissertation, I critically reexamined my participation as a member of the reporting team at the *Los Angeles Times* that won a Pulitzer Prize, the profession's highest honor, for its coverage of the 1992 L.A. civil upheaval that I call the 1992 LA riots/insurrection/*saigu*. The tripartite term reflects how different participants viewed the event. For the dominant white supremacist society, as reflected in the *Times'* coverage, the riots were an eruption of violence perpetrated by Blacks; for African Americans, as reflected in the Black press, the violence was a justifiable response to the initial state-sanctioned police assault on Rodney King and the equally violent court acquittal of the four police officers who had been charged with using excessive force. For Korean Americans, who call the event by its date ("*sa-i-gu*" representing 4-2-9, or April 29th), the riots reflected the U.S. government's disregard for and abandonment of Korean immigrants who suffered a disproportionate amount of the damages, a total loss of 2300 small businesses and nearly $400 million. Upon ruminating over and analyzing the newspaper's coverage during the course of five years, I concluded that it had been shallow and racist, and, that as one of the few Korean-American reporters, I had been played to create a multi-racial façade while delivering a dominant narrative that supported White supremacy, the police, and the law. As C. Wright Mills might say, it was a "terrible...magnificent" lesson (1959, p. 5).

When I started teaching at BMCC in 2007, there were more terrible, magnificent lessons to learn. I thought I had an awareness of poverty in New York City, having worked as a reporter in the city for six years, covering some of the city's poorest neighborhoods and schools; furthermore, I had studied social inequality in my doctoral coursework, and, as a graduate student, worked on various CUNY campuses, including Bronx Community College. However, working full-time as a professor, teaching four or five classes a semester, dealing with as many as 150 students in a single session, I became much more acutely aware of how crushing poverty was in the city, especially for our students whose median household income was $28,400 in 2017. I've had students who lived in homes without electricity or water. I've had students who were homeless (typically, they disappear). I've had students who were fleeing domestic abuse and living in a shelter. I've had students who have stolen food to survive. Presently I have numerous students who don't own a desktop or laptop computer and write their papers on their cell phones, later printing them out in the campus computer lab.

There are so many students who are indelibly imprinted on my mind. I remember a young woman who immigrated from Yemen to the Bronx at the age of 10. She described having to climb up giant mountains for hours with her sister and cousins to attend a faraway school, back in her homeland. When she turned 14, her parents sent her back to get married. Her much older husband constantly pressured her to quit high school, which she finally did. When she was in my class, she was 22, and already had four children, with the eldest, 7. She was critical of the patriarchal culture that had married her at a young age, and in the process of divorcing her husband and pursuing a college degree.

I remember a 20-year-old Chinese American woman who had immigrated to the United States with her family ten years earlier. Even though she'd been here for some time, her command of spoken and written English was weak, having spent most of her time among Chinese-language speakers. She had come to my office to get help on her final paper. She said she worked in a nail salon from 9 a.m. to 7 p.m., which was better than the restaurants, where you worked from 9 a.m. to 11 p.m. or later. She said her dad, a restaurant worker, didn't understand why she was going to college, and that he wanted her just to work and to earn money. "He's old-fashioned, and he doesn't know why I'm going to school," she said. "But I'm young, and I think I can do more…"

I remember a young Filipino woman who was undocumented. She had graduated college in the Philippines, then worked in the hospitality industry there. She felt frustrated by the limitations of the work and the low pay, and eventually came to the United States and overstayed her tourist visa. Her first jobs were cleaning motels in the south. Eventually she came north to NYC and was studying, hoping one day to be a nurse. It was unclear how she would get there.

I've seen them graduate and move on to new challenges. I have a former student who is pursuing a PhD in ethnomusicology at an

Ivy League university. Another student graduated from Brooklyn College, worked as a high school teacher for Teach for America in Memphis, Tennessee, and is starting a PhD in literacy studies at Middle Tennessee State University this fall. Another is beginning an MA in gender studies at UCLA. There are also students who transferred to private, elite colleges, then struggled, dropped out, and disappeared. We need to hear all these stories.

In the nearly fourteen years since I started working at BMCC, as the result of listening to my students' stories, I've radically altered my approach in the classroom. When I first started teaching in 2007, I was stunned by the classroom behavior and literacy skills of many students. Initially, I blamed them for their low level of academic work; then gradually, I realized that their academic struggles stemmed from a complex confluence of social issues, social forces, and challenging circumstances, rooted in an unequal, unjust society and the ongoing historical inequalities faced by the poor, the racialized, and immigrants. As just one piece of evidence, consider the *New York Times'* uncovering of former President Donald Trump's tax evasion scams, for which he has yet to pay a penalty, in light of Trump's relentless scapegoating of immigrants and other racialized minorities as draining this nation's public resources.

Hearing about my students' lives, I wanted to learn more. So, in my introductory sociology classes, I developed a final paper assignment that requires them to investigate their family history and evaluate their personal experiences in school over the years. It's been fascinating to learn about their struggles and journeys. For far too many students, their public-school experiences have been a failure—whether due to overcrowded, underfunded conditions; insensitive teachers and administrators; a dehumanizing lack of personalized interaction; a heavily policed environment; or the school-to-prison pipeline. This awareness has led me to open every class, by saying, "Thank you for being here. And, thank you for being here on time…" For our students, racism and economic injustice are incontrovertible facts of their lives.

There is the fantasy of the liberal university, a place of free-wheeling critical thinking and hyper-political correctness. Yet, the reality is that the American public university has been under attack and seriously defunded over the last 40 years due to neoliberal efforts to disinvest in and privatize public goods. Meanwhile, the turn to emphasize career training—rather than a critical liberal arts education—as the goal of college seems a deliberate pushback to the radical student activism of the 1960s and 1970s that desegregated campuses and led to the creation of ethnic studies programs, a history in which CUNY students have played critical roles. The current right-wing efforts of state legislatures in numerous states to ban the teaching of Critical Race Theory (CRT) in public schools and universities is the latest, most frightening attempt to silence any discussion of racial inequities in this nation (Goldberg, 2021). While elite universities may still maintain the liberal arts' educational ideals of cultivating broad minds and engaged citizenship, many public colleges, especially community colleges, are being redesigned into job training institutions to exit as quickly as possible. Yet, today, more than ever, we need to cultivate critical perspectives to counter these assaults and to make decisions that benefit the children of the whole people, instead of the marketplace and "the 1 percent". We need to always be asking questions, to always be seeking solutions. We need to be awakened to the problems of injustice and inequality, again and again, until they are changed.

It is important to know that the assault on public higher education, as well as CRT, is happening around the world (Goldberg,

2021). Since the start of the 21st century to this day, there has been an increase in the number of student protests, globally. In Germany, students have organized massive protests against neoliberal efforts to impose market reforms, such as imposing or raising tuition, and viewing education as a private good rather than a public one. In the UK and in South Africa, students have been fighting to "decolonize" education, demanding for Black and minority ethnic voices to be included in the academic canon. Students are also being attacked by the state, whether the 43 missing young men who were witnessed being kidnapped by police in Iguala, Mexico, in 2014, or the ongoing crackdown against students and professors in Turkey.

My years at CUNY radically altered my perspective of society. Interacting with radical and subversive professors and students, and considering with them the society in which we live—through a close, critical reading of past and current social theorists—has played a significant role in effecting that change. I deeply value the practice of critical inquiry embedded in higher education and believe wholeheartedly that it yields benefits for humanity as a whole.

The public university must be fought for. The stories of CUNY must be told and heard.

References

GOLDBERG, David Theo. (2021, May 7). The war on critical race theory. *Boston Review*. Retrieved on June 10, 2021, from http://bostonreview.net/race-politics/david-theo-goldberg-war-critical-race-theory.

GRAEBER, David. (2014, May 30). Savage capitalism is back and it will not tame itself. *The Guardian*. Retrieved on June 1, 2021 from https://www.theguardian.com/commentisfree/2014/may/30/savage-capitalism-back-radical-challenge.

MILLS, C. Wright. (1959/2000). *The sociological imagination*. Oxford University Press.

WOLF, Zachary B. (2019, July 13). Yes, Obama deported more people than Trump but context is everything. *CNN.com*. Retrieved on June 10, 2021, from https://www.cnn.com/2019/07/13/politics/obama-trump-deportations-illegal-immigration/index.html.

YANCY, George, and bell hooks. (2015, Dec. 10). Bell hooks: Buddhism, the beats and loving blackness. *The New York Times*. Retrieved on June 1, 2021 from https://opinionator.blogs.nytimes.com/2015/12/10/bell-hooks-buddhism-the-beats-and-loving-blackness/.

Contributors

Sylvia Beato-Davis is a writer and an educator whose work revolves around the phenomenology of the body, the politics of linguistics, and post-colonial identity; she has been published in the poetry journal *December*. She earned her MFA in poetry and translation from Queens College.

Teronia Campbell (TSC performer) joined College and Community Fellowship in 2009, and participates in both the Academic Support Program and the Theater for Social Change Ensemble. She holds an MA in rehabilitative counseling. Teronia currently works at Odyssey House, a nonprofit helping people recover from addiction.

Regina Bernard-Carreno holds degrees from John Jay College, Columbia University and The Graduate Center. She is an associate professor in the Black and Latino/a Studies Department at Baruch College. Dr. Bernard has published three books about race, education, feminism, and social justice.

Nancy Cardwell is a psychologist and doctoral lecturer in the early childhood education graduate program at the City College of New York with expertise in neuroscience; child development; unconscious bias reduction; and racially, culturally and linguistically inclusive classroom practices in urban settings. Her research examines the interplay between culturally based knowledge and the professional knowledge of teaching among early childhood teacher candidates from diverse backgrounds. She began her teaching career as an early childhood teacher in central Harlem and later joined the graduate faculty of Bank Street College.

Sandra Cheng is an associate professor of art history at New York City College of Technology. She has served as a faculty leader for City Tech's First Year Learning Community (FYLC) program, and continues to teach FYLC courses.

Grace M. Cho is a professor of sociology and anthropology at the College of Staten Island and an alumnus of The Graduate Center. She is author of *Tastes Like War* (2021) and *Haunting the Korean Diaspora: Shame, Secrecy, and the Forgotten War* (2008).

Wanett Clyde is a collections management librarian at the New York City College of Technology. Her research investigates the intersection of fashion studies and Black history.

Lisa Dazzell received her BA in psychology and Africana studies, with a minor in health education and promotion, from Macaulay Honors College at Lehman College. She is currently in a doctoral program in counseling psychology at Iowa State University, where she is studying race, risk, and protective factors in low socioeconomic, predominantly Black neighborhoods, and the stigma associated with mental health in the Black community.

Mery F. Diaz is an associate professor in the Human Services Department at the New York City College of Technology. Her work focuses on the minoritized, racialized, and gendered school experiences of young people, and social justice issues. She is a long-time faculty participant of City Tech's First-Year Learning Community initiative. She is co-editor of *Narrating Practice with Children and Adolescents* (2019), and is on the editing board of *Affilia: Journal of Women and Social Work.*

Abby Dobson is a sonic conceptual performing artist/composer, activist and scholar. She received a JD from Georgetown University Law Center and a BA from Williams College before accepting her artist's calling. Artist-in-Residence with the African American Policy Forum and NOW-NYC Board President, Abby is passionate about music as a tool for transformative change. Her CD, *Sleeping Beauty: You Are the One You Have Been Waiting On* received rave reviews. She was a 2017 Create Change Fellow with The Laundromat Project and performs with Black Women Artists for Black Lives Matter.

Michelle Fine is Distinguished Professor of urban education and psychology at The Graduate Center. Her publications include: *The Changing Landscape of Public Education* (2013), with Michael Fabricant; *Charter Schools and the Corporate Makeover of Public Education* (2012), with Michael Fabricant; *Revolutionizing Education: Youth Participatory Action Research in Motion* (2008), with Julio Cammarota; *Muslim-American Youth* (2008), with Selcuk Sirin; *Becoming Gentlemen: Women, Law School, and Institutional Change* (1997), with Lani Guinier and Jane Balin; *Working Method: Research and Social Justice* (2004), with Lois Weis; and her classic *Framing Dropouts: Notes on the Politics of an Urban High School* (1991).

Bryanna Flores, a mother of two kids, loves reading, writing, and spending time with family. Her favorite genre is mystery. Currently, she is working as a concierge with Emblem Health, and plans to become a paramedic. She is a graduate of Borough of Manhattan Community College.

Selina Fulford (TSC performer), who returned to society in 2009, is currently employed as an MSW coordinator and has worked in the homeless shelter system since 2001. Selina has earned three MAs with College and Community Fellowship's support, and is inspired to further obtain a PhD in social work. She is an advocate for social justice.

Maya Garcia is a writer, poet, and researcher from Minneapolis, Minnesota. She received a BA in English and Puerto Rican and Latino studies from Brooklyn College, and an Advanced Certificate in Labor Studies from The CUNY Graduate Center. Garcia has received fellowships from VONA (Voices of Our Nations Arts), the Watering Hole, and Brooklyn Poets.

Constance H. Gemson was an adjunct lecturer at LaGuardia Community College. Currently, she organizes a writing class for CUNY academics, and is active in the Professional Staff Congress, the union for CUNY faculty and higher education officers.

Karen Goodlad is an associate professor in the Department of Hospitality Management at New York City College of Technology. Specializing in beverage management, she teaches an array of courses preparing students to become leaders in the hospitality industry. Her work as a faculty coordinator of City Tech's First Year Learning Community initiative, as well as a learning communities' teacher, brings high-impact practices into classrooms across the campus.

Yvette Heyliger is a graduate of Hunter College and Queens College, and an award-winning playwright, producing artist, educator and activist. Author of *What a Piece of Work is Man! Full-Length Plays for Leading Women*, she has also contributed to various anthologies and recently returned to the stage as a solo artist in her first one-woman show, *Bridge to Baraka*.

Katherine Sweetness Jennings is a self-identified poet. With the support of College and Community Fellowship, Katherine earned a BA in sociology; and an MA in professional studies from New York Theological Seminary. She is also a credentialed alcohol and substance abuse counselor (CASAC), and a member of the Theater for Social Change Ensemble.

Jasmine Kasheboon Khoury is a Palestinian-American from Long Island, New York. She graduated magna cum with a BA in anthropology from the City College of New York. She has researched mental illness and dis/ability amongst Palestinians within the CUNY Pipeline Program and the Mellon Mays Undergraduate Fellowship.

Rose M. Kim is an associate professor of sociology at the Borough of Manhattan Community College and a co-editor of *Women on the Role of Public Higher Education: Personal Reflections from CUNY's Graduate Center* (2015) and *Struggle for Ethnic Identity: Narratives by Asian American Professionals* (1999).

Christine Kovic studied at The Graduate Center from 1990–1997, during which she participated in the student strike of 1991 and anti-war protests. She is a professor of anthropology at the University of Houston–Clear Lake, and her current research addresses the intersection of human rights, health, and immigration, with emphasis on the organizing efforts of Latinxs in the United States, Central American migrants crossing Mexico, and the impact of enforcement policies at the U.S.-Mexico border.

Philip Kreniske is an assistant professor at the HIV Center for Clinical and Behavioral Studies at the New York State Psychiatric Institute and Columbia University. Kreniske concentrates on the impact of socioeconomic factors and digital technology on adolescent and young adult development in the United States and sub-Saharan Africa. He earned his PhD from The CUNY Graduate Center, where he created a digital network, and then studied the ways that first-generation and low-income students used the network to generate a system of support in their transition to college.

Shirley Leyro is an assistant professor of criminal justice at Borough of Manhattan Community College. Her research focuses on deportation effects, including the impact of fear resulting from the vulnerability to deportation. She is currently working on publishing the results of a funded research project exploring the impact of deportability on the sense of belonging and membership among CUNY noncitizen students.

Jose Lopez was born and raised in New York City. He received an associate degree in sociology from the Borough of Manhattan Community College.

Linda Luu is a PhD student in American studies at New York University and a graduate of Hunter College. Linda organized with the Coalition for the Revitalization of Asian American Studies at Hunter (CRAASH) and is the curator of a CUNY digital history archive collection on the fight for Asian American studies at Hunter.

Katherine McCaffrey is a professor of anthropology at Montclair State University. She studied at The Graduate Center from 1989 to 1999 and participated in the student strike of 1991 and anti-war protests.

Her research interests focus on social inequality and violence, its consequences, and resistance to it in Latin America and the United States. She examined a multi-decade-long movement to evict the U.S. Navy in her book, *Military Power and Popular Protest: the U.S. Navy in Vieques, Puerto Rico* (2002). More recently, she has been conducting participatory action field research with new immigrants and refugees in New Jersey.

Denise McFarlan (TSC performer) returned to society in 1993. Since then, with College and Community Fellowship's support, Denise earned her BA. She joined the Theater for Social Change Ensemble in 2006. Denise is hoping to return to school to earn her MA in social work.

Robin McGinty received her PhD in Geography from the Earth and Environmental Sciences program at The Graduate Center. Anchored in the political subjectivity of formerly incarcerated Black women, her dissertation "A Labor of Livingness: Oral Histories of Formerly Incarcerated Black Women" is situated at the intersections of Black feminist thought and carceral geographies that re/imagine the 'living prison' experiences of formerly incarcerated Black women. Robin McGinty is a 2022 American Council of Learned Societies (ACLS) Leading Edge Fellow.

Charles R. Menzies is a professor of anthropology at the University of British Columbia. His primary research interests are the production of anthropological films, natural resource management (primarily fisheries related), political economy, contemporary First Nations' issues, maritime anthropology and the archaeology of north coast British Columbia. He has conducted field research and has produced films involving north coastal British Columbia, Canada (including archaeological research); Brittany, France; and Donegal, Ireland. He is a member of Gitxaała Nation on BC's north coast and an enrolled member of the Tlingit and Haida Tribes of Alaska.

Nina Angela Mercer is a cultural worker. Her plays include *Gutta Beautiful*; *Racing My Girl, Sally*; *Itagua Meji*; *A Road & A Prayer*; *Gypsy and the Bully Door*; and *Mother Wit & Water Born*, a trilogy, including *Between Whispered Blood-Lines*. Recently, Nina collaborated with filmmaker Toshi Sakai on "Invocation for Jose Antonio Aponte," a video poem. She is co-founder and co-director of Ocean Ana Rising-www.oarinc.org. Nina is a doctoral fellow (Level II) of theater and performance at The Graduate Center. She holds a BA from Howard University, and an MFA from American University. She teaches at Brooklyn College.

Chamutal (Tali) Noimann is associate professor of English at Borough of Manhattan Community College, where she is the founder and coordinator of the Children and Youth Studies AA Program. Her primary areas of research are Victorian Children's Literature, fantasy, game pedagogy, Neo-Victorianism and Other Worlds theory. Her articles have appeared in various publications, including *College English Association Forum, Topic, The Washington and Jefferson College Review*, and *Children's Literature Association Quarterly*. Currently, she is an elected member of the Children's Literature Association's Ethics committee.

Yolanda Johnson Peterkin (TSC performer) has been working to serve people with criminal justice histories for over a decade. Prior to her current role as chief of housing community activities at the NYC Housing Authority, Yolanda was director of operations for reentry at the Women's Prison Association. She and her peers published the article titled "Life Capacity Beyond Reentry: A Critical Examination of Racism and Prisoner Reentry Reform in the U.S." in *Race/Ethnicity*

Journal: Multidisciplinary Global Contexts. She received her MA in social work from Hunter College.

Lee Painter-Kim is a nonbinary and queer biracial Korean and White American. A current graduate student and a fellow in the cultural studies program at Claremont Graduate University, they hold a BA in English with a concentration in literature, language, and criticism from Hunter College (2018) and a BFA in Painting & Printmaking from Virginia Commonwealth University (2012).

Peggy Lou Pardo was born in Barranquilla, Colombia, and received a BFA from City College. She is a member of the Motion Picture Editors Guild and works in TV and film editing.

Lavelle Porter is an assistant professor of English at New York City College of Technology. He holds a BA in history from Morehouse College, and a PhD in English from The Graduate Center. His writing has appeared in venues such as *The New Inquiry*, *Poetry Foundation*, *JSTOR Daily*, and *Black Perspectives*. He is the author of *The Blackademic Life: Academic Fiction, Higher Education, and the Black Intellectual* (2019).

Mariah Rajah is a native Guyanese who immigrated in the early 2000s. Since graduating from the New York City College of Technology in 2017, she has gone onto becoming a copywriter in the pharma industry, where she has been a leader in helping create entry-level opportunities for BIPOC writers.

Javier Riveros, a child of Colombian immigrants, was raised and still resides in Jamaica, Queens, New York. Currently a first-generation college student at Hunter College, Javier will soon become an elementary school teacher to serve the diverse demographic of children in New York City and use his position to instill ideals of social justice and equity in today's youth.

Jaime Rodriguez is a proud Puerto Rican from Brooklyn, New York, who is legally blind and has a passion for politics. He is currently an undergraduate at Hunter College, having received his AA in sociology from the Borough of Manhattan Community College.

Edna (TSC performer) is the regional director at a not-for-profit mental health agency in New York City. She received an MSW from the Hunter College School of Social Work in January 2009, and her MSW license in December 2014. Edna aspires to open a program that would address the myriad of issues that arise for incarcerated women and their children. She has been a member of College and Community Fellowship's Theater for Social Change and The Writer's Group for over twelve years.

Ashwin Satyanarayana is an associate professor with the Department of Computer Systems Technology at New York City College of Technology, where he serves as a faculty leader for City Tech's First Year Learning Community program. He is also currently serving as chair of the computer systems technology department.

Emily Schnee is professor of English at Kingsborough Community College where she teaches composition and what remains of developmental English. She is a graduate of the urban education doctoral program at The Graduate Center. Her research centers on issues of justice and equity for community college students.

Jennifer Sears is an assistant professor of English at New York City College of Technology, where she is a faculty leader for City Tech's First Year Learning Community (FYLC) program, as well as a dedicated FYLC instructor. Also a fiction writer, she received creative writing fellowships in 2018 from the National Endowment for the Arts and the New York Foundation for the Arts.

Samrah Shoaib is a queer desi femme and a recent graduate of Brooklyn College, where she double-majored in sociology and women's and gender studies. Her research seeks to reimagine the ways in which queer Brown girls can use art as resistance.

Emily Sohmer Tai is an associate professor of history at Queensborough Community College, and a Queensborough representative to the University Faculty Senate.

Cynthia Tobar is an artist, activist-scholar, archivist and oral historian who is passionate about creating interactive, participatory stories documenting social change. An alumna of Hunter College, Cynthia is an assistant professor and head of archives at Bronx Community College, where she creates socially engaged art programming and leads community-based archiving and storytelling projects.

Jason VanOra is a social/personality psychologist and professor of psychology at Kingsborough Community College and The Graduate Center. His research addresses the ways in which narratives can be used to reveal resiliency, identity, and "wisdoms" among persons living within conditions of both marginalization and hope.

Maria F. Vera was born in Cholula, Puebla, Mexico. At 10, she immigrated to the United States and has lived in New York City ever since. While attending the Borough of Manhattan Community College, she was the first woman president of the BMCC Dream Team. After holding different positions at the New York State Youth Leadership Council, the first undocumented, youth-led organization in the state,

Maria is their current dream team network coordinator and supports undocumented high school and college students to organize in their communities. Maria attended John Jay College of Criminal Justice and majored in Latin American and Latinx studies and minored in gender studies.

Vallaire Wallace is a second-year PhD student in English at the University of Virginia. She graduated summa cum laude with a BA in English from Queens College in May 2020.

Alison Wong received her MA in anthropology of food from SOAS University of London, and her BS from Macaulay Honors College at Lehman College. As a writer, she examines her experiences with Chinese-American identity politics and her relationship with her heritage and food. She currently lives in London and New York.

9 781645 042389